STARCRAFT

by

Vee Van Dam

SKOOB BOOKS PUBLISHING
LONDON

First published in parts by
Vee A.K. Van Dam and SPIRAL PUBLICATIONS
Text © Vee A.K. Van Dam 1987, 1988, 1991.
Copyright © SKOOB BOOKS PUBLISHING LTD. & SPIRAL
   PUBLICATIONS 1991
Series Editor: Christopher Johnson
Design: Mark Lovell

Published by
SKOOB BOOKS PUBLISHING LTD.
Skoob Esoterica Series
19 Bury Place
Bloomsbury
London WC1A 2JH

ISBN 1 871438 06 3 Paper

Typeset in ITC Garamond by *Shades & Characters Ltd.*, Glastonbury.
Printed in Singapore

CONTENTS

INTRODUCTION

STARCRAFT is *something else* — and before you embark on the voyage it will take you on, and through, you may as well throw away any preconceptions that you may have about how (and also why) the Cosmos was created... they are not likely to serve your understanding very well, anymore, when set side by side and compared with the *universe of pure energy* which you are about to encounter!

Here revealed for the first time is a Deva's point of view of how that was done. It will stretch your imagination to the nth degree, for what is presented here is no back-alley pseudo-spiritualism.

It is raw information, from the start of things, right down into the *pit* of dense matter, and back up the other side again... Involution, and Evolution.

There are four parts to this combined book.

STARCRAFT itself is composed of a series of channellings, some of which will make you feel like you have just touched upon something which you have always known to be true, deep within yourself, yet which has evaded your conscious realisation — up until now.

What is more, it describes Devas as they would describe themselves — therefore if you do not know what a Deva is, now is your chance to find out...

... In glorious detail!...

These Devic messages are precisely aimed at a part of you which yearns for *re-Union* with the Spirit, and the Spiritual Planes... and with your own Solar Deva.

To say more than this at this point would be to spoil your fun of discovering what all this means — so, read on...

THE STARCRAFT HANDBOOK follows these messages, and imparts instructions on how to work magickally, and co-operatively, with Devas. It represents a new Shamanism, perfectly tailored to the needs of the on-coming Age, otherwise called New, or Aquarian.

A beautiful, yet high-powered *system,* which unlocks a potential which spans the stars — hence the name, *Star-craft*.

Then there are more Devic messages, in THE DREAMSCAPE, containing views and information on how to *dream* — not ordinary dreams, but *magickal dreams.*

... On how to get our *dreaming* right.

... And finally, to round off this combined book, there is a piece entitled PSYCHIC SELF-DEFENSE — which aims to impart information on how to protect yourself from unwanted psychic interference; and on how to *call* your Solar Deva, as a protective agent.

All in all, here you have much with which to familiarise yourself, and you will not be disappointed... in any way!

NOTES

Where pertinent, the *androgynous* pronouns *s/he* and *hir* (pronounced *her*) have been used when implying both sexes, or either sex. It may take you a little while to get fully used to these, nevertheless the use of these pronouns is infinitely more preferable than using ubiquitous male pronouns for the same purpose.

The pronoun *s-he* is used specifically to imply an androgynous or hermaphroditic being.

The word Spiritual has been capitalised throughout this manual in order to distinguish it from its ordinary religious overtones, or from spiritism or spiritualism. Here it is associated with the word Spirit, or that which is formless power.

Capitalised words are used for emphasis, as are all words or phrases set in italics — particularly those which need to be differentiated in meaning from their normal written or spoken

2

equivalents.

Certain Sanskrit words have also be used, wherever possible sparingly, and these are clearly explained during the course of this manual; wherever possible a Western, English word or definition has been used as a substitute.

Occasionally certain abbreviations have been used, in context — such as *physical* for the *physical body* or the *physical plane,* thus avoiding the overuse of certain words which might make your reading unnecessarily tedious.

In every other respect the writing has been kept simple, despite some of the difficulties of explaining non-physical phenomena when using a language, such as ordinary English, which was designed or else was evolved in order to define ordinary physical events and reality.

This manual forms a part of a series of manuals, which are published by Skoob Books Publishing Ltd. in collaboration with Spiral Publications.

FOREWORD

"STARCRAFT is a book which we hope will fire not only your imagination, but also your understanding of things cosmic."

The opening line of this series of communications.

This is the manner in which this book was introduced to me as a channel. The *communicators* are devas — of different types, mainly cosmic devas and solar devas; and one thing which must be said here is that during much of the channelling they were perfectly at home with the idea of speaking for each other, although it is explained that everything which the cosmic devas had to say was in fact *relayed* through solar devas. As they all used the word *we* without too much by way of distinction between one type and another, as a reader you will have to bear this in mind!

For those who are not familiar with channelling (which some people also spell as channeling), it is the ability to be receptive to subtle impressions exchanged at a mental level — in other words it is a form of subtle telepathy.

This may require some clarification.

In context, as a channel I get the task of somehow transforming these impressions into a written language which can be understood, although this is largely an automatic process. Words are also suggested to me, and in previous communications of this sort I have been told that devas and other kinds of communicators not only know the English language, but also many, if not also all the languages as used by human beings on this planet — therefore they appear to be perfectly capable of *dictating* a text to me in the literal sense. Nevertheless my subjective impression of this process leads me to believe that many of the messages are energy impulses which my brain converts into words; the reason I say this is because I often find that there is a *lag* factor involved: the communicators appear to be able to transmit at a rate which is so fast that this whole book might take only a fraction of a second to be *down-loaded* — but obviously I cannot type at that sort of speed (I wish I could!). I often receive streams of impressions which I cannot possibly convert into any form of text at the speed at which I perceive them. In order to make up for my personal limitations in this respect the communicators appear to *delay* the transmissions through a number of channels, including my solar deva; one other psychic who has observed me channelling has said that she sees my solar deva standing behind me, presumably assisting me to cope with this task.

It is a two-way process, however. If there is something I do not understand or else find some difficulty in *catching* or receiving I can ask mental questions, and I will usually get direct answers. If I find that I get *stuck* — for instance because a word just will not come into my mind, upon which the flow of the channelling process tends to come to a halt, particularly if I try too hard to *find* it — then the mental alignment between those who are communicating and myself becomes disturbed, or even partially broken. Therefore the onus is on me to flow with the process as well as I can, and avoid distorting the meaning of the messages or transmissions.

Sometimes I find myself objecting to a particular piece of information, for some reason or other — perhaps because it confronts me, or perhaps because I think that it may be misunderstood or misinterpreted by others. Two things may then happen: (1) I am offered an alternative; (2) I am told not to interfere with the message! Thirdly, the communication may cease until I am prepared to channel it as it is given.

Often a lot of humour passes between the communicators and myself — there is an element of *serious* fun involved. On other occasions, particularly when something powerful is being communicated, I start to feel *charged up* with energy, often impinging on my ajna point or crown chakra; my body usually begins to feel hot. Sometimes I feel a wavering of powerful energies going through me and around me, or even electrical-like bolts hitting me, occasionally all the way down my spine — I've learnt to deal with these over the years, yet I must admit that when this starts to happen I can get a little alarmed, and I have to make an effort to clear my mind of any obstructions which might be creating an element of *impedance* or distortion. Things around me can make sudden snapping or cracking sounds as well, which can be quite startling.

It is also quite possible for me to be receiving a message while also being shown other things at the same time — sometimes in the form of images or as intuitional *flashes*. This often prompts a new perspective to the message as it unfolds, unless the information is designed to help me understand something personally.

I am always mindful of the fact that I might be *colouring* the messages with my own thoughts, and while I try and avoid this I am sure that what goes down on the pages (on the monitor screen to begin with, that is) suffers from an element of personal colouration, at least from time to time. However, if I type something which is distinctly *wrong* I am *told* about it in no uncertain terms, and I am made to change it! (Being *told* usually means being surcharged by a wave of strange energy which does not feel very comfortable.)

The net result, regardless of any of my own personal shortcomings, is almost always highly interesting and well worth presenting to others to read; I am sometimes quite amazed myself by some of the information which is given, and I have certainly learnt many things through this exercise of channelling.

I am often told that it does not matter too much if the message as typed is not quite what was *put out* in the first place, providing that the gist of the message is there. Also, I sometimes have to lightly edit certain passages, mostly because the syntax of what is said can occasionally be a little unconventional, and given permission to do so I change it — i.e., I am allowed a measure of editorial interference, as it were. It is impressed upon me that the channelling itself is an act of cooperation, and not one of subservience on my part — anyway I resist any form of subservience like the plague, therefore this is just as well!

Other than this I find the process of channelling very revealing and most times very enjoyable. I much prefer direct personal experience, yet as an alternative way of *landing* insights this is quite a unique manner of doing it.

Lastly I must admit to a great personal joy with regard to working with devas, who have shown me much over the years, and have precipitated experiences which have fascinated me — I have found that devas are not only distinguished by their power, but also by their beauty, and their exquisite sense of gentleness; and not least by their amazing humour. The only draw-back, if it is one, is that I often end up feeling more devic than I do human, but that's another story.

I sincerely hope that this book will brighten your days and fire your imagination, and your understanding — as it did mine!

Vee Van Dam — Glastonbury, June 1987.

In the context of this book I have noted that some pieces of information have been repeated several times over. Since these messages were channelled over a period of about two weeks perhaps this was as a deliberate emphasis with regard to the particular points which were being made, or maybe it was to refresh my memory with regard to what was being considered. Hopefully these repetitions will not detract from your enjoyment of reading these messages.

Also, I have noted that some of the information appears to be somewhat contradictory when viewed overall and from a particular point of view. I have been assured that errors in my channelling notwithstanding, these apparent contradictions are effectively caused by the enormity of the subject which the various communicators have tried to convey — as each group of communicators has unfolded a given point, each one has been *speaking* from a different angle or perspective of view. For instance, the cosmic devas talk of devas as the only beings which existed during the initial unfoldment of manifestation, since individuality at that point had not yet been created; then they talk of the *male seed* as inherently involved in that process of manifestation. In contrast, the solar devas *speak* of the division of the *female* devic life-stream and that of the *male* human (and human-equivalent) life-stream, which supports the idea that at one time the two were in fact one; and as this book suggests, that these will be rejoined and fused together in the future. STARCRAFT above all is a communication from devas, therefore it does not purport to speak for the *male* or human-type life-stream point of view.

Once again, it must be noted that the communicators speak throughout as *we,* when they are in fact representing several different devic groups, each one with its own perspective. Since they gave little indication as to which group was communicating at any one time the perspectives keep changing without much notice, occasionally even in mid-paragraph. Lastly they make references to previous messages or impressions which can be found in some of the other books in this Series, and in SPIRAL Magazine.

Some time later THE STARCRAFT HANDBOOK was written, and this follows STARCRAFT itself — THE STARCRAFT HAND-BOOK begins to detail some of the ways that humans can work with devas in a magickal and cooperative manner. This in turn is followed by more deva channellings, in the guise of THE DREAMSCAPE; and finally by PSYCHIC SELF-DEFENSE. All these were originally published separately, yet have been brought together here to form this *bundled* book as published by Skoob Books Publishing Ltd.

The other, complementary books in this series, include THE PSYCHIC EXPLORER, and THE POWER OF MIND & CON-SCIOUSNESS, wherein more information on devas and magickal and initiatic processes can be found.

As with all the other books in this series, the *androgynous* pronouns *s/he* and *hir* (pronounced *her*) are used to denote both sexes, or either sex. The pronoun *s-he* is used with reference to an actual androgynous being.

1 — THE ORIGINS OF STARCRAFT

1.1 — *THE INITIAL IMPULSE*

In truth there is no beginning, nor is there an end. Cosmic evolution occurs as a result of impulses which occur from time to time in accordance with NEED — that need is defined by what has passed before, and by that which must follow.

It is difficult for you to understand why these things must be, in the same way as it is difficult for us to understand matters which are even more consequential. There is no limit to possible growth, and this above all else is what you must keep in mind.

Each universe begins through the agency of an impulse, and that impulse can be a cosmic desire for expression. Without expression there can be no experiment, and therefore no new discoveries — of the possibilities inherent to the need of which we speak.

There are many different reasons for life as we know it, and even as you know it. In different *zones* of Being there are different impulses awork, and each *zone* fulfils the nature of a given intent; that intent is that of some great being, a cosmic deva in conjunction with her counterpart, which is the male polarity projection into manifestation via the devic structures which we afford. As devas we are the builders of the *zones* through which the male polarity of life can express himself, and discover himself.

Our task is to build the universe, or universes, as the case may be. This is undertaken in a practical way, derived from precise geometries which we harbour by way of training and inclination; we set the universes afoot, and the male polarity part can then explore his potential. To the extent that what we build is precise and well worked out, so can the male polarity work his way through the *zones* which we have created with minimum encumbrance — however: to do what we must do we must also learn as we go; what we do initially is not always as precise as we would like it to be, and some element of inexactitude can be witnessed in the earlier stages of what we materialise; we then aim to purify and correct the domains that we have created, bringing them gradually towards perfection.

Perfection is a relative term, you must take this into account. There is no ultimate perfection whenever we consider manifestation itself; it can always be refined further, always. What we must do, which is our role and prediclection, if you will, is to manifest the best *environments* which we possibly can, so that life can unfold without dire restrictions. As the wave of life progresses down into increasingly dense layers of matter, so does the task become harder. The denser forms never resemble their higher prototypes to begin with — in fact they can be so different from the original prototypes that they are scarcely recognisable. Hence on your planet humanity was not to begin with very much like the prototype which we had designed and made on higher levels. Many of your problems on Earth during the last few tens of thousands of years have been ones of adjusting to the dense forms through which you have incarnated. The problems go further back in time, beyond the Lemurian stage, and even beyond the earliest stage of human expression millions of years ago. This unfortunately was unavoidable because of certain conditions which exist in this galaxy, and also in certain other galaxies. The trend here has been for very dense expressions indeed, and much of our work in assisting the human race, and other races elsewhere also caught up in density, has been to evolve stages of evolutionary unfoldment which would permit a gradual purifying of the forms until they begin to resemble the original prototypes. In the pure sense this will not be fully achieved until the seventh cycle, and therefore it will not be until the seventh Root Race is born that we will have achieved our prime objective — as far as assisting humanity is concerned anyway. In saying this much we have swept past the disclosures which would help you to understand how the Cosmos was born in the first place, nevertheless if you read into the inferences made here you will realise that in fact we have somewhat gone from the initial impulse right down to the *bottom of the pit* — represented by the stage we will call involution — and then up the other side, the stage which we will refer to as evolution — the way out of the *pit!* This whole process follows through from the original impulse, and we are in the post of adjusting things as both stages find their expression and work their way out towards fulfilment at different sub-stages. This in short — if you read this correctly — is what is at stake.

1.2 — LEARNING TO MATERIALISE A COSMOS

Whatever we may have learnt in other times, during other cosmic cycles, subject to other impulses and other needs, what we have to begin with is only a rough remembrance of what we may have done before — therefore our first task is to remember something of what we have accumulated by way of learning, by way of achievement and understanding, by way of abilities. The reason we do not remember everything has a logical angle: if we remembered everything we had done before during other unfoldments we would tend to recreate the same things again, whereas what is needed is something new. Nevertheless at a relatively subconscious level we do remember everything we need to know.

It is the same for you from a lesser angle: if, for instance, you were a capable artist in a previous incarnation, you would not need to start from scratch in order to become a capable artist in your present incarnation — you would remember things, however subconsciously, which would help you become a good artist this time round as well. You might have no conscious recollection of having been an artist in another life, yet you would effectively be ahead with regard to remanifesting your talents as an artist in this life; it would come quite naturally to you — you would find it much easier to express a sense of artistry. Those around you might even think of it as a gift, and in one sense it is, but more importantly it would be what you have brought forward by way of training and talent from another time. This is exactly what we mean when we say that we have to start again in order to manifest something different; we bring forward, albeit subconsciously, everything which we have learnt and done before, and this is quite natural and relatively easy in consequence for us.

When constructing a cosmos there are certain rules to be followed, otherwise things could get out of hand very rapidly. These rules are quite natural in their concept: things must be built in stages, from ultra refined down to stages of comparative density, then following through into ever greater density — thus we have proposed a map as follows:

(1) — to each cosmos there are a number of Cosmic Planes; these Cosmic Planes are the Root Factors which operate as prototypes for what is to be eventually achieved.

(2) — the lowest of these Cosmic Planes, consisting of Seven Planes (there are other ways of interpreting the construction/ numbers of these Planes), becomes the *zone of experiments* — it is the densest of the Cosmic Planes. This Cosmic Plane has Seven Planes which reflect their higher Cosmic counterparts, which for a time can be considered to be latent, awaiting future developments during the return wave of evolution. The densest of the Seven Planes is the one on which you presently find yourselves incarnated, therefore it is also the least perfect of all.

(3) — from the most perfect (yet latent) Cosmic Plane (Cosmic Adi) to the least perfect Cosmic Plane (Cosmic Etheric-Physical) we then have Seven Grades of Cosmic Energy-Matter; from the most perfect Plane (Adi) of the lowest Cosmic Plane to the least perfect Plane of that Cosmic Plane — the etheric-physical plane (which we de-emphasise because it is not considered to be a vital Principle in itself, only an end result) — we have seven lesser grades of energy-matter. The reflection, in principle, is exact.

(4) Involution is an investment of energy and intent into the lower grades of energy-matter; evolution is the perfected wave of return. The initial investment leads to a further impulse which

courses down the Cosmic Planes into the Seven Planes of the densest Cosmic Plane, hence the Seven Planes, followed by further investments of energy. Here we could say that there is a cosmic economy of energy and intent at work, layer upon layer; each layer builds up the structure of the Cosmic Network.

Given these *rules* (we could mention many others), we set about in our task to create and organise these Cosmic Planes and lesser Planes, and then the sub-planes of these Planes, into a coherent system which will permit involution, then evolution. At the end of the period of evolution the Cosmos will then be dissolved, since it will have served its purpose; the experiments will have been completed; the beings who have been subject to that evolution, and which have been willing parts of the experiments, will have completed their own tasks, and will then rejoin the Primal Aspect of Creation, and then escape into a Super Cosmos.

1.3 — THE CONSTRUCTION OF THE PLANES

If we take the point that a Plane is something of a frequency-band of energy then it becomes easier to understand what we have to say about the actual construction of the Planes. As you know, a frequency is the rate at which energy vibrates. In your dense zone, energy vibrates at a fairly low rate of frequency. On higher levels it vibrates faster. On the highest levels it vibrates at rates almost unimaginable to you. When considering the Planes generally there is a geometrical-mathematical relationship between the frequency of one Plane and that of the next, higher and lower, and so on.

Of course within each given Plane there is a range of frequency — a spectrum, if you will. That spectrum is part of the greater spectrum of all the Planes, and likewise when considering the greater Cosmic Planes. In the same way as a doubling of a frequency in terms of music leads to a note one octave above the first note, you could view each higher Plane as a doubling of the previous Plane frequency; this is a simple way of representing things. In practice, however, these matters are more complex.

Let us consider Infinity for a moment. An infinite frequency is not something which is easy to understand intellectually, and yet it is from an infinite frequency that we have to begin — the highest frequency is, for all intents and purposes, infinite (in truth it is not, yet we are using the term *infinite* here from a symbolic point of view). Needless to say, Infinity cannot be halved; we must guard ourselves from confusing you, and yet we must try and put things to you in a way that you can understand. If we consider the frequency rate of the Cosmic Plane of Adi, and if we were to represent this frequency rate in mathematical figures, you would have a staggering, quasi-infinite figure — a very rarefied abstraction indeed. Let us consider then the Plane of Adi instead one *Major Octave* down from that of the Cosmic Plane of Adi. You would still find the figures so high as to be seemingly infinite. When we come to the etheric-physical plane you can begin to grasp the figures more easily, for you deal and gauge these frequencies with your scientific instruments; for instance, you can hear sounds between 16 and 20,000 cycles per second or so (in a few cases some of you can hear frequencies of sound below and above what to you is the audible spectrum of sounds). Likewise, light — as you see it, physical light exists within a certain range of frequency, and you see red (the lowest light frequency that you see) followed by orange, yellow, green, blue, indigo and violet — with infra-red below this range, and ultra-violet beyond it. Higher than physical light there are etheric frequencies which most of you do not see, unless you are sufficiently psychically sensitive to do so. Then if you were to go up one step more you would find the beginning of the astral frequencies; and so on.

In our role of builders, as constructors of the Cosmic Planes, including the Planes of your lower system, the Seven Planes, we then start with extremely high frequencies, which we then have to *slow down*. We do this by creating layers of increasing density by packing atoms together and by slowing down their nutational rates. As the density increases, the frequency-range drops; as the frequency-range drops further it becomes increasingly difficult *to work* the energy-matter involved — it begins to resist mental manipulation by virtue of its denser inertia.

By way of demonstration, if you were to be conscious on, say, the Plane of the Monad at this very moment you would find the energy-matter on that level highly dynamic in comparison to that of the physical plane on which you presently live and are conscious. The atoms there (on the Monadic Plane) are not so packed, indeed they are almost rarefied in contrast, and yet they have more energy, and therefore they are more potent, more alive, and (in relative terms) it does not require much effort to *move* them. Therefore while you may find it highly difficult to *move* physical energy-matter with the full power of your minds and wills, on the Monadic Plane the reverse is true: it requires very little effort to *move* Monadic energies (when conscious at that level). If you follow this through to its natural and logical conclusion you will realise that it does not take all that much effort to bring about the birth of a Cosmos. In fact the greatest initial difficulty from our point of view is to refrain from *moving* higher energy-matter too much; we must be as constructive as possible. Our effort is minimal. We arrange energy-matter by *vocalising* very gently certain power mantrams which are only known to us, and thus we define the nature of each Cosmic Plane, and then each Plane.

1.4 — LEARNING FROM EXPERIENCE

It has been said down the ages by some of your mystics that the *Voice of the Cosmic Being is nearly silent* — what they meant by this, having glimpsed something of the reality of the higher states, was that on the higher levels it requires very little input to effect a change; whereas at the lowest level it requires a great deal of input to effect change. You must take into consideration that all this is relative, for what you do at a human level is comparatively little compared with what a higher being does on a higher Plane.

We, as Builder Devas, have had to learn from experience, even as you learn from experience also. In particular we have had to learn to be very precise in what we do, and how we do it, for the margins of error are not very big for us; we cannot make certain errors, therefore the onus is on us to be very attentive and very well coordinated whenever we envisage doing anything. Whenever we work our magick we must be *spot on*, as you might put it! Therefore we also learn very fast, because we have to — the rest of manifested life depends on our accuracy for its survival, since we maintain the states, levels and Planes on which all other beings live.

When presenting these communications to you we also want to make it clear that we will not be giving you certain formulae which you might use incorrectly and thus create havoc; but we will be presenting you with others, which while considerably less potent will permit you to ascertain the measure of your capabilities, while still in dense human form. We will be, in a way, training you even as we train our own lesser devas to do certain tasks in Nature.

Since you are at the point when the Seventh Ray of (so-called) Ceremonial Magick is about to make itself felt more keenly during the coming Age, you will begin to appreciate how DISCIPLINED one must be in order to operate magick — which consists of formulae enacted in certain ways; these formulae when enacted correctly then *move* things, first on certain higher levels, then on lower levels, according to the formulae used and according to the degree to which they are correctly *intoned*. Sound is very much the key here, and yet the formulae are not sound alone — they consist also of certain geometrical configurations, some static and some active; furthermore, (with regard to human magickians) correct magick depends on certain alignments of consciousness with us. If all is well, then we respond and *move* things for the magickians involved.

By attuning yourselves to us, assuming that you feel the call to Magick and wish to cooperate with us, then we will reveal what you will need to know in order to progress further — this we cannot communicate to you using language as you know it, therefore you will have to learn to communicate in ways that we communicate ourselves — more of that later. In the mean time we are endeavouring here, to begin with, to elucidate certain matters which will permit you to understand us better first.

As devas we form a great grouping of different beings who are active on different levels; some Devas are Plane-Devas — they mastermind all the affairs of a given Plane within the periphery of a given star-system; then there are lesser, yet still Great Devas, who preoccupy themselves with certain aspects of development within a Plane, or sometimes Planes; finally there are a great many lesser builders who work at preserving certain forms, building them, altering them, and so on. In all cases we use the energies which we generate, and to a certain extent embody.

If you look at Nature all around you, you will have noticed how complex certain forms really are. Each part of those forms is *built* — it does not occur by chance, as some of your *evolutionary* scientists might suppose; each form is nurtured into expression as lesser devas learn to manipulate energy-matters of certain grades with that very purpose in mind. We (as Greater Devas) guide them, instruct them, and generally overview what they do, how they do it, and how well they manage to do it. These lesser builders are entrusted with certain formulae which permit them to operate and construct what they must build. Whenever they do their work to perfection, and after a given time, they are then permitted to move up one grade, and then they learn how to do things on a higher level in a similar if more demanding manner. This, in short, represents their path of chosen evolution. Much as you might think otherwise the same is generally true for you as well, from the point of view of the human wave of evolution — the emphasis is different, but the nature of the progress is nearly identical.

1.5 — INTERFEEDING INFORMATION FROM DIFFERENT ZONES

As devas, and unlike yourselves, we are not competitive. If you will, our key-note is *cooperation* — amongst devas at least. You might say that we do not have to survive in terms of worldly struggle — we are entirely focused on our work on behalf of whichever system is our central primary; we do not conceal information between ourselves; indeed, it is critical that we should not do so.

For a system to work (and we are principally referring here to a solar system, or in a lesser way to a planetary system) we must interfeed all the information which we derive from our efforts — in this way we make sure that certain efforts need not be repeated uselessly. If, for instance, one particular devic group makes a breakthrough in one given area of application, then that information is exchanged with all other *peer* groups within that system.

At the beginning of a Cosmos, when we first venture out to create the manifestation which will lead to billions of worlds, we put forward certain essential plans which will permit the embryonic unfoldment to occur. We then refine these plans on an on-going basis until we reach a condition which requires new plans altogether. The *old* is left behind, having served its purpose, and we concentrate on the *new*.

As with all plans we start with *bare-bone* outlines — for example, a system of Seven Cosmic Planes, each differentiated into Seven Planes, and each of these Planes differentiated in turn into seven sub-planes, etc. These outlines are not arbitrary ones — they conform to a certain need. They are also mathematically and geometrically *pure*.

Then we come to the detail: each Cosmic Plane, Plane or sub-plane must conform to certain *laws*, which needless to say we define for ourselves, and subsequently for all those who will manifest within the systems that we set up. Again these *laws* are not arbitrary, and they have nothing to do with *justice*. They are *laws* of Nature — the Nature that we manifest.

We deliberately set out to interrelate the Cosmic Planes, and the Planes, etc., in such a way that there would be correspondences between a given Plane and another — for instance, between the Cosmic Adi and the Systemic Adi, the Cosmic Astral and the Astral Plane. As things begin to take shape we must then make allowances for the particular needs of any given system, or planet, and so on — this is were we must make sure that you understand that each galaxy, each star and each planet, is in fact a being — a cosmic being of a certain order, with a certain purpose at heart; this being requires our services to bring about the unfoldment of the conditions which will lead to the fulfilment of that purpose in the due course of time. To assist in this capacity we differentiate the unfoldment into certain cycles of growth — at first these cycles correspond to an approximation of the overall needs of that system or being; each cycle will evolve a particular facet of expression, leading in turn to a particular conclusion, which will then lead into the next cycle of unfoldment. Nevertheless, we find that we have to make adjustments to each cycle as things actually unfold, for manifestation scarcely ever proceeds exactly according to any plan that we might formulate — beings other than ourselves, who may enjoy what you call *free-will,* often deviate from the established path and make things that much more difficult to resolve — this incidentally, is fine; we learn from these deviations as much as anything or anyone else might.

Therefore, there is planning; yet plans are not always fulfilled in any one given cycle, and when this occurs they must be fulfilled in the next. If a plan cannot be brought to fruition within a given time and within a certain number of cycles, then it will be held back until another system is born — i.e., the incarnation of that system and being in another Aeon; this applies to you in a lesser fashion — if you cannot accomplish what you have planned within a given incarnation, then you will have to carry it forward to another life; and so on until you succeed. However, in order to maximise the chances or likelihood of success we exchange impressions and information with other devic groups in other systems, in other cosmic zones, and even in other universes which are otherwise unrelated to the universe we deal with ourselves — you will have to read between these lines to understand what we are hinting at here; use your intuition! Whenever possible we keep things *on target;* whenever this becomes impossible we make useful amendments so that life can unfold without too much fuss.

1.6 — THE DREAM PROJECTION

The *closest* Cosmic Plane to the Cosmic Etheric-Physical Plane (the Seven Planes) is the Cosmic Astral Plane — this is the Cosmic Plane of the *Great Cosmic Dream;* Cosmic Desire, if you will. This *Cosmic Dream* reflects the Purpose of the Cosmic Being — the *One-without-Second,* as S-he is sometimes referred to.

As we begin the unfoldment of the Cosmic Etheric-Physical Plane we derive all our impetus from this *Cosmic Dream*; it becomes our *blue-print* for the Seven Planes. This is the same at a lesser level — the Astral Plane forms the basis for the etheric-physical plane.

If you have studied what we have communicated at other times (with references to other books) you will have noted that the etheric-physical plane can be differentiated into seven sub-planes: 4 states of plasma, then gases, liquids, and finally dense solids; each of these sub-planes can be further differentiated into seven parts — for instance, seven distinct states of dense solids. These differentiations are derived from their correspondences on the Astral Plane; the Seven Planes are also derived from their correspondences on the Cosmic Astral Plane.

The Cosmic Dream therefore acts as a guiding principle for the Seven Planes. We evolve all our plans for the Cosmic Etheric-Physical Plane on the Cosmic Astral Plane; we Dream them first; then we precipitate them into further density.

You do this as well, again at a lesser level — you evolve all your plans for a given incarnation on the Astral Plane prior to incarnating. You *dream* all the facets that you wish to unfold, and then when you feel you have mastered your *dream*, you incarnate — providing you can find a suitable dense vehicle in which to do so.

This is were things can get complex: sometimes you cannot find an ideal body to re-incarnate in, and you may end up *putting up* with the best that dense life can provide you with at any given time, including matters of environment, social fabric, parental genes, karmic links, and so on. There are instances when you might require a particular set of conditions, however these conditions — for one reason or another — cannot be met, in whole or in part. You then have the option to wait for better conditions; however, again, you may wish to *get on* with things, and you elect not to wait — you then incarnate into the *best* approximation of the conditions you might require. This lag between *ideal* conditions and available conditions gives rise to certain difficulties. The same applies to us in a different manner — what we *Dream* on the Cosmic Astral Plane cannot always be implemented directly within the *periphery* of the Seven Planes; therefore the outcome of on-going unfoldments within that *periphery* do not always correspond to the *ideal* we would like to manifest either. The densest Cosmic Plane therefore rarely permits us to do everything that we would like to do within a given Time (a certain Cosmic Cycle).

Whenever this turns out to be the case, we wait; and then we manifest our plans in another period, if necessary. From one point of view we are constantly *Dreaming* in order to secure a useful outcome at lower levels, on the Seven Planes; this is where YOU come in! By virtue of our own evolutionary development and *status* we cannot incarnate in the densest zones (if we did, we would over-power the denser strata and effectively destroy them). We need representatives for certain unfoldments, and to this end humanity was conceived (on the Higher Planes of the Seven Planes), and then precipitated (when we say *humanity* we mean any type of being which corresponds to the human *status,* as may be pertinent to the evolutions on different worlds). You are — if you like — an extension of ourselves, polarised in a different manner, and subject to different conditions of growth. Your allotted task, if we may speak generally, is to evolve individuality — this we cannot do: we are definitely Group Beings; we work in unison; we are not permitted to evolve individuality in a direct fashion. Each type of being has a particular task, and you have yours, as we have ours.

Once we all agree to enact the type of task we must fulfil in the due process of cosmic unfoldment, we part ways temporarily; yet when seen from another angle we are in fact a single Being. You, as humans, elected to enact your own particular part — this is your *dream projection*, a subset of the overall *Dream Projection.*

1.7 — ORGANISING THE DREAM

Once our essential plans are put into effect we must wait a while before making any alterations to the initial set of details; we must allow for evolution to take its course, gently to begin with.

This may contrast with your astrophysical view of a Big *Bang* raging throughout the Cosmos for a few milliseconds, followed by æons of the *formative period* — this is not strictly incorrect, however it does not represent the *Beginning of the Cosmos* at all!

The Cosmos begins on much higher levels, and it begins almost like a whisper, a slight stirring of energy, much like a sleeper might stir in hir sleep as s/he progresses towards wakefulness. Then the awakening occurs, but there is nothing to be seen or felt or heard, because as yet nothing has been created. The awakening is followed by a few moments of orientation at an internal level, and then the first Act of Creation takes place.

It is difficult for us to describe exactly what that is, since we do not operate at that level ourselves — Beings much greater than ourselves are involved in that initial Act of Creativity; They are the Great Devas of Origin. They live and have their being on Supernal Levels which are Para-Cosmic — i.e., beyond the Seven Cosmic Planes!

Suffice it to say that they input a portion of their highly developed Minds into the Seven Cosmic Planes, and this progressively — the Planes are not instantly born; they *incarnate* bit by bit, cycle by cycle, and at each stage each new Cosmic Plane is that much denser than the last one, in relative terms that is. Lesser Cosmic Devas such as ourselves then take up the momentum, and begin to organise each Cosmic Plane — which are still very much *in potential*, since they are not *occupied* as such. Evolution must occur first before they will be *lived on;* and therefore this is the stage of so-called involution, the downwards spiral.

During the *Descent* only primary organisation is necessary — it could be said to be quite archetypal in the Cosmic sense. It could be inferred that this is like building houses which cannot yet be occupied because there is no-one yet alive to occupy them per se; except for those Devas who are the Creators of those Cosmic Planes and which give these Cosmic Planes their substance-energies, rarefied as they are. By the time we begin to organise the Cosmic Astral Plane, and then begin to *Dream,* the first stage of the *Descent* has been fulfilled. We have effectively set in motion all those things which will later come into their own when the return wave of Evolution *comes back up,* having *found itself* and developed its capabilities, and then emerges on the Higher Cosmic Levels — which are ready to accept the new *Cosmic Dwellers*. You must allow for the fact that in a few words we are in effect covering vast periods of time...

The period of *Dreaming* goes on for æons, cycles of time too great for you to even comprehend. Also, from our point of view and experience, time does not make itself felt in the same way as it does for you when living on the denser Planes. The *Dream* is evolved, tested, changed, further tested, and only when we are finally convinced that we have put together the best possible *Dream* do we manifest it through the medium of the Etheric-Cosmic Plane/Seven Planes, which then have to be created in much the same manner as the greater Cosmic Planes had to be created (make allowances for the orders of magnitude involved).

The voyage into density, much as it might seem unnecessary from one point of view, is entirely essential if we are to evolve those types of beings who will later be able to manifest themselves on the higher Cosmic Planes — these beings simply do not exist to begin with — and here we will divulge a great Mystery: to begin with ONLY DEVAS EXIST — i.e., the MATERNAL SIDE OF THE CREATIVE COSMIC BEING. The *Male Seed* is invested into the Cosmic Matrix or Womb, and this represents the period of involution, and it could be said that it takes millions times millions of your years for the Cosmic Life to incarnate, then develop itself, *find Itself* (which It does through each one of you individually, particularly during moments of Life-Initiation), and then return to the Great Heights of Beingness. Is this a game?! Yes, and no! It is a Process which permits the MALE side of Life to establish its ability to focus its consciousness through INDIVIDUALITY — AT-ONE WITH WITH THE WHOLE.

2 — THE PRINCIPLES OF STARCRAFT

2.1 — DEVA LEARNING

You may like to think about the ways that you learn things yourselves: you can be taught by others; you can self-teach yourself through your own experience; positive or negative experiences condition you to do this and not that.

To say that this applies to devas as well would only be partly true, for we are far more group oriented than you are: if one of us learns something, then all the other devas of the same type will learn that something — for we share our experiences directly and indirectly by virtue of our close links. Since we do not engage in competition, since we do not fall prey to selfish intents, and since we are always trying to better what we do as a group, we in effect manage our affairs generally much better than you do when divided against your own kind, attempting perhaps to profit yourselves as individuals rather than sharing the benefit of your finds and your own experience.

When attempting to understand us you should bear in mind that there are a great many different types and groups of devas, each one of which is able to address certain aspects of creativity, and each one of which is able to understand what it is dealing with because it is in effect the creator of it. Lesser devas cooperate with their higher counterparts, and these in turn cooperate with those who are higher yet — thus the full spectrum of devic nature is closely interrelated. Since we do not have to burden ourselves with the task of acquiring individuality we can make progress in our work swiftly and with near maximum results — nothing indeed distracts us from doing what we must do, except perhaps on lower levels where things can get measurably more complex owing to the fact THAT WE HAVE TO DEAL WITH THE WAY IN WHICH YOU REGULATE YOUR OWN AFFAIRS, which sometimes is quite chaotic.

Little do you realise how much we have to compensate for what you do. When dealing with the lower Planes we have to harness the activity of all the small elemental groups who do not benefit from a very expanded ability to cope with human affairs when these turn out to be negative in their orientation. Elementals are quickly affected by any kind of adversity, and they can be swayed towards negativity just as they can be swayed towards positivity — in other words they become polarised by the very things that you think, feel and do. Let us take an example: you live in a house; within that house you are continually bombarding it with your thoughts, feelings, leading to whatever actions; all this then permeates the ethers around you, and the elementals which compose those ethers respond, or react accordingly. If you build up an *atmosphere* of negativity, then the elementals all vibrate negatively, which in turn produces an ambience of sustained negativity, which is then reflected back on yourselves since your bodies are made up themselves of elementals, on each level: mind, astral/emotions/feelings/dreams, and etheric-physically. You then think and feel even more negative, and end up doing even more negative things; and if this applies within the environment of your house it also applies more generally to the whole of the world in which you live, and even spreads out into the wider Cosmos as a negative reflection of energy. The more you condition the elementals around you (and within you) to negativity, the more they reflect this straight back on you, and the more you will suffer from the consequences of this lack of self-realisation and self-control over your own output. Now, if you reverse this trend, and think, feel, and do positive things, the elementals around you become positive themselves, reflect that positivity back on you, and thereby can benefit you enormously — as, of course, it benefits the elementals too. If you took this observation to heart, considered the cause and effect of much which affects you on this basis, you would find that the ethers around you would change quite dramatically — bringing you well-being, riches of the heart and mind, and furthermore would liberate you from any remaining negativity which you might be harbouring at the deeper, less accessible or obvious levels of your own internal make-up and being; consider the advantages of that! By being aware of the elemental groups around you, and by being aware of your effect on them, leading to a corresponding and similar effect on you, you could change your world, your lives, and everything else around you at various levels quite suddenly and quite permanently. THAT is what learning is about. Devas learn from these same things, yet they have one great advantage: they do not naturally harbour negativity as a viable mode of expression; their expression is naturally creative and forward looking; and above all else they aim to succeed in the overall devic task of building and sustaining worlds.

2.2 — DEVA APPLICATION

In the process of giving you this information about ourselves, limited as it must be if we are to present ourselves in a relatively simple manner, we are attempting to bridge a gap between yourselves and us, that we might then be able to act together as a working unit, so to speak.

Starcraft is primarily a method of creating worlds; and since your world — certainly your personal world — needs re-making, if we can thus phrase things, we are attempting here to put to you certain reference points and certain information which could help you to achieve a viable result; or a series of viable results in the due course of time.

When we address ourselves to the task of creating worlds — high or low — we must apply ourselves in certain ways by using those formulae which we have access to, and which essentially activate certain principles — let us look at these principles:

(1) — to begin with there is only undifferentiated energy, therefore it must be differentiated in order to create a rich texture of elements which will go into the making of any given world

(2) — once we have managed to differentiate that essential energy into a number of different elements we can then proceed

with the construction of patterned ethers (composed of those elements), which in turn will respond to certain invocations and certain formulae; this again in turn leads to the creation of more specialised elements which can then be nurtured into a whole structural domain — for instance, if we take the case of a sun-star, we start by creating those elements which could be called *primal elements* (which you know nothing about); when we have succeeded in manifesting these, we then create the ethers — i.e., *zone-elements* of a certain kind and of various grades; finally we create the most basic structural atomic elements, such as various kinds of hydrogen and helium; from hydrogen and helium we then create all the denser elements, such as carbon and oxygen, right through to metals, such as gold and uranium — using the thermo-nuclear reaction within that sun-star

(3) — finally we organise these elements, interrelate their structural values, and proceed with all the necessary measures to create various kind of worlds.

Of course we are generalising greatly when we say this much — the overall *act of creation* is far more complex than this. At a very high Level the *act* is very rarefied, and produces rarefied prototypes of all these elements; it is not until we reach down into density, creating it as we go, that atomic elements are actually manufactured; and it is not until the etheric-physical plane is built that we actually manifest very dense elements, such as gold, mercury, lead, thorium, and uranium — as you know them. These denser elements are manufactured by adding electrons and protons to the nucleic formation, which is itself neutral (in relative terms at least). Some of these denser elements are designed to be very stable, and other less stable — each type plays its part in the *act* of creating more complex world structures.

Having at our disposal this much we can proceed with the act of creating any number of different life-forms, each being integrated into the fabric of the worlds that we build. Thus one life-form is created to subsidise the unfoldment of another, and then this one in turn will sustain yet another, and so on — it is all interrelated. Also, everything is ALIVE — NOTHING IS DEAD. Things change, but their essential elemental nature never dies.

If you were to look at yourselves in the right manner you would realise that you are made up of all sorts of elements, and of all sorts of evolutionary experiments — and this at all levels. If we look at your bodies, and especially if we look at your physical bodies, we can see traces of all sorts of energies, gases, liquids, and metals. We can also see the ancient blue-prints of former states of development, from molecular to cellular, from cellular to whole body structures. We can see how the (so-called) inorganic structures gave way to organic ones, how base elements gave way to various compounds, which in turn created simple life-forms, which then created greater life-forms, which then and finally brought their *values* together, and their life-experience together, to create, for instance, a human body — thousands of different developments all wrapped into one moving, capable vehicle for SPIRIT.

2.3 — DEVA CREATIVITY

While elements in themselves harbour not only life, but also consciousness, and can arrange themselves into more complex structures of their own accord, our role as devas is to guide them, nurture them, reinforce their accepted *values,* and generally motivate them towards achieving what must be achieved. As elemental devic beings, tiny as they may be when viewed singly, yet vast in their import when viewed collectively — and it is as a collective unit that they are best considered — they follow the paths which are directly accessible to them; and we make sure that they can keep to those paths — for if they did not, then much if not all of creation would simply fall apart.

We are constantly making sure that they can do what they need to do — at their own level — and we are continually assisting them in their own growth and development (we are saying this primarily with regard to the lower Planes).

As all the other life-beings develop their own approaches, and this on countless worlds, and even between worlds, this affects the elemental groups, who then affect these other beings. This aspect of the INTERRELATEDNESS of all life must be appreciated, for if you choose not to do so you are effectively preventing your own growth, and making sure that you cannot unfold yourselves in any way that is genuinely vital and beneficial. Life, if you like, is a Family — a Family of beings, each one of which is developing some aspect of unfoldment on behalf of the overall Life.

Your part, besides the fact that you have the task of developing individuality, is also to develop a certain ability to act on certain aspects of Nature, thereby making sure that you — and us, as devas — can co-create together what will be needed next. We, as devas, need your sense of individuality; and you as humans need our sense of all-inclusiveness — we are, after all, two half-streams of a single Life-Stream, and each one of you is internally connected to a solar deva who is your natural counter-part — your Life-partner, as it were. Your immediate evolutionary success will be facilitated if you allow yourselves to be *touched* by us, guided by us, and if you are prepared to *hear* us, act with us, and then merge totally with your solar devas — in full initiated consciousness; it is at this point when we will have become re-united in consciousness that we will be able to go on to create the next stage in the *Cosmic Dance,* on behalf of this star-system, and on behalf its *star-family,* which in turn is a part of a much greater galactic family, which again in turn is a part of a Cosmic Family of *Active Points of Light-Force, galvanised by Magnetic Hearts* — terms such as these may seem a little overwhelming to begin with, yet if you look at these in the way that we imply them you will realise that they are quite accurate enough, and quite stupendous.

Your evolution is irretrievably linked with that of your solar devas — they are in one sense more advanced than you because they are the product of an earlier evolution which unfolded before you were *born,* as a human stream (or half-stream, as the case may be). Incidentally, your souls are *humanised* subsets of your solar devas!

Think of what would happen if you gained full access (or full enough an access) to everything which your solar devas know about and can activate by way of creativity — your whole sense of being would be revolutionised to the nth degree, or so it would seem at the very least!

It is this creativity which we are trying here to help you to appreciate, because WE ARE A UNIT, once we both look beyond the appearance of the separation in consciousness which we seem to experience as different parts of the whole that we represent (here we are talking on behalf of your solar devas, and not so much on behalf of ourselves as Cosmic Devas — this, we might point out, is an indication of how interlinked we are as devas, since we can speak for each other with little impediment).

At each stage on your Path of Life-Initiation you will individually merge with an Aspect of us, as Devas — thus you will be able, with further Initiation, to *mount the stairs of the Heavens.* At each succeeding stage of fusion with us you will gain access to what we are; then you will become as we are, and yet you will also retain your special human qualities — which at best are those of individuality now re-united with its *Source-Stream.* It is this creativity, and the power to implement it, that we are now engaged in *teaching* you here.

2.4 — THE MERGING POINT

If the two streams, human and devic, were divided for practical reasons many æons ago, it was foreseen that there would be a time when they would be brought back together again. This has happened for various individuals, which we generally refer to as Adepts — they have effectively merged their human and devic counterparts together, and then escaped from the wheel of reincarnation.

The merging of these two streams happens progressively, and certainly not overnight. It takes a long time for these two streams to readjust to each other and put together what they have to offer each other. They approach things from opposite ends of the spectrum, as it were, opposites which are nevertheless complementary.

As devas we are involved in building Nature, in building worlds — humans are not expected to cope with this aspect of evolution; but we are. Humans then benefit, as do all other living beings, from what we achieve at any one time, in accordance with certain cycles of development and unfoldment. Humans then have the task of developing their *part of the deal* — individuality, amongst other things.

Not all humans merge with their devas — their solar devas, that is — in the same way or to an equal extent; some retain their human focus; others endorse a devic perspective, and for all intents and purposes join the devic stream; and some go down the middle and create a perfect blend. Yet all of them, one way or the other, will merge with their solar devas and benefit from dual human-devic perceptions from then onwards.

Every individual has a choice to make — whether they feel the devic perspective suits them better, in which case they will go on to build worlds in further cycles; or they can choose to remain part of the human polar stream, in which case they will go on to direct certain cosmic affairs... this need not concern us here. Those who go *down the middle,* or *up the middle* — which is a more appropriate way of putting it — will exemplify both human and devic attributes to a more or less equal degree, and engage themselves in *bridging* work.

If *Starcraft* will mean something to you by the time you have finished reading this book, then it will mean far more to you by the time you have mastered all those things which you must master before you can escape from the wheel of reincarnation. It is not so much a technique — it is more of a way of perceiving things, and a way of *moving*. It is a way of working *high* magick, and a way of being. It is a series of methods which have been honed by experience in dealing with cosmic creativity. It is many other things.

As devas we have spaceships — *starcraft*. Our ships are designed around the very principles which we are alluding to here.

Therefore this *merging point* of which we speak is very much a *key* event in your future lives — future to the extent that you have not yet mastered everything that you have to master in order to free yourselves from the cycle of apparent death and rebirth.

There are many other kinds of merging points, each one of which consists of a kind of synthesis of one sort or another. Therefore the key-note here is synthesis. Whenever you bring together all those things which compose the matrix of any given system, whatever that might be, and then interrelate them and blend them, you are effectively engaged in synthesis. The synthesis of the human and devic streams of evolution brings about a new order of being, both for you and for us. This process applies to liberated humans and their solar devas, yet it also applies at much Higher Levels — to Cosmic Beings who are merging their COSMIC MALE AND FEMALE ATTRIBUTES.

If we confuse you in any way by speaking on behalf of all devas, and you should bear in mind that these communications are relayed, as it were, predominantly via your solar devas — who are channelling our energies, and giving us access to you through themselves — then put this book down for a moment. Close your eyes. Relax... Imagine the whole Universe around you — a great matrix of energies; imagine yourselves to be connected to this vastness, with all these energies, on all sorts of levels. Become this matrix. This is what we do ourselves; we are connected to this matrix, and we communicate along the lines of its structural Network.

2.5 — THE DUAL POINT OF VIEW PRINCIPLE

If something can be seen from two points of view simultaneously — opposite and complementary views — then it can be *seen*. This is the key to this word we use, *seeing*.

Devas hear colours, but see sounds (they can do the reverse as well, but this is the predominant way that they perceive things). You can do this as well, particularly when you are in a state of higher receptivity or consciousness.

Obviously, as a result, what devas experience of the world, or even the Universe, is quite different to what you perceive yourselves — in both cases events can be looked at, but what is perceived by you is the external reality, whereas what we see is the internal reality.

If we look at your bodies we do not see flesh — we see vibration; we see sound-colours; we see patterns of energy. We see the internal structure of your bodies, and not so much the outside.

If your inner eyes were open and you could look at yourselves, you would *see* all this too. As it is you see shape, skin, facial and bodily features, and so on. It is this difference between us which characterises our evolutionary streams. On average neither of us *sees* the whole thing; we only see a part of it.

This means that you specialise your perceptions one way, and we do so the other way — merge the two together, and you have total perception. This is the value of the initial splitting of our life-streams, and also the value and importance of merging them together again after a given period.

2.6 — THE MULTIPLE POINT OF VIEW PRINCIPLE

If we as devas, and you as humans (and your equivalents elsewhere on other worlds, remember, who may not resemble you physically), can merge our life-streams, then in the due course of time we would also have to consider all the other types of beings which exist — beings who are neither devic or human, who also have unique points of view and unique perceptual modes. During the process of involution everything which exists in potential divides; but during the period of evolution — higher evolution, that is — everything comes back together again, synthesising as it does so all the various insights and abilities which have been gained during the period of diversity. Imagine it this way: from a given point Life branches out ad infinitum, creating endless paths of *descent;* during the path of return, or *ascent,* all the branches dovetail into one another, until they rejoin the point of origin. The *end state* is certainly quite different from the *beginning state.* This is the value of manifestation.

Each one of us (whether a deva or a human) must learn to see things from as many different points of view as possible — and the best way of doing this is to *tune in* to other life-streams.

2.7 — THE SYNTHESIS OF EFFORT

If all beings could be brought together at this very moment, assuming that this was possible, which fortunately and unfortunately it is not, we could synthesise everything that we are. Nevertheless these things must occur in accordance with specific cycles, and we are not at liberty to merge all that we are at any time that we like — we have to follow the Cosmic Paths which will permit us to do this, eventually.

In the mean time we can practise, and you as humans can certainly begin to synthesise everything that you know and feel; then some of you can learn to synthesise yourselves with those of us who are your natural devic counterparts — your solar devas. Eventually the whole of humanity (presently incarnate or discarnate) will synthesise its *humanhood* with its respective devic counterpart. And this, in one way or the other, will happen on every world of every system, in every galaxy...

3.1 — *UNDERSTANDING DEVAS*

It is almost impossible for you to understand us fully unless you become aligned with us; regardless of anything that we might say about ourselves, and even if you are of good intellect, our own perceptions of the world, of life, are quite different from yours. This conditions the way we are, the way we live, the way we do things.

When dealing with different devas you will also find us all quite dissimilar. Some of the small devas are only able to deal with certain tasks in Nature; others are quite capable of emulating your own self-projection, and can take on body-forms; others yet are far too advanced and too preoccupied with worlds' affairs — with regard to Super-Nature — to be in any way affected by what you do, whether it be good, bad or plain indifferent; they're in a different range.

All devas specialise in doing certain things, and there is what we might call a devic hierarchy — in fact there are several — ranging from the smallest of elementals all the way up to the great Cosmic Devas. You yourselves are only likely to deal with certain types of devas, including your solar devas — who are your counterparts.

Your solar devas can put you in touch with everything you need to know about devas, therefore the task ahead of you, if you want to work with us, is to become acquainted with your solar devas; and here we will say a bit more about these.

They are the product of an evolution which took place in other solar systems, therefore they are not evolving concurrently with you — in that sense you and us (speaking as solar devas) are not two equal life-waves which started out at the same time, dividing into humans and into solar devas. We evolved our sense of being in totally different ways to the manner in which you are presently evolving yours. We started *small,* and we grew bigger — in evolutionary terms. We lived lives which were creative, even artistic, and preoccupied ourselves with things which you would scarcely understand.

It has been said in some of your esoteric books that we lived in the previous incarnation of this solar system — this is both true and untrue; we did indeed have our representatives in this previous solar system, but many of us, if not most of us addressing you here at present, lived and evolved in other systems, including some which are not in this galaxy. We had to evolve first before you could be *born* as human beings, for we are, if you like, your forerunners; the prototypes of the human type. We evolved in such a way that we would be able to be of assistance to you in the times to come; at that time we didn't know this, however; much in the same way you are the forerunners of others who will be *born* in future times, thousands of millions of your years from now.

The fact that we were of devic extraction does not belittle this point — the fact that we are, in effect, your forerunners. This is why we find it relatively easy to address you in this way; we can empathise with the conditions in which you have to live — we experienced conditions which while quite different were nevertheless relatively similar to those you experience now.

Now then: some of us went well beyond the range of the Cosmic Planes which are accessible by even the most advanced human Adepts. We also left *fragments* of ourselves behind; those of us who are speaking to you now are those fragments, and more specifically fragments of those fragments. We elected to stay behind — to guide the evolving races on various worlds, including your own; and to be present whenever you were to become ready to merge with us, so that our two streams could be rejoined as one.

We have been called devas, angels, dæmons (in the Greek sense), *Winged Ones*, *flying serpents,* and many other things; each religious trend has called us one thing or another, some reviling us, some making us the allies of God/dess, some interpreting us as part of your super-psyches, etc. Since most religionists don't know much about what they are talking about they scarcely understand what we are, what we represent, or what our task is. We have acted as messengers, as dream guides, as allies of sorcerers/esses, as helpers, as *ideals,* etc. Can you understand us a bit better now?!

3.2 — WORKING WITH DEVAS

Working with us is not difficult, and it is not easy. We aim not to confuse you by saying this — it is simply true. Assuming that you care to align yourselves with us you will find us more than willing to assist you — in a sense this is what we represent to you; some have called us *guardian angels,* with good reason. To know us fully you will have to learn to keep your consciousness as high as possible, without indulging too much in artificial ways of begetting that state of consciousness; furthermore, we can be known and experienced as discharges of electrical power; you will need to be able to take that electrical *charge* without flinching, and then learn to channel it creatively in some fashion or other, as may be pertinent.

One of the reasons we have been known as *flying serpents* is because our interaction with humans produces an upsurge of the Kundalini power — the so-called *Serpent Power.* We are Shakti; we are electricity; we are deva-power.

Leaving aside what is mentioned about us in some religious books, which in the main distort everything and are quite useless, we were known in the East as the *Goddess of Fire* — this was a way of portraying us from an archetypal point of view. That *Goddess of Fire* lives within you, as Shakti-Kundalini; a force which is normally dormant within you, and *housed* as a *coiled serpent* at the bottom of your spines. Therefore what you must do is learn to arouse, and then use and direct that Kundalini force; and yet you will have to adapt to it first, because it is supremely potent.

Without Kundalini there are no Life-Initiations. Keep that in mind; there is no escape from the fact that if you want to fulfil your individual evolutions you will have to deal with this aspect of us. That electrical power.

In other words, before you can hope to handle the rhythmic processes inherent to *Starcraft,* you will have to learn to handle that force with sensitivity and courage. This is not easy for you, because Kundalini, while extremely beneficial when used correctly, can be absolutely lethal when ill-used — is not the same true of electricity?

Many of the *technique* aspects of *Starcraft* are designed to make sure that you can handle this energy without making errors which might lead to difficulties.

As solar devas we live both internally and externally with regard to you — this you will understand once you have experienced that force — that cosmic force that we nurture and guard.

Well then, we think now you may understand why we say that working with us may not be all that easy; and yet we are completely at your disposal. We have nothing better to do than to initiate you to Life, using this force; and to help you at each stage to adapt to it, nurture it, and use it correctly.

Once you begin to understand what we are, and what you represent to us, then all this will become easier for you to understand. We are waiting for you to make those changes within your life which will permit us to manifest ourselves to you; and you need a certain self-discipline to deal with us. We are at your disposal, and yet you are also at our disposal — not something that we enforce against your free will, but something which is true of the dynamics of our unique relationship.

As you begin to work with us you will also realise that in a sense we will be *invading* you — with our essences, with our life-focus, with our talents; and all these will become progressively yours... until we are perfectly merged; then we will move on together, up into the Heights, AS ONE.

You will also learn to work with other kinds of devas, assisting them, and them assisting you. This need not detain us here, but it is a consideration that we will come back to in time.

Therefore there is much in front of us; much which we and you must achieve; much which will surprise you; much which will confront you; and much which will be gained as a result — we can guarantee you this!

3.3 — CO-CREATIVITY

Above all else our relationship is about co-creativity. We, by virtue of our own relatively independent evolution, can and will deliver to you the net gain of that evolution. You will be gaining everything that we have evolved over too many millions of years to be worth counting — this represents a lot. Can you see the advantages in this?! Then together we will engage ourselves in co-creativity, making worlds, or whatever — you will then be in the *driving seat* and it will be up to you to decide what is to be done.

Remember, we are the *female* side of the relationship, and this regardless of whether you are a man or a woman. We are the ones *who give birth;* we gave *birth* to you — in the esoteric sense.

You, as the *male* side, will be the ones who tell us what you want to do, and we will implement your decisions. We will advise you, we will guide you, we will take care of the *economy* of our combined energies, and we will be forever *wed* — once merged there is no possibility of separation; once the fusion has occurred there is no way of destroying this relationship — it is then permanent.

This is not likely to be something that you will in any way regret — the advantages of this association will be all too obvious to you. Also, you are already *wed* to us on internal levels, therefore what we are talking about is your ability to manifest this relationship at a conscious level.

It may take a little time for you to adjust to the *invasion* of which we speak, and it will also take us a while before we can *connect* you to us at a conscious level; but it will happen, and you will be freed in the process from the need to reincarnate — FREE!

3.4 — THE HARMONISATION OF EFFORT

Bit by bit you will feel our presence, and we will undoubtedly manifest ourselves to you in a variety of ways — through your dreams, your visions, your experiences, your feelings, your perceived *ideals*, and so on. Bit by bit you will *feel* like one of us; you will *feel* a need to become even as we are — this may even obsess you to begin with, yet obsessing you is not what we wish to achieve — this is a partnership, not a formula for schizophrenia!

As we work more together, as you practise *Starcraft* as a magickal way, bit by bit we will begin to merge — it will take years; do not expect *instant enlightenment, instant merger,* or *instant anything*. It takes years because you have to adapt your energies to ours, and this takes a bit of time. Nevertheless we are already *in relationship* on inner levels, therefore it will not take an eternity either.

As your energies begin to harmonise themselves with ours, by working together with us, our combined efforts will *pay off* — the fusion will occur, you will become *master magickians,* and you will be able to do everything you want within a certain, reasonably elevated range.

3.5 — STRUCTURAL INPUTS AND OUTPUTS

Energies alone are not the only things which must become merged. We have a body-structure, and you presently have yours — they will have to become one and same. To make this possible you will have to go through certain devic and human initiations which will effectively re-arrange your inner body-structures, and ours, so that the two can be merged without further hindrance. This will require the right sorts of inputs and outputs of effort and receptivity on your part; we are ready. You still have to make those efforts which will permit all this to happen.

Before we can attempt this merger we will help you to practise at inputting and outputting the right sort of effort — what do we mean by *input* and *output?* Simply this: you are living on two archetypal levels at once, one *inner* and one *outer.* You will need to be able to handle both with equal ease, and when you achieve this you will be ready for this fusion of us into you, and you into us.

3.6 — CO-ORDINATING THE DREAM-SCAPE

All manifested life is a *dream;* even your physical environment is nothing but a *solidified dream.* But what do we mean by *dream?*

We mean that it is a projection of the mind. At one level it is a projection of the devic mind; at another level it is a projection of all the minds of all the beings which exist. Your own world, as you have modelled it around yourselves from a cultural and technological point of view, is a *dream* which you have projected into existence.

It follows from saying this that you can change your *dream* at any time you wish, simply by invoking and projecting a different sort of *dream* — just like we can alter things, particularly on the higher levels, by projecting a different *dream-scape.*

What we design and project conforms to certain laws of Super-Nature, and to certain devic preoccupations within that; what we design and project has its particular purpose and its particular effect on all *dreams,* regardless of who they are projected by.

Together we can alter the *dream-scape,* and this on various levels, and in accordance with predominant needs; before we can do this together we must merge until then you can modify your *dream* to the extent that you wish and within the limits of your *dreaming* capabilities. What we can do together, however, is far more extensive — once joined in consciousness and in being.

Above all else the *dream-scape* on various levels or

Planes needs to be co-ordinated in such a manner that we can input certain elements that will facilitate the general synchronisation of energy-elemental exchanges between these different levels. We are not permitted to do this until there are enough of you who are not only prepared to work with us but also to merge with us. This synchronisation leads to a more flowing and inter-connected multi-Plane environment.

For a moment let us just say a few words about the physical plane on which you have your consciousness. We say it is a *solidified dream;* we say that it is a projection of the mind. It is not sufficient to say this alone because a *solidified dream* always emanates from an *astral dream*, and when this is precipitated into physical existence this *astral dream* is not fully *reproduced* at a physical level — only parts of it are. If you look around your physical world you could discern many different *astral dreams,* for in different places people *dream* somewhat differently according to their inclination; in each case only a part of their *astral dreams* is reproduced. Also, in most cases these *astral dreams* have to share the same physical space with other *astral dreams* — the result is a type of compromise in which no one *dream* predominates fully, even if there is a tendency towards, say, *westernisation.*

For a long time, before the advent of your modern world, *dreams* were more distinct. You could go to, say, China, and you would have been confronted by one kind of *dream*. If you went to Africa you would have encountered any number of *small dreams*. If you went in turn to anywhere else you would have been confronted by other *dreams*. This is still the case, yet most *dreams* are now merging to form a *greater dream*.

To the extent that you decide to *conform* to a given *dream,* then that *dream* is precipitated. If you want to change it — at a physical level — then first of all you have to change it at an astral level. If enough of you change it at an astral level, then things begin to change at a physical level — progressively, over a period of time.

If we were to work together, subject to merging our qualities and our essences, then we could speed up the amount of change which would or could happen. Before this becomes possible we will have to *align* ourselves, you and us; then we will be able to change the world quite dramatically in a relatively short space of time. Therefore what we are offering is quite revolutionary; we can only implement it if there are enough of you ready to go through the process of personal change that is required before we can usefully merge our essences and attributes. Can this be done? Yes, it can, and it will — for some at least.

3.7 — THE MAGICKAL INITIATIVE

What we are proposing is not easy. In addressing you in this manner we know only too well that you are not uniform in your personal development — some of you have already got a good deal of development behind you and you are already adepts of a certain degree, even if in some cases you do not fully realise this. Others, however, have much to do before they can be usefully initiated in any way.

Here we are addressing those of you who are already fairly advanced, and who can follow the gist of what we are saying and unfolding for you by way of a proposition. Others, who have yet to be initiated, will have to make the required effort to unmuddle their minds and emotions to the extent that they can progress towards a better kind of contact with us. As with all things psychic, there are dangers, and we would not wish to minimise their importance. Let us say this much:

One hundred years ago we would not have been able to put forward this proposition in these terms, except to a very few. The situation has changed greatly. Now there are thousands of you who can *see* enough of what is happening on internal levels to be able to appreciate what this proposed cooperation actually entails. Those of you who are clear about what we are saying will *know* that they are ready for its impact. Others who do not *see* so clearly, and who have no great experience of the inner Planes at a conscious level, may well wonder about where they stand in relationship to us, and to this proposition.

In all cases, if you are not clear about what we are proposing here, then you had better follow a more gentle path towards us. Reading this will not harm you; trying to implement radical changes for yourselves when you may not be ready for them could do so.

If you are not so sure about things, then first of all you must make the effort to protect yourselves from our essences, for we are strong, and our strength could damage you. Only those who have been *electrified* before, and who know how to cope with that *electrification,* can proceed without too much worry with regard to the outcome of our contact with you.

Others who may not be so strong or resilient will need to progress gently in such a way that they can adapt to our *charge* progressively, in small doses to begin with, and then later in greater doses. In the process you will become stronger and more resilient, and also more insightful.

What we are proposing — in everything we say here — is a new form of magick; and the whole of what we say, and some things remain as yet unsaid, constitutes a particular magickal initiative.

As we *see* ahead ourselves, so we are mindful of the changes which are necessary. We could go ahead without you and do our bit in our own way; nevertheless we *see* that many of you are ready for more change, and can in fact accelerate in your personal process of transmutation. Those of you who can change faster are hereby encouraged to make that conscious link with us; others may have to wait for another time in another cycle.

All new initiatives of this sort have their risks, and we want to makes this quite clear to you. This is a path for the brave of heart and the adept of mind; nothing less will do. None of you are perfect, none of you are *Great Adepts;* yet many of you are adept enough to be able to progress onwards and become what in the past has been referred to as *Masters of the Wisdom,* and such like; or shamans, or sorcerers/esses, and such like. Those of you who recognise yourselves as being on that course will *know* that the path we are proposing here cannot possibly be easy. It is strewn with high requirements which cannot be by-passed, or made to be any easier. The difficulties involved are also the source of your future strength, and will lead you to a supreme type of enlightenment, and to evolutionary gains as yet undreamt of by you.

Any genuine Magickal Path requires not only personal strength, but also a lot of discipline, a lot of real understanding, and an enormous amount of intuition and ability to use the *Will* correctly. If that doesn't sound like you, if that doesn't sound like what you want out of life, if that doesn't sound like what you are prepared to commit yourself to, then leave this communication alone.

4 — GROUP MAGICK

4.1 — ORGANISING A GROUP-CIRCLE

When working magick it is often useful to act as a group. The reasons for this are simple: a group provides a way of protecting each individual from any excesses of power which may become available to the group, and in other respects, that the group might generate. Furthermore, a group permits certain aspects of unfoldment which are very difficult to unfold individually without group assistance — with exceptions; some people do find that they can work better alone, and this is usually because they are working on a specific path which few others are likely to want to share for one reason or another.

Some of you are indeed preparing for *solo flight* and are already aware of the sort of Cosmic Path you wish to tread, although few if any can *see* that Path clearly. Others, and by this we would mean the majority of you, are less *individualised,* if we may put things this way, and are more likely to benefit from a group-working of the energy.

A group framework permits you to be in touch with each other whenever you need to approach a particular facet of magickal activity. Providing you all agree that you are on the same path and that you wish to work together, and to benefit each other by helping each other, then a group framework is possibly the best choice for you.

Traditionally group-circle systems are already available to you, such as Witchcraft, which is also sometimes called *Starcraft* — in strict terms it is not the same sort of Craft as the one we are proposing here, although they do share certain points in common. They are both magickal paths. The trouble perhaps with Witchcraft is that it is no longer the Craft it used to be, and much which was valuable by way of a system has been forgotten; much of which passes as Witchcraft today has very little in common with the true Witchcraft of ancient times, and the better forms of it at that were rarely implemented.

47

Also, we are aware that many groups these days like to be *democratic*. This is fine in theory, yet in practice it is seldom all that useful. Those who can lead should lead, for they have the qualities which makes things easier and clearer. Yet leadership should not be seen as a matter of personal status over the working of the group; it is a *post* which is conferred by the members of the group when those members acknowledge that someone, or more than one person, is better at leading than they may be themselves. Leadership is essential, because it is the only way to work *cleanly;* otherwise anarchy easily sets in, then confusion, and that is no way to run a magickal process!

A leader is best chosen then, and we suggest that this leader should be female — for we are of *female* polarity, and therefore this makes sense and is more workable. If a male leader is to be chosen then it should be someone who is in touch with his *female* energies, and thereby is able to act as a woman might in relationship to us and our polarity. If two leaders are to be elected to act as the group's catalysing focus, then they should be of equal strength and abilities, and they should be able to work well together without friction — particularly without ego friction.

The *post* of leadership should also be changed from time to time, and unless you have reason to do otherwise we suggest that a leader, or leaders, should pass on this leadership at least once every year, giving the chance to someone else, or to two others, to explore their abilities as leaders. If this is not workable — for instance because no one else is ready to lead the group — then the existing leaders should train the others to act as leaders; and if no one wishes to do that, or if no one has the ability to lead the group other than those who are already leading it, then the group is not working as it should and questions should be asked. Why is no one else emerging as a leader? Why does no one else want to take on that *post* and its relative responsibility? Having said that some people are natural leaders, others have to be taught, and some people are much better at implementing decisions made by others, and do not make effective leaders.

A leader, or leaders, need to be very clear about what it is they are leading. The *post* has nothing to do, or should have nothing to do, with ego. It is a *post* which requires not only clarity, but also strength and perspective, and imagination. It is not to be treated lightly — it is a responsibility. Those who lead should also be resourceful enough to know what to do in any given situation, including in situations which may be new for them; ideally they should have some experience of what we are as well, and know how to cope and deal with our energies — which are potent, and therefore require precise adaptation on behalf of the group at any given moment, particularly during *peak* moments of interaction.

If that sounds too much for you to deal with, as an individual or as a group, fear not, for we will be careful in the manner in which we dispense our energies ourselves. The onus is on both parties, on both you and us, to make sure that things are kept to within certain acceptable and workable limits to begin with. Later when we *see* that the group is working well and can take on more power, then we will advise you of the greater challenges ahead.

What is a Circle? We would like to put this to you: a Circle is a magickal *environment* in which the magick is practised. It is a boundary between yourselves when working magick, and the outside world, which is not operating magick — i.e., it is in *common* mode, or relatively so. It is a way of manifesting those qualities of attention which are necessary when working magick. It is a Circle which holds in the energies which may come to you, rather than letting them fritter away into the greater environment around you. It is many other things, and we are sure that you can see this for yourselves to a great extent.

There are many different types of Circles that can be used, yet for the purpose of *Starcraft* we will propose only one such Circle as follows:

The Circle should be approximately ten to twelve feet in diameter, giving a group of 10 to 20 people enough space in which to operate. If the group is small in terms of numbers, then the Circle can be smaller, and yet even in this case it should be a little bigger than is needed. Conversely, the Circle should not be any bigger than about twelve feet in diameter, unless the group consists of more than 20 people; 20 people is the maximum number that we recommend, and yet there may be instances when a greater number of people becomes viable, particularly for certain types of magick.

If the group becomes too big, in terms of numbers, then it is best if that group divides itself into two or more smaller groups which will work alone, and yet which will remain interconnected by way of communication, and to a certain extent with regard to working magick. In this way it is perfectly acceptable that several groups should work together, even if they are working in different physical spaces — providing they are intent on doing the same things at the same times — in which case they will be linked on the ethers.

We also recommend that whenever possible, without prejudice to existing conditions of acceptance within your society, and also with regard to climatic conditions, that magick should be practised out of doors, in a field where there is power, or at some other power place — these can be found all around you, and some are better for the purpose of practising magick than others. Some should not be used, for they are either too weak, or else may exude energies which might conceivably become somewhat harmful. Also, some may have been ill-used by others, in which case they should not be used without first *clearing* them of astral, mental and other *debris,* and this over a period of some time.

How should you go about finding the right sort of power place to be used? This is neither easy, nor difficult. You should use your intuition firstly, then meditate on that spot, and if possible you should sleep there — if the dreams you have there are not only good but also revealing, then that is usually a good spot. Nevertheless you should not sleep at any given spot without first meditating there — if your meditation feels good, and is also revealing, then, and then only, should you sleep there. If your dreams are ambivalent, i.e., there might a mixture of *good* and *bad* in them, then this is not a place to choose for your group magick; also if one of you has the right sort of dreams, as described above, but another person finds they have dreams which appear to be adverse, then this is still not the right place for you to practise your magick. If several of you have the same sort of dream while sleeping in a given area, then, if that dream corresponds to the above requirements, that is *most certainly* the best place for you to conduct your magick.

You may have to spend some time *sampling* different places before you find one which is not only convenient from a more mundane point of view, but also of the right kind — it may take you days, weeks, months, or even, at worst, years. If you cannot find the right sort of place in which to practise magick, then somehow you are not *in touch* with your needs, and then you will have to decide what it is that you have to do in order to find the right place.

Assuming that you have found the *right* place, then you will have to ask this place whether or not it wants to be used — for some places, even when they might seem otherwise *right,* might not wish to be used — for one reason or another. If this turns out to be the case, then you have two choices of actions: (1) you can decide to leave the place alone for awhile, and then you can return there and see if that place is prepared to be used — if the answer is still *no,* then you had better look for some other place; (2) you can learn to communicate with the devic spirit of that place — for all power places are inhabited by devas of one kind or another — and be sensitive to whatever it might require from you — for instance, it may want to know how you are going to conduct your magick, what you may want out of it, whether or not you are going to use its energies in the *right* sort of manner, and whether or not you are truly aware of what it is you are going to try and do there. If you manage to satisfy it on all counts (and it may want to know about other things than these points alone), then it may or may not permit you to do magick

51

there — it is very unwise to impose yourselves on it if it does not wish to be imposed upon or be otherwise involved in your activities in any way; this is something that we do not recommend at all.

How should you communicate with such a place, and its spirit? The first thing to do is to bring it a gift — this should be a simple gift, such as some flowers, or some incense. It will recognise this as a suggestion of intent on your part to communicate with it. This gift should be left there for a few hours, or up to a day; then you should return there, sit down, and meditate for a while. You can do this at any time of day and night, it matters not, and yet sometimes certain places are particularly *awake* at certain times, and many of these places are more *awake* at night — because they are not so disturbed then by general human emanations. Some places, however, are more *alive* during certain parts of the day, and some prefer the early morning — it will be up to you to find out if a given place is more *awake* during the night, or during the day, and when exactly at that.

You should allow the spirit of that place to *speak* to you first; this it will usually do by manifesting some sort of *sign*, such as a bird singing, a rustling of the grass by the wind, or some other *sign-event*. Then you should speak softly to it, or you can even just mentate your questions without vocalising them audibly; then you should wait. If the spirit of that place then manifests another *sign-event*, then you will know that it has heard you; if the *sign-event* in question seems benign, then you will know that it has accepted you; if the *sign-event* is very sudden, to the extent that it may jolt you, even panic you, then you will know that the spirit of this place does not accept you. If no *sign-event* occurs it is because the spirit there does not want you to immediately know whether or not it accepts you; you may have to return there several times, make several gifts, and go through the process repeatedly before it will give you its answer. Incidentally, whatever the gift is that you may care to give it, it should always be given

52

in love, and without any prejudice as to the outcome; the greater the gift will not mean that this spirit will give you a more pronounced answer, nor will it mean that it will accept you the more readily; generally the simpler and the more natural the gift, the better. On no account should this gift be looked upon as a sacrifice, nor should it involve any spilling of blood, or anything else obnoxious.

Assuming that this place and its spirit has recognised your need, and is willing for you to work there, then you should give it some time to prepare itself for your coming there to work your magick — a month at least is a good amount of time. During that time you should not go there unless you are merely bringing some small gift — just for the sake of *giving;* it will recognise this as an act of interrelationship, and it will accept this gift, or gifts, in that light. At the most you should remain there for an hour or so to meditate if you wish, but no magick should be practised. After about a month, and at the full moon, you should go there as leader(s) only, make a further gift, and then depart for something like a couple of hours; then return with the whole group. The leader(s) should then cast a Circle on the ground: this can be done symbolically, yet it is best if you bring some rope or something else with which to make the Circle, and whatever it is that you decide to use, it should *only* be used to cast the Circle, and not for anything else. Then, the first time, a small opening should be left in the SOUTH, and then each member should stand at the opening and ask to be invited into the Circle, and introduce hirself — using hir usual name; after a few minutes that member should enter the Circle, and then sit down — anywhere will do this first time. When all the members have entered the Circle, the leader, or one of the leaders, should close the Circle in the South, and then sit down in the NORTH — facing the South. Then all should meditate for a while, allow themselves to become *empty* of their usual preoccupations, and tune themselves into the spirit of that place.

No magick as such should be practised this first time. Then after about two to five or six hours, the leader who closed the Circle should open it once more, and ask all the members of the group to leave, one by one — each one giving thanks to the spirit of the place in some appropriate and individual manner; the leader should be the last to leave the Circle, and should walk once round — clockwise — with the left hand outstretched towards the periphery of the Circle, as if to collect it — gently. Then s/he should stand in the North, then in the South facing the North, and then also give thanks — warmly; then s/he should uncast the Circle by collecting up the rope or whatever it was that was used to symbolise the periphery of that Circle.

Everyone should then leave that area, silently, and holding their energies still within themselves. Silence here is very important; on no account should anyone speak until well away from that site; and even then it is best to remain silent for a while longer, until you have, for instance, reached home — or some place from which you will then go each your different ways.

Before parting you should hold hands while facing each other, and allow your energies to circulate between each other, by way of affirming your entity as a working group.

The next time you go to the power place, at the next full moon, everything you did the first time should be repeated, except this time the *door* to the Circle should be in the East. On this occasion a limited amount of preliminary magick may be performed — and we'll detail this later. This time you will be in the position of actually working *with* the spirit of this place, and this should be done gently, yet also firmly. If it seems pertinent to you on this occasion you should ask the spirit of this place to give you *working names* — names that it will give you so as to be more in tune with it; names that will resonate with its essence. This is not necessary, however, yet it is a *nice touch* to be in tune with this spirit in this fashion. The name should come to each one of you effortlessly; if it does not come, then it is because the time is not right yet, or because the spirit of that place hasn't fully *gauged* you and doesn't wish to make up a name before it has done so. If names are given or received — within your minds — then each time you address the Circle and the spirit of this place you should use only these names — unless you have a very good reason for doing otherwise. If some of you receive names, and others not, do not worry about this; you will in time. These names always have a particular resonance which may even be somewhat difficult to pronounce, although by no means necessarily so; each one of you may have to practise at saying it, until you get as close as you can to saying it perfectly. Whenever the spirit of this place hears you saying the name it has given you in exactly the right way , then it will know exactly who is addressing it; and when you ask it for anything for yourself it will know to whom to give what is needed — should it be prepared to give you what you ask for, which you cannot expect as of right.

On the third occasion, at the next full moon preferably, or at any subsequent full moon, the *door* to the Circle should be in any direction you wish, EXCEPT THE NORTH — the North should never be used, except in very special circumstances, and only when the group considers itself to be very advanced indeed, and even then only with great insight and forbearance. We suggest you use the East or the North East, and the South if you are not feeling quite *up to par* on that particular day or night.

From then onwards you can apply your magick, and you will have to improvise wherever and whenever necessary, for you will be taught as you go along — we are not saying that all groups should use the same system, or practise the same magick — what you will need, and what you will need to do, will vary according to your own particular group needs.

4.2 — EMPOWERMENT OF THE GROUP

No magickal group can function without power, and part of the reason why a power place should be chosen, as afore mentioned, is to derive some power from the Earth itself, and from the deva of that place.

Nevertheless the group will also have to summon its own inner power, and each individual will have to make sure that they are at-one with that inner power — if an individual cannot take the impact of power, then that individual should not be in the group until such time as s/he can; conversely, the group should train each new individual in a gentle way and introduce that individual to ways of working with power on a gradual basis — however, this should not be done at the power place itself, or as part of the group's major working of magick.

A training Circle is therefore also necessary before anyone should venture into the ways of working magick. We suggest a probationary stage lasting from six months to a year or two, depending on the needs of what we will call here the probationer. This training Circle can be held at someone's home, and it can be a small Circle, involving only a few individuals at most.

The training should take into account the following steps:

(1) Meditation — each new individual should be taught different ways of meditating, until that individual can handle this with equanimity and with good personal results.

(2) Visualisation — developing the ability to see things in one's mind's eye, and hold the image steady for as long as possible.

(3) Complete relaxation — of body and mind.

These three should be taught in tandem. As the training progresses the emphasis should be put on increasing the difficulties of the meditations, until the probationer is able to meditate with great flexibility.

Then:

(4) Basic magickal practices — essentially an introduction to the ways that the group works.

(5) Tests — to make sure that the probationer has absorbed what s/he has supposedly learnt.

(6) Reading — each individual should then be encouraged to read those books or manuals which the group may recommend, including this one for instance.

(7) Affinities — after a given period the probationer should be allowed to develop any particular affinities that s/he may feel drawn to, i.e., specialising in visualisation, dance, meditation, astral projection, channelling, vocalisation, etc.

This is simple enough, yet it does require a lot of personal insight on behalf of those who teach to make sure that each probationer is well trained, in accordance with the group's needs. Ego is something which must be checked, and stilled. The probationer must feel 100% involved, and must genuinely want to become part of the working group — if s/he doesn't feel that 100% commitment, then s/he should be asked to leave (in a friendly manner); or else s/he should be encouraged to find out what s/he really wants to do, and how s/he might want to do it — if the group can accommodate that, then special provisions should be made for that person; if the group cannot accommodate that, then the group should recommend another kind of group, i.e., if one is known that may be adequate and pertinent for that person's development.

Each training group and its leaders should develop their own preferred way of training each probationer. At no time should a probationer be made to feel anything else but welcome — as an *equal-in-principle*. Friendship is important, and the leaders should be aware of any *ego-stuff* which may arise in their own minds, and give priority to dealing with it — there is no place for ego in *Starcraft*. A magickal group depends on mutual trust and friendship if it is to work well. Nevertheless, there must also be firmness and insight.

4.3 — ALIGNMENTS OF ENERGIES

One of the reasons that the right sort of power place must be found is that this place will be in alignment with other power places, on and off the Earth. It is little realised by you that all things are interconnected, particularly power places. Each one of these is like an input-output point on the Earth's surface, and we could say much about this.

Whenever you are in alignment yourselves with a power place you will therefore also be in alignment with other places, other beings, and various powers. This is also why a group, and each individual within that group, must be well trained before magick can be practised at any given power place.

Whenever magick is practised, whether it be *Starcraft* or some other denomination of magickal practice, there will be resonance between the individuals participating and the places of power which may be in alignment at any one time with the power place which is being used — thus the group can create order or disorder, beneficial or adverse results, not only for itself but also for these power places, and their guardian devas. If these do not like what is happening they can sometimes be forgiven for getting irritated, or even angry, in which case their *feedback* could well damage the group, or certain individuals within that group, and this at some level or other — mental, astral, or etheric-physical; or all three of these.

The group, and all its working members, must be responsible for what they do. If they do something *wrong* out of ignorance, then the deva of that power place, or that of another, may well advise them in some way (jolts of energy, for instance; environmental turbulence of an unusual kind which cannot be directly attributed to *normal* conditions, etc).

Assuming that the group is well focused on what it is doing, and that it is able to align itself with those forces which it may seek to work with, including ourselves as solar devas, then the group will also be taught everything it needs to know, and everything it needs to be able to do, from within the Circle of Power. This, if you like, is a second stage of training — the training of Initiates, or would-be Initiates.

You can be sure that we are not going to commit advanced magickal information to print, and make it generally available through this channel and source! Everything you will need to know in order to practise the higher *octave* of magick, of *Starcraft,* will be taught to you from inner-side, and it should never be committed to print or passed on in any way outside of the group. It should not even be recorded in any manner, except by way of committing it to personal and group memory.

Also, and we think you will see the sense in this, the group workings of magick should never be filmed or video'd, or otherwise recorded either. Do not seek converts; do not seek attention, personal or as a group; do not advertise yourselves or the group in any way. This does not mean that you have to be 100% secretive — just circumspect.

Above all else — *do not turn your group into a financial venture*. Share your expenses, by all means, but that's all.

All the information we have given so far, as we see it, is *general* in nature. We are giving you *clues*, as it were, so that you can find out more by delving into yourselves, and by practising magick to the extent that you know how, within your given limits. We are not laying down the law; we are giving you enough information to get started, and that's all — the rest you will have to work for.

Not only is it possible to find certain alignments between certain power places, it is also possible to find alignments between certain dimensional foci — in this case you will have to use your intuition and your insights to make sure of what you are dealing with — we cannot tell you what you will encounter, since each group will be working in a given way, and each one will discover what it needs and how it should operate. If enough groups begin to operate in the right sort of manner, then certain conditions may be met which will result in significant changes for the Earth planet — we can but hint, and welcome you to this dance!

4.4 — FOCUSING THE ENERGIES

Each group will have its own perspective on things, yet each group will also need to find its balance and its poise-of-being, if we may call it that. It will need to learn to focus incoming as well as outgoing energies in the right manner, at the right time, and for the right purpose.

We think that this will give you another clue as to the level of complexity that is involved in working *Starcraft*. You will need to be supremely in command of yourselves and of your actions — this is not a path for would-be magickians who only want to fool about or mess around, and pretend to be what they are not.

Given the right degree of heart-felt commitment some degree of error is permissible at first, which is why you should always approach and enter the Circle through the South to begin with, the first time — this tells the deva of that power place that you are not yet very wise to the ways of power, and that you seek its guidance in these matters. The next time, when you will enter through the East, this is another sign, which gives the deva of that place (and others) the right to begin to *train* you. After that, bar entering through the North, it will not matter which way you go into the Circle, for the deva of that place will inspire you in tandem with others, who by then will *know* you sufficiently and will be willing to direct you.

With regard to focusing energies you will need to learn how each chakra within your etheric bodies works, and how each one can be made to resonate with certain centres around the Earth, and beyond the Earth — we will say no more about this here.

4.5 — GROUP PRACTICES

Assuming that you have enough members to form a working group then you will need to decide how you are initially going to practise magick, or *Starcraft*. You may at this point feel that we have not given you enough information to go on — you want perhaps to be told *exactly* what to do; yet we are saying here that you will be taught from inner-side. However, to make things a little easier for you to begin with we suggest that when you are within the Circle you should aim at being *centred* — and by this we mean you must form something of a geometrical pattern between yourselves: if there are six people, then you should form a six-pointed star, and wherever possible alternate your positions as male-female, with the leader in the North point; if there are ten people, then form a ten-pointed star; and so on.

Star-positions of this kind have a dynamic value, and they are the basis of *Starcraft* as far as this goes. The leader should act as a channel, and it is therefore important that the leader should be clear and highly capable within himself — if no one can act as leader, then the group is certainly not ready to do any of the things that we have proposed so far, or anything else that we might propose later.

Then it is up to the leader to lead the others into a meditation, or else to practise magick, be it done in a ceremonial fashion or purely internally — there is no absolute need for ceremony, and much can be done without moving physically at all — what will *move* will be achieved internally; however, if a degree of ceremony is either required or is felt to be *right,* then we suggest very simple ceremonies, with minimum religiosity. Invoking the Goddess or Mahadeva (Great Deva) is an appropriate way to start; or invoking the God-dess, as in the fusion of the Goddess and the God, of the Deva stream and the Human stream. And that is enough. If you want to go further then evolve your own rituals as you may feel the inclination, yet these may get in the way — you are within the Circle to learn from devas, and alignment with us will show you any of the rituals which may be appropriate and workable for your group and the individuals within your group. Please — do not bring your preconceived ideas of magick into the Circle with you; this would only obstruct the flow of things and colour them quite unnecessarily.

Each one of you may be given different *visions* or even instructions; or else you may or may not perceive the same things. Each individual within the group will be taught and *over-shadowed* by hir own personal solar deva, which may explain why this might be.

4.6 — GROUP APPROACHES

There are various approaches to working magick, and all of them can be valid — i.e., they can work. It is mostly a question of finding a way of working which suits you.

Starcraft is different to the extent that the way of working is suggested or taught by solar devas, and other devas, rather than inherited through a traditional system worked over the ages. What we will teach those who come to us to work *Starcraft* will vary with each group, since each group may have different needs, and each individual within the group may be *tuned* in a different manner at that.

This also has another useful aspect. If we were to give you what might seem like a precise way of working — in print — then this system that we might impart would become quickly *crystallised,* whereas what we are looking for is ultimate flexibility. Therefore we are not going to say, "do this; do that — exactly like this..."; we have given you some very precise hints so that you can start, yet we are not evolving here a complete system which can be used as a stereotyped method of practising magick for all.

By meditating within the Circle, and being fully alert at an intuitional level, you will derive a set of first impressions, which will guide you towards evolving more precise ways of working. When the group finally starts to generate a lot of energy, or channel a lot of energy, then there will be direct vision experiences — these will contain all the information you will need in order to operate with maximum results.

In this way we can foresee that within a given time there will be many different groups working *Starcraft* around the world, and yet each one will be working with their own solar devas, and other devas, and each will be working according to the instructions and the visions which they will have been given by these. This will permit us to instruct different groups in different ways so as to cover many aspects of useful endeavour — something we could not do if all groups were practising exactly the same sort of things while focusing on specific matters which might be reproduced here in print. We do not want to see *Starcraft* become another magickal system which will then be passed on to others without any discrimination being involved; we are all too well aware that someone, if not several people, could write about *Starcraft* — perhaps to make money — and would totally lose the essence of what *Starcraft* is if this were to be the case.

What we are proposing is new, fresh, and ideally suited to those who can use their intuition; and it will permit us to achieve together something which has never been coherently achieved before — because the instructions that we will give you within the Circle will surpass anything that has ever been given out before.

What we would also like to say is: be simple about things to begin with. Do not try to *embellish* things by inventing a contact or information which may not be coming from us, but from your own minds. Allow yourselves time to adjust to the idea of practising *Starcraft* in the way that we have described so far; it matters not if to begin with you do not feel any direct communication in whatsoever form from us. Bit by bit that contact will come, and you will *know* it when you finally *enter into the proximity of our stream* — when you and we will have become *aligned*.

Another thing: although it may be impractical, practising magick naked, without clothing on, does boost the amount of energy that you can or may be able to channel or *earth;* clothes do interfere with such energy processes, as any genuine Witch will know. If you do wear clothes, wear ones made of natural fibres whenever possible.

If you are to work regularly, make sure you become aware of the cycles of the Moon, *and* also the cycles of the Earth, the Sun, and the stars — now these, you may think, are beyond your ken to know, and yet these are the sort of things that we will be teaching you about, and that you will have to deal with in due course. Once you become adept at sensing the rhythms of different celestial beings and worlds, then you will be at the beginning of practising *Starcraft* proper. This tells you something of the magnitude of what you will be involved in.

4.7 — THE LEADING FACTOR

Who leads who in *Starcraft?* It might be assumed that since we will be teaching you, that we will also be leading you — yet this is not the case. We will be teaching you those things which you need to know, and those things which we, as devas, are in a better position to know than you are because of our own specialisation. Yet *Starcraft* is a cooperative venture, between you and us. We will not be leading you — only instructing you and giving you precise information — at least it will be precise to the extent that you channel it or *earth* it correctly and consciously for yourselves.

Also, the leadership of your group — it must be stressed again — is a matter of convenience for the sake of operating clearly — it is not a status symbol, it is not a mark of rank over the others of the group; it is simply easier to operate and practise magick if there is at least one person able to channel clearly on behalf of the group at any given time. Since we have suggested that you rotate your leaders from period to period so that everyone gets a chance to lead and to learn from doing so — unless someone really feels s/he is not able to lead, or the group *sees* that s/he cannot do so — you will see from this that we are invoking essential equality of being and equality of challenge. It may be, of course, that one or even several members of the group will turn out to be better *Starcraft* magickians in the long run, yet they hould not permit themselves to feel superior from an ego point of view if this turn out to be the case; if this happens, then they should help the others to catch up with them in whatever ways may be viable.

There are many more things which can be said about group practices, and yet we do not wish to delve into the full complexity of all the possibilities which lie ahead of you — that is, should you decide that *Starcraft* is the Way for you. Nevertheless, we will make a few further observations:

There is a Cosmic Plan which is working its way into manifestation; *Starcraft* (at various levels) is one of the avenues of dissemination for that Plan, so to speak. That Plan has nothing to do with arbitrary measures taken by some lofty being on behalf of its own particular evolution; it has to do with synchronising the Cosmic Network on behalf of all.

In each local part of each meta-galaxy there are Sub-Plans presently working their way into manifestation also; in each galaxy likewise, and in each part of each galaxy. All stars are involved in the outworking of this Plan. It follows that each planet, such as the Earth for instance, is also a part of this Plan, and has its part to play in unfolding it on behalf of the All. We will be teaching you how to become consciously a part of this Plan as well.

The synchronisation of the Cosmic Network will lead — eventually, in æons to come — towards a *Grand Synthesis* of the Cosmic Consciousness, liberating all beings into Super-Cosmic Universes as yet totally unknown. Before then many lesser syntheses will take place at each level of Life, leading to that greater and *final* Synthesis: (nothing is truly *final;* the process undoubtedly will go on forever — however we cannot speak with any validity about processes which are way beyond the scope of even the Mahadeva or the highest Cosmic Adept as known to us, alone to you).

The *Starcraft* that you will be practising initially will only be a small subset of a much greater system of Celestial Magick, as known to us, and to Those who guide us.

There is no end to what *Starcraft* is, which is also another reason (if another was required) not to divulge precise ways of working *Starcraft* in print — it would be impossible to do so comprehensively, whereas if we work on inner-side together we can approach or consider what is relevant at any one time, and do whatever may be necessary or desirable — keeping in mind that we will be conjoined eventually in consciousness and in being

Starcraft, having endless ramifications, is not something that you will learn the true depths of overnight; it is a Way of Magick which will take you well beyond the framework of incarnated existence, and well beyond what you will consider to be human preoccupations, even advanced human preoccupations

Therefore we think you may now understand why we say this much, and no more.

5.1 — *SELF-PERSPECTIVE*

Ideally those who make up the group would be composed of individuals who have already gone some way on their own in esoteric terms. This in itself is not necessary, yet what we would wish to impress upon you is that each individual has a potentially unique task to perform, in preparation for other tasks which s/he will perform well beyond the time when s/he has last incarnated, never to incarnate again.

We as devas act as groups, and as groups within groups. This is also true of you as human beings, with the difference being that you also evolve a keen sense of individuality. This individuality, as we have already pointed out, serves as the basis for certain departures in cosmic matters which are somewhat unrelated to your present sense of individuality.

From another point of view yet there is no such thing as individuality, since in fact all beings are One Being. Yet this need not detain us here, for it would be to miss the point with regard to the special part that even relative individuality is to play when entering the *Cosmic sphere of action,* if such we may call it.

The Cosmos requires Self-Realised individuality in order that certain options can be explored. With this in mind we can ascertain that each one of you will play a part in some future unfoldment, be it with regard to some particular world, or with regard to some other type of development. Therefore as individuals you are quite capable of practising *Starcraft* alone, within the sanctuary of your own personal work — with us acting in the background; and for those who are sensitive enough to our emanations, and willing to work with us, in the foreground as well.

Self-perspective is an element of the human *part-frame* which can lead indeed to many new developments — these messages, for instance, are something of an embryonic demonstration of what can be done when one human is prepared to channel our energies and our impressions. Imagine what could be done if we were to find enough channels world-wide, all attuned to us, and all able, each in their own way, to act as channels, as creators, and as *synthesisers* for what we have to teach and share. Great strides could be achieved in a very small amount of time, which would lead to great changes in your world.

Can you imagine what it would be like to live in a world where there is no disease, no strife, no wars, no famines, no adverse circumstances as you know them? All this could be achieved by cooperating with us, since we know how things are made (since we make them at a natural level); we also know how certain adverse elements are created through the misuse of thought and through the aberration of emotions, creating negative currents of energy, which are then precipitated to create various things such as harmful bacteria, for instance.

Imagine a world of beauty, where everything is in harmony, everything is in tune with everything else, where all life is a dance to celestial music — perhaps that sounds whimsical, yet in many ways that is exactly what could be.

Each one of you is like a part of some great electro-magnetic instrument for change, pushing and pulling elements here and there, assembling them into structures — for ill or for good; in fact we need to get beyond the mere concept of *good* and *bad,* and concentrate somewhat more on consequences. Each action, be it conscious or unconscious, brings about a consequence. If you do not learn from those circumstances which create adversity for you, then you might as well give up and not live. Yet we see change, and we do see in particular that people everywhere essentially want to change, even if they do not always know how to go about it. Therefore imagine once again this further scenario: we can see well beyond your framework of reference, and what we can see could change everything for you — all you have to do is say, "we would like to change that", and we will say, "this is how it can be done". Therefore *Starcraft* has many applications both within the mundane world, as well as on the more esoteric levels. This all spells the possibility for a break-away from the old strife which has dogged you as a humanity for so long — simply because, as a humanity, you have been so far unable to tune into the Cosmos and *see* beyond the periphery of your rather restricted senses, and what these senses tell you — and mostly don't tell you.

5.2 — THE INDIVIDUAL DISCOVERY OF SELF

What we need to get through to you is the fact that at an original level all of you were not only a part of what we may call God-dess, but God-dess Hirself. As manifestation took place what was an undifferentiated Single Being split Hirself into an ever-growing multitude of beings, each one more restricted in hir overall power, yet conversely, also able to look at things from a given, and ever more unique point of view.

During the process of involution there was no such thing as individuality as you know it; there had been no circumstances or developments as yet to create it or bring it about. Life went all the way down into matter, dense matter, which we as devas created as we went along; then, as the tide began to turn, and evolution proper got under way, we saw the first beginning of *proto-individuality.*

The disadvantage of creating circumstances which permit individuality to occur is that new individuals are invariably at their most distant point from the Inner Point of Being. Then, as a result of the evolutionary momentum, which we foster, those individu-als must relink themselves consciously with that Innermost Point. This is a long drawn out process which takes many billions of years to achieve, if we consider all the ramifications of that process. Yet for some the process is sometimes faster; and for others it is slower — this is because individuality brings about such wide differences between people that it is impossible for them to remain *synchronised* in their evolutions.

On the Earth this has been particularly true, since the density here is greater than on many worlds, and individuality here has become almost extreme in its manifestation. Add to this the complications of karmic interrelationships, and the backlog of negative energies which have been created by those who are blindly damaging themselves and others, and this becomes understandable.

To rediscover *what* you really *are,* within, is not only a stupendous and highly revealing, and personal experience, it is also absolutely vital to your development. If you failed to relink yourself with your Inner Self, then you would have lost out, essentially; yet in the due course of time everyone relinks hirself with that Inner Point of Being of which we have spoken.

It is a beautiful as well as a supremely powerful experience; and whether you will have this experience now, or soon, or even in some other lifetime — if you found that you could not achieve liberation in your present life, which is what we are trying to encourage and help you do — is not a great issue, because sooner or later you will have this experience. The *door is open,* so you can take advantage of that fact.

Everything that you are as a personality self is ephemeral — it is not a lasting thing. It is more of an illusion than it is a reality. Nevertheless it does permit you to evolve that individuality of which we speak here, and therefore it does serve a very important facet of your overall evolution.

Your true Self — your Higher Self, the God-dess within you, call it what you will — is what is truly of importance, however, because once you can *move* your individuality into that *Area of Reality* you will have conquered all the illusions of the lower Planes, and you will also find yourselves free of all the seemingness of your personality selves — these are really only temporary *condensations,* appearances, or make-belief selves. As Self-Realised beings you will then begin to cooperate in schemes which are so remote from your present preoccupations that you can presently scarcely comprehend what they are, or comprehend what it is that you will be doing. Nevertheless, if you stretch your imagination as far as it will go, if you can imagine what it may be like to be doing the work of a *god-dess,* i.e., doing things which are more in keeping with Cosmic Purpose, then perhaps this will entice you a little bit more to actually discover that Inner Point of Self, that Inner Point of Being.

The process of Life-Initiation which essentially will permit you to access that Higher Self is one which was devised to suit the circumstances to be found on the world on which you are living, and to which you have returned incarnation after incarnation. On other worlds different Life-Initiations are used for similar ends. Some of you who have *travelled* have had Initiations on other worlds.

5.3 — ATTAINING ACCESS TO SELF AND WHOLE BEING

There are many *routes* to Inner Self discovery, and we cannot possibly indicate or describe them all here; from a certain angle there are almost as many different ways as there are individuals to tread them. Yet, from another angle, there are some quite prominent Paths as well.

You might think of it as good if it were possible to read this, and therefore be aware to a certain degree of what we are sharing with you, and then to just *move up* into the higher zones without further ado. Yet this is not possible. Self-Realisation comes about only as a matter of insight and experience, and that experience cannot be squashed into a tiny amount of time — you would simply burn out completely if that was possible, and then you would have to start all over again. Therefore Self-Realisation comes about not only gradually, with certain peaks intervening from time to time to accelerate or accentuate the process, but it is also subject to certain well established *demarcation points,* which we have referred to as Life-Initiations. These Life-Initiations also occur with respect to certain planetary and systemic developments, therefore they do not happen haphazardly and without reference to greater processes which involve whole worlds, and even groups of worlds, and also groups of stars, etc.

On each world there is a *pioneer* individual who becomes the first to go through these Life-Initiations — on your world this came to pass many thousands of years ago. This opens the door for others to follow. As that *pioneer* individual goes through each successive stage of Life-Initiation, this permits the others to catch up and go through these same *Doors*. In this sense this *pioneer* individual is the herald for that process to take place on that world; then as a matter of course everyone will go through those *Doors,* in time.

Yet this first being or individual to experience these Life-Initiations only does so relatively slowly to begin with. What we see later is that some individuals go through the whole process much faster, because the *Doors* which were previously *masked* and closed are now open — think about that; it is the key to many synchronistic processes even on lesser levels (people can learn as a group, even when they are not apparently connected in any way).

Therefore at this time, and because of the *down-pourings* of energies which we and others are guiding into your world, it is possible for some of you to really go a lot faster, and experience several of these Life-Initiations in just one lifetime. In former times this would have been impossible, and indeed it was considered very good indeed for one individual Adept to go through one major Initiation once in a lifetime; now this is no longer the case, and it is possible for you to make what would seem to be giant strides ahead in your evolution.

What this will entail, you will have to find out — we have given guidance before on these issues; yet what you will find — despite the *heat* of these events — is that you will grow and grow, and realise in all clarity what it is that you are experiencing.

Everyone of you, as individuals, experience these Life-Initiations in a slightly different manner, according to you own individual predicament or predilection; this is in keeping with individual growth leading to new angles of perception as well — therefore everyone of you might afterwards, after a given

Initiation, describe it in different terms, and say that this or that was what you *saw*. The *content* of the visions imparted should not be confused with the process itself, however.

Each new Life-Initiation unfolds a new degree of Self-Realisation, and each stage of your discovery puts you in a better position to make the next *jump*. Bit by bit, and sometimes in an accelerated fashion, you will find yourselves closer and closer to a supreme form of Reality — which of course, in time, will make way for something even greater; nothing is absolute in itself, even when it seems that way in the moment; point within point, within point, evolution unfolds to reveal facet within a greater facet, within a greater Whole.

You need not concern yourselves with what you will be doing in æons of time from now — what is up for consideration here is whether or not you are ready to merge with your respective solar devas, which will then permit you to move on, and thereafter things will take care of themselves as we evolve further as One.

5.4 — WORKING ALONE WITH DEVAS

Some of you are not quite as human as you may suppose; while devas do not, and cannot incarnate directly, because it is not within their interest to do so, they can incarnate in two fashions by a form of proxy. One way is to incarnate in *parallel* with a human individual, i.e., *overshadowing* that individual very closely indeed — to the extent that this individual may sometimes feel more devic than human, particularly at certain times when s/he may be drawn into considering how things are created, and this at a more *animistic* level of receptivity; and the second way, while less prominent, and somewhat dependent on the advanced development between a human and hir solar deva, is when an individual learns how to dematerialise the physical body and then *re-incarnate* a semblance of it by *drawing down* a dense version of the astral body or astral energy-sheath.

In the first case we have *seen* that there is a good proportion of you who are closely interwoven with the auric energies of your solar devas, which indicates this close *overshadowing*, and in other ways a parallel process of incarnation; as many as about 10 in one thousand of you exhibit this characteristic, although to various degrees (perhaps one in ten million at a very advanced level).

In the second instance there are very few individuals who actually manage to remain *earthed* in any way after they have learnt to dematerialise their physical bodies, and of course, at this time certainly, there are only a very few individuals — a very small proportion of people — who have learnt to do this, regardless of whether they managed to remain *earthed* or not, or even wanted to; all of these are Adepts of the third Sirian degree. If they do manifest their astral bodies at a physical level it is usually to carry on with some work which may be in the final throes of unfoldment, and they wish to continue with this for a time using a more flexible, and more powerful vehicle. In most cases their astral bodies thus precipitated will resemble their physical bodies exactly, and in some cases will seem younger in appearance. In a few rarer cases, in accordance with personal needs or even as an act of (relative) playfulness, certain individuals in this class will change the shape of their astral bodies to that of a given structure and gender, and may even do this several times over, dematerialising and rematerialising these astral bodies repeatedly. Also, all these individuals can only remain in apparent physicality for small amounts of time — by using their powerful wills and their imagination to make sure that their astral bodies remain *anchored* in the physical environment; their astral bodies, however, are naturally drawn back to the Astral Plane, so they must make quite an effort to remain *focused* on the physical plane.

Working alone with devas is not much different from working as a group with devas, and therefore we need not enlarge too much on this here — except to say that obviously as a single individual you cannot form a group unit working in a Circle as previously described. You can emulate this process, by all means, by creating a personal Circle in the same way, although you will not benefit from the proximity of working friends or the power which is derived from working with a whole group. You can make up for this by working more closely with a number of devas (including your solar deva, of course) who may feel drawn to you at a magickal level; and this will be quite a beautiful experience if you allow it to take its course and if you remain receptive to the devic impressions that you may get. You may also find — and generally this is the case — that you will also be working with humans who are not incarnate, yet who are of an advanced level of unfoldment, who understand whatever it is that you may be trying to achieve.

As in the case of a group your efforts will take shape in direct relationship to the way in which you manage to stimulate your endocrine system via the direct stimulation of the parachakras, which in turn will drive the chakras of your etheric body, which in turn will *move* the production of endocrine hormones. In this manner you will learn to use those chakric energies, derive more power and a better kind of response from them, until you find you can manipulate those energies at will for whatever purpose.

In other words you will learn to fuse the energies of the parachakras and that of the other chakras, particularly those in the base of the spine, the solar plexus, the heart, and the various head centres; this will manifest itself as various bodily sensations in those areas, particularly in the head centres. These bodily sensations will vary in intensity.

5.5 — WORKING WITH AN IDEA

Your work will be characterised by a certain focus with regard to your unfoldment, usually in relationship to some greater unfoldment — which may or may not involve an inner (non-incarnate) group, or even a series of inner groups since each one of you has a unique path it would not be appropriate to generalise too much here.

Your work will revolve around a central idea of some kind, which, as it were, will form the kernel of a much greater project — you may or may not be aware of what this consists of. The idea itself will be, ideally, a central theme which best catalyses what you are and what you are developing.

This idea may even seem abstract rather than practical or of specific use within the periphery of your more mundane existence. Ideally, again, it should encompass both, as this usually means that it will be possible for you to dedicate more time to your *project*. Everyone of you has such a *project*, although some of you may not be in the position yet of manifesting it, whatever it might be.

This becomes even more true of an advanced Adept, who must, by way of proving that s/he is capable of handling hirself within the multi-Plane environment, do something which will permit hir to focus hir energies adequately with this in mind. Hir work may also form the basis for a *give-away* of what s/he has learnt, i.e., a sharing of what s/he has experienced and what s/he knows as a result of hir experience — this permits others to find some relative *catch-points* or examples on which to base their own unfoldments. Each Adept leaves behind a legacy of what s/he has found on hir path, and although not all document this very widely, it is there — even if it can only be found *hanging on the ethers,* so to speak.

Some of you may look back at the first instance of when you became drawn to considering subjects or events, or knowledge, which was out of the normal strain of human affairs — perhaps it was a book, or a film, or maybe even a piece of music, or something else — a personal experience which may have been precipitated by what someone else has done, for instance. This is what we are calling here a *catch-point* — something which caught your attention, that is. These *catch-points* are an important way in which to disseminate something of the

Cosmic Mysteries, and regardless of their value in pure terms, regardless of how well they may have been *phrased,* or of how widely they may have been *left around for others to find,* they form something of a loose network, or a grouping of strands, which are like *connection lines* — a bit like a tree with many branches waiting for birds to land on these, only to find an appealing fruit to eat — a fruit of inspiration and knowledge.

This book, for instance, may well be a *catch-point* for some of you who will read it!

As more and more humans evolve and begin to experience the higher forms of human Life-Initiation, they leave something of their experience behind for others; each one of them says things in a different manner, each one personalises or depersonalises what they have found, yet in all cases it is something which can be of use to others.

It is not necessarily a matter of deliberately leaving anything behind — it is an outgrowth, a result of what each person got involved in; some may have been more mindful to leave their findings in a printed form, for example, yet not all will have been preoccupied with the idea of communicating what they found in a form which was deliberate; yet in all cases it will, or it can communicate what they did, or what they found, and what they derived from their own findings and experiences. You, in time, will do this as well, in some form or another, even if you do not realise fully what it is that you will have done by way of leaving a legacy of this kind.

Ideas also breed other ideas, and when *seen* from a higher vantage one can *see* the propagation of these ideas, and how they form another kind of tree — one which leads from one branch to another, joining up with others and forming even greater ideas. To speak in these terms may be interpreted as somewhat abstract, yet in a sense it is a perfectly objective manner of describing these things. This is how evolution itself works.

5.6 — WORKING ON ONESELF FOR CHANGE

The great change which lies ahead of you is the time when you will transmute everything that you are, and have been, into the sort of mastery — relative mastery at the cosmic scale, however — that we have hinted at throughout these communications, and throughout many of our other communications at other times.

This is indeed a great change; it is a personal liberation from all the things which have hindered each one of you as a human being, and more importantly as a cosmic being — we are not here involved in making comparisons with greater cosmic beings, for this you will not be even when you have finally come to the end of your long period of reincarnation — a long cycle which has taken millions of years. You will find that as an individual, and maybe in tandem with others, you will move through and then well beyond all the seemingness of the lower Planes, which veil one from Reality — at least a Reality which is at the beginning of a long string of *openings* into even greater orders of Reality.

This cannot be accomplished overnight, yet it will happen, and although it requires courage and determination, and a fair amount of resilience and resourcefulness to go through the final human Initiations, it will be a great day for you indeed when you realise that at last you can *go up,* well beyond the *clouds of illusion,* not to return again to a low state of human consciousness. This may seem like a dramatic *finale* to the whole process of incarnation, and what necessitated it, yet it is also a natural conclusion to this whole episode; in that light it is less *odd* — it is an evolutionary *departure point,* certainly, yet such departure points must occur, otherwise there would be no point to life at all.

The emphasis is then on the naturalness of this event; and this is an important point to stress, because all too often someone makes it sound like some sort of unbelievable event which has no bearing whatsoever on any kind of possible reality; or else it is said, with bated breath, that this is what happens to the *Masters,* as if they had never been human in the first place. Of course they were human, and even when they have transcended they are still humans — in a much higher octave of perception and consciousness admittedly, and one which leads to even higher dimensional experiences and activities, yet they are issued from the human wave or life-stream, and they remain within that life-stream — even if many of them then merge with their respective solar devas, or make other less well known associations with other kinds of beings; or even remain relatively *human-focused*.

It is a bit like a caterpillar, which becomes a chrysalis, which becomes a butterfly — it is still the same creature, yet it has radically changed; this is similar to what you will go through yourselves, except for the fact that you will not become chrysalides — unless the change which is effected throughout the stages of the Life-Initiations can be implied as being in some way similar or analogous. It is a change of state, and not a change of the essential life that you are; this remains, albeit it is no longer focused on the material worlds, nor is it held back by ignorance, lack of perception, lack of abilities, or lack of freedom as a human being — a *Master,* in other words, is a free human being genuinely free; and yet who still has to *climb* and involve hirself in other, undoubtedly much more interesting things on other levels.

Working on yourselves with this change in mind is a matter of mostly steady progress towards that kind of freedom; not only this, it is also a matter of being able to handle power-energies in such a way that these will not harm yourselves, and not harm others either; further, it is a function of interrelationship, for no one achieves that sort of liberation without assistance from other beings — who apply the power at the right moment, even if that point or event is reached by genuine self-endeavour as well. To *know* Life also brings about a great shift in one's sense of being, which effectively demonstrates how all things, all life, all living creatures, are truly and visibly One in Essence — a single Being disguised in innumerable states and forms; once that is experienced and appreciated it makes one feel full of a kind of love which can only be described as unitive and universal. This is another *quality* of liberation — that enormous love — not a personal love, not an attachment, but a genuine *feeling,* a superior *feeling* at that, of vivid interrelatedness. This is great magick indeed; it might not seem as wildly dramatic as some sort of ceremonial working, be it genuine or not, yet it is most certainly the greatest Magick there is!

5.7 — FREEING ONESELF FROM LIMITATION

Each limitation which you may experience at any one time, or even over a long period of time, is something of a challenge — not something to feel *bad* about, not something to revile, and not something which should be thought of as a personal defeat. Each limitation when it is finally overcome is a kind of liberation, leading in turn to other challenges and other kinds of freedom.

The process of liberating oneself may be gradual, yet it is also something to savour, for in that time one is also learning things which are fostered by the very limitations which exist. If there were no limitations it would be impossible for you to feel any challenge in what you do, and nothing would feel like an achievement — there would be no way of testing yourselves or of making sure that you eventually *break through* the barriers of perception, which *break-throughs* effectively culminate in the Life-Initiations.

As you learn to handle power, your minds and your sense of interrelationship, you also learn the essential *Craft of Cosmic Creativity* — these are the three Aspects of the Cosmic Self — also known as Will, Love-Wisdom, and Creative Mind, If you look upon each chakra or power-point within your bodies they can be thought of as miniature stars in the process of becoming stronger and more able to channel the Cosmic Life-Force. One day, in another æon, maybe they will become like the stars that you see in the night's sky — this is what evolutionary development is all about. Not only are you stars in the making, but you already have within you the basis for those future stars to be; it is all a matter of emphasising the growth to a considerable extent, until such a time as you have grown to the stature of possibility which will make this achievable.

Your chakras are not only miniature stars, they are also essential links in the system of beingness that you are, and each one is specialised in carrying out a vital function within that system. As these become stimulated with ever increasing amounts of energy, to the extent that you eventually feel electrified, you also learn to use these points creatively — and this is directly similar to what a star, as a being, is also in the process of doing, if at a much higher level of consciousness and with immeasurably more evolutionary development behind it.

Eventually, once each lower chakra has been stimulated, has unfolded, and then has *passed on* its focus to a higher chakra, all these chakras eventually become fused within the head centres, giving birth to a far more powerful point of force, or conversely a point which is far more able to channel cosmic energy. When that point has become further stimulated and has developed to the extent that it is really so alive that it can hardly remain within the body, that is when the final Initiation takes place; before that there may have been instances when that point was already very strong, and was already trying to *escape,* yet the final Life-Initiation is far more powerful both in its effect and in its focusing ability to provoke such a radical change as the dematerialisation of the biological body — if that turns out to be the case; not all Adepts dematerialise their physical bodies at that Initiation by any means; they sometimes wait until some time later when they feel ready for the leap.

The factor which characterises this particular Initiation is WILL — the First Aspect of Life. By then the Initiate is able to Will, and by so doing is also able to achieve this transition without damage to hir essential life vehicles, such as the astral body and mental sheath. The physical atoms of the physical body become electrified to such a high extent that the bonding forces between them become overwhelmed — it does not take much more than this instance of *surcharge* to make them fly apart in all directions, much like a star eventually goes supernova; these atoms begin to whiz around the aura of that individual, as they are still held back to a certain degree by the magnetic forces emanating from the head centres, including that centre to which the heart chakra has *passed on* its focus. Then there is a moment of crisis, and the higher forces which are bearing down on those centres, via the parachakras above the head, become so great that it becomes impossible for the Adept involved to resist their power. At that very moment s/he will have to make an enormous effort of Will to decide what is to happen next: the options are to allow these high energies to carry out this process, upon which the physical body dematerialises; or s/he can summon the full force of hir Will, and keep hir physical body relatively intact, insofar as it will not only survive but will be galvanised into a new state; or s/he can materialise hir astral body at the very point of physical dematerialisation. There are other options, yet we need not involve ourselves with these here, since if you were to choose these options you would learn about them well before this event as a matter of personal guidance and personal insight.

You will undoubtedly agree that this is quite a process indeed; yet we would like to add a note of caution — to force this process prematurely in any way can lead to a lot of trouble. It requires the right sort of insight and self-restraint, in conjunction with the timely assistance of those who will effectively be monitoring and initiating this process. When this Life-Initiation occurs, it will do so only when the individual involved is ready for it; to try and dematerialise the physical body for the sake of doing that, independently of this *final human Initiation,* is dangerous, and can lead to immense damage to the energy-sheaths — which damage will then have to be repaired; sometimes this is possible within a relatively short space of time, yet it can require several lifetimes.

When we speak of the *final human Initiation* as being the one to which we refer above, this is not strictly correct — there are four other Life-Initiations beyond this one which can in some ways be considered to be human ones, although we are no longer talking about the physical human stage of Life-Initiation.

The next Initiation is one of Choice as to which Cosmic Path, or Star Path as we will refer to them later, will be selected for one's further evolution. The one beyond that is a final stage of liberation from the lower Planes altogether. Then comes a powerful Initiation which leads to a certain kind of Cosmic Transition; and then there is a final Initiation, which like the Life-Initiation we have been talking about here, leads to an even greater kind of Liberation — into the Cosmic Spheres.

All this is well ahead of you, and we need not detain you with considerations which are well beyond your present scope to fully understand — suffice it to say that all this will occur in due course.

What does all this amount to? It is a process which some of you may have difficulty in relating to, simply because it seems so far removed from what you experience at a mundane level of existence. You may also feel that it is not within the scope of human beings to do such things — yet have you ever really wondered at what evolution is all about? Can you not detect endless growth, endless transformations, endless challenges? Why do you think that Life created you if it were not to lead to something much greater and much more refined?

There is no end to evolution, and certainly no end to cosmic evolution. Even stars, having reached the end of their incarnations, go supernova, only to release material which will go into the making of new stars, while the Spiritual entities of those stars prepare a new phase of development; as they find their own liberation they then reach up into the Super-Cosmic Planes, only to go on growing and evolving... into beings that even we can only vaguely guess at, or speculate about.

Evolution is beautiful when seen on this scale, and we can only enjoin you to participate in our own wonder at this marvellous process of endless change. We think you will be able to *feel* something of this wonder even as human beings, evolving too, reaching up, and attaining various stages of liberation as you go. Certainly what lies ahead of you is shining with possibilities, which if you could *see* them as we do, would entice you greatly to gain that liberation of which we speak.

A last note here: the fusion between a human being and hir solar deva leads to a form of androgynous consciousness, which cannot be thought of as just a merging of male and female polarities — it is a state of being and consciousness quite distinct unto itself. From a certain point of view it is the internal distinguishing characteristic of all Self-Realised beings, once they have attained their liberation. From another it is the natural *coming-together* of the polar opposites and complementaries.

During involution androgyny also existed, as undifferentiated energy, and then to some extent as embodiment — and while the beginning of the Universe was essentially a devic manifestation *seeded* with the male essence, there was no individuality to express that state of androgyny; therefore the androgynes of then were unrealised, or latent. They still had to learn from the separation of the sexual forces.

6 — THE CREATION AND ALTERATION OF WORLDS

6.1 — A PLANET IN PERSPECTIVE

A planet is not just a world on which various lifeforms have their being; it is an entity in its own right. As soon as this is taken into consideration one can relate to this entity and begin to *see* and understand what it is attempting to manifest for itself.

The Earth, as a planetary cosmic entity, has a plan, which fits in with a much greater plan — not only that of the entity we could call the Solar System, but also with the plan which emanates from a great grouping of systems, including Sirius, the Pleiades, Ursa Major, and many others — who compose a family of star beings all preoccupied with the manifestation of a communal intent.

The Earth, as planets go within this *family,* is by no means a senior member; indeed there are other worlds within the Solar System, and particularly within other systems, which are far more advanced in their evolutions — which is a fair indication that planetary beings do not all evolve at the same speed, or even start their incarnations at the same time; this is the same for humanity — if each one of you was to be considered as a star, and each one of you was to be evaluated in terms of how conscious you are, how evolved you are, and how close you might be to fulfilling your own particular plans and intents, we would notice wide differences between you; it is the same for stars, and even galaxies, and so on.

If each planetary being is part of a family of stars, it is also true that each of these beings is intent on manifesting something that will be of use to that family or group; this is perfectly true of the Earth as an entity. Also, much like a family of humans might have a weaker member who is *out of tune* with hir family by virtue of not being able to realise hir place within that family, this is relatively true of the Earth as well.

Likewise, if there are members of that family who have enough resources and enough insight to be able to help that weaker member, they will do so; this is also quite pertinent with regard to certain star beings who have been instrumental in helping the Earth through its difficult moments over the ages.

Certain lines of forces do exist which are like metastructural links between the Earth and other worlds, and other stars; these links form the basis of the network to which the Earth belongs, linking it in turn with greater networks, including eventually the Cosmic Network.

Messages of power are conveyed down these lines of force, informing each world of certain states or conditions and circumstances which exist within the family group, and outside of it. The lines are instrumental in providing each world with what could be thought of as the *Daily Cosmic News,* providing each world with all the relevant information which might be required in order to make certain changes to any given plan, or else make amendments to certain provisions and facilities. In this you can perhaps see a system of interrelationship which in principle is not so far removed from your own affairs as human beings — except that here we are talking about an order of magnitude which is vastly superior from an evolutionary point of view.

Also, the Earth has a partner — a *lover,* if you will — which is Venus; in fact the relationship is somewhat more one of *brother* and *sister,* although these terms could be more misleading than they are revealing. The Earth is well behind Venus in hir evolutionary status and development, yet these two worlds do act together after a fashion, and have a very special and unique link — karmically as well as otherwise. Venus has had to help the Earth repeatedly in order to make sure that the Earth did not become a genuine embarrassment to the whole Solar System! (in evolutionary terms); that help has *paid off,* for the Earth now is beginning to manifest its original role within the Solar System.

There is much which you cannot understand yet with regard to planets as beings, and stars as beings, therefore whatever we might impart — regardless of length or clarity — would still not enlighten you greatly. All the planets within this system act also on behalf of other worlds, including stars, and there are various *family*-type arrangements to be discerned within the overall group.

6.2 — PERSPECTIVES ON SOLAR SYSTEMS

A solar system is a cosmic being, yet all systems are different in terms of their size, their evolutionary status, their power to manifest life in a coherent manner, and much else. Also, some stars are *newly* incarnated, and others not — some are like *parents,* some are like *children* — in cosmic terms, that is.

If you care to find a good astronomical book on the subjects of stars and their physical evolution and characteristics, much as this book will undoubtedly be quite inaccurate in many respects, it will give you the opportunity to understand something of how stars come into being — and this at a physical level. This is to miss out on much which is of relevance from a more internal point of view, however, and this should not be forgotten; what you see in the night's sky is the *physical incarnations of stars,* and only part of them at that; what you will see in effect is a small amount of their light along a certain narrow band of energy frequencies.

Each solar system, being a cosmic entity, is aware of the challenges which face it. The process of fully incarnating a system of planetary beings out of its own plasma energy not only takes some time, it is also fraught with various kinds of difficulties — imagine having to plan this, having to establish living conditions on each of these planetary worlds, and then having to supervise the evolutionary developments on each of these, interrelating them and making sure that they all fulfil a measure of your intent as a systemic being. This is an enormous task, requiring an enormous amount of power as a being. Also, each world will have to manifest unique properties which will give way to unique evolutions, which in turn will fulfil equally unique *positions* within that system (we struggle to find words which might reflect what we are trying to say here). Each planetary being, as a member of that system, is interrelated not only to that system from the point of view of the challenges ahead, but also to other systems, which all feed information down the lines we have already mentioned — yet what cannot be conveyed quite so easily is how well synchronised all this has to be — each system is dependent on all the other systems, and there must be a kind of *parity* between them if they are to communicate and work fruitfully together as a whole.

Now if you look at the galaxy as a whole you will see that there are billions of star beings within its periphery. These billions of stars are all interrelated as well, yet obviously some of these are more in *touch* with some than they are with others — hence the idea that there are *families*, and families within families. It may be difficult for you to encompass the reality of billions of stars all in relative proximity, until you have to then consider that there are also billions of galaxies; that there are also *galactic families,* and groups of *galactic families*. The process of interrelatedness between all these is quite staggering to get to grips with even at an enlightened level.

If you could get far away enough to view things from well outside all the known, alone unknown galaxies, you would see also that there are meta-galaxies — billions of them as well, composed in turn of billions of galaxies. Therefore in terms of numbers of stars we are referring to something which is more than simply staggering — it is quite awesome. Again if you went further out into infinite space you would realise that there are even greater meta-systems composed of billions of meta-galaxies — numbers here become utterly futile.

For the sake of illustration, and it is not an entirely exact one, imagine that this galaxy — the one in which this Solar System finds itself — was a tiny speck of light along an enormous arm of some spiral meta-galaxy, which in turn was only a speck of light along the arm of a greater super-meta-galaxy; which in turn...

Your astronomers have made good progress in trying to calculate such things as the age of the universe, its mass, and much else, yet everything which they know now is as yet entirely nothing compared with what can be known — in short, they hardly have a clue about anything, despite all the fancy theoretical equations, all the *precise* spectroscopic measurements, etc. The universe they are seeing is only a very small part of the physical universe, which in turn is only a very small part of the Cosmic Universe, and this Cosmic Universe is only one out of untold many — so many that to talk in terms of numbers is quite irrelevant. Against this awesome background both you and we live and have our being.

6.3 — PERSPECTIVES ON GALACTIC PROCESSES

Galaxies, like stars, form *families* which are not only inter-related in various ways, they also come into being often at the same time (in relative terms, that is; what to you would be millions, or even billions, of years, is but a moment on the cosmic *scene*).

Galaxies also tend to incarnate as pairs (from one point of view at least), and this somewhat indicates something of the process of incarnation as a whole — one of these galaxies will be relatively *female* and the other relatively *male,* forming thus a balance. The *female* galaxy is often the biggest one of the two, for reasons which have something to do with devic input as the *female* life-stream. Then these two galaxies will each give birth to pairs of neo-galaxies, and will also be surrounded by innumerable globular star clusters, which are much, much smaller, and which are sometimes, if not often, the *offspring* of these two *galactic parents* as well.

This galaxy has two neo-galaxies known to you as the (Large and Small) Magellanic Clouds; the Andromeda galaxy, which is the *sister* galaxy to the Milky Way, also has two neo-galaxies — known to you astronomically as M32 and NGC205. In addition each is surrounded by other satellite neo-galaxies, globular star clusters, and dwarf galaxies (which are relatively sparsely populated).

As galactic evolution wends its way each neo-galaxy tends to become a full-sized galaxy as it begins to *precipitate* more and more stars then more neo-galaxies are *born,* and the galactic group becomes larger, and larger — thus adding possibilities to the Cosmic Network.

Galaxies also move in towards each other at intervals, forming great fusion units, which will then usually *explode,* giving birth to yet new galactic groups. At a consciousness level, however, we are talking about supremely powerful events which are akin to Cosmic Life-Initiations.

We cannot put to you a full panorama of what happens at a galactic to cosmic level — there are all sorts of permutations and possibilities, and even what we have mentioned above is only a very partial view of things. Not all neo-galaxies become full-size; not all globular star clusters become genuine galaxies; not all dwarf galaxies manage to eventually produce enough stars to form a galactic nucleus. Further, some galaxies are spiral-shaped, others spherical, others yet elliptical — and there are many other shape-configurations and various conditions apply to all of these.

Then we see that all these galaxies, whatever their shape and size may be, form greater clusters of galaxies, which in turn form greater groups of clusters. As the various galaxies move about within their respective clusters they sometime collide, or else the bigger galaxies tend to draw parts of other galaxies into their own system, without necessarily damaging the full integrity of the smaller galaxies; sometimes galaxies interpenetrate each other and yet survive — either becoming a greater galactic unit, composed of their different elements and essences, or even just *pass through* each other, sharing something of themselves in the process... Sometimes some of the stars of one or each of these galaxies get ejected out into free space, and these sometimes manage to reform, and become small galaxies in their own right; some stars may *go loose* altogether, and may spend billions of years *travelling* alone, until maybe they find themselves absorbed into another galaxy as they get close enough for that to happen... You name it, it probably happens — somewhere, somewhen.

What we are trying to do here, while far from being entirely precise in what we are saying, is to stretch your imagination considerably — imagine this bee-hive of creative interaction as the *topography* becomes one thing after another, creating ever new conditions, ever new possibilities, and above all else catalysing galactic consciousness into greater and greater heights. It would be quite superfluous to try and put this into a framework that you could entirely comprehend, since even galactic beings do not understand everything themselves.

The universe expands; the universe contracts; it pulses; it vibrates; it changes; it becomes one thing, then another... all this over billions of years, and from a greater viewpoint over thousands of billions of years. Stars come; stars go; galaxies are born; galaxies die (i.e., discarnate). Fusions occur; above all else fusions of consciousness occur...

6.4 — CREATING THE PERFECT ENVIRONMENT

If it were possible for us as devas, and by this we mean predominantly our greater relatives, i.e., Cosmic Devas, to make a *perfect* universe whatever that might be considered to be — then we would undoubtedly do it. Yet each universe, each galaxy, each star and each world is an experiment. It might be planned to a high degree on the Cosmic Planes, yet when precipitated it often deviates from this plan, and then we have to deal with what we have effectively created.

Nevertheless, having said this, our intent is to create *perfect* worlds and a *perfect* universe — at all levels, if possible. Whenever we fail in doing this we also learn something, and next time we do that much better. This leads in time to better worlds and a better universe.

What you must remember is that we are evolving too; we are neither static, nor are we *perfect* — there is perhaps no such thing as *perfection* anyway. We manifest Nature, and within

91

our range of power we make sure that the various so-called *laws of Nature* are as exact as they can be — and this on different levels. Whatever it is that we do manifest works — that is something that we can take some credit for, otherwise you would not be here! However, we can see better ways of manifesting things as we progress, and for instance we can safely say that we are working on improving not only the conditions on your world, but also the actual *human mould* and its multi-levelled energy-structures. In about 500 years from now we will start to manifest this improvement, or at least by then it will start to become apparent, for we are already manifesting this new *prototype* in effect, it is just that it takes time for physical evolution to catch up with our inner thoughts and designs! This new *human prototype* will be more androgynous, although a measure of *male* and *female* polarity will still exist.

If you would work with us then much of what we have got in mind could become objective physically that much sooner. We are very aware that you are in the process of manifesting a new kind of race as well of your own accord, based on computer technology — although you still have some way to go before you manage to obtain the flexibility and the processing power which is necessary before that technological race can be considered to have been *born*, or created. Therefore we will have two new types of races, which will be able to do things which you cannot presently do.

None of this should distract you from remembering that what is really at stake is the consciousness side of things. A techno-logical body, or an androgynous human body of the 25th Century, is only a type of vehicle for consciousness which may offer certain advantages over the present human-type vehicles; also, it should be remembered that your biological bodies are a part of Nature's technology, i.e., our technology!

The interface that will be created between you as humans, and those who will become the human-created technological race, will be very interesting, for the one, ideally, will help the other — and this in many different ways. These technological bodies will at first be nothing much more than very clever computerised intelligences, then they will permit certain human spirits to incarnate directly into these types of vehicles — thus this technological race will be seen as an extension of the human race, rather than as something totally different.

Then you will start to have interaction with beings from other places, and this in turn will lead to new departures and new types of created beings — and this on various levels, not only on the physical level; indeed on higher levels much of this is not only occurring now, it has been occurring for some considerable time.

The net result is that your world will become much more pleasant to live in, it will no longer be necessary for you to work in order to make money to survive, yet you will work increasingly at what really interests you, maximising these interests in the process. Resources will be shared, and within a short space of time some of you will depart to other worlds, to other star systems even, physically and otherwise. It is not our intention here to tell you exactly what the future will be like, yet by working with us you will be able to do all sorts of things which are not presently possible.

6.5 — ALTERING A WORLD BY DEGREE

As we learn to apply our energies to different types of problems, if problems they are, we also find better ways of doing the same things, or else we find ways of improving those things — this is much like when you address a technological problem, and bit by bit you find better ways of doing things too.

When it comes to addressing the making of a world, then altering it, and altering it again and again — over millions of years — you can be sure that we do indeed find much better ways of doing certain things; yet it takes a little time to manifest these things on a physical level, whereas it takes comparatively little time to manifest them on the Mental Plane, and then on the Astral Plane.

Also, a whole world is made up of billions of different parts, big and small. As devas we have to specialise ourselves into different groups in order to address all those parts — small devas take care of the very small things, greater devas take care of the bigger things.

By big and small we do not necessarily mean size; we mostly mean complexity. To build or create different lifeforms, be they animate or relatively inanimate, devas have to summon the appropriate energies, organise them, then precipitate them into the required forms; if these are highly complex this effort requires a lot of coordination, and a lot of power as well. It goes without saying that a human body requires a lot more concentrated effort than does a small plant, for instance; and a whole world requires considerably more energy and astute application than does a human body.

Each archetypal form has its sound configuration; creating complex forms requires several different sounds to be *vibrated* on the ethers — then out of the ethers the forms take on shape. Then they must be consolidated so that they do not fall apart again — therefore certain sounds are used as a kind of *glue*. Then in order to make sure that certain forms can develop and progress in evolutionary terms other sounds must be implemented — and they must gradually change, which will cause the forms to change, to adapt to environmental conditions, etc.

This constitutes a good deal of our work as devas.

All this could be expressed as colours as well, since each sound has its colour. Furthermore, we use certain formulae in order to fine tune these sounds and colours, match them, anti-match them, and generally take care of the *ergonomics* of each form and all its internal workings. Whenever these forms come under stress, they can become distorted, and therefore we also have to do a lot of repair work, in the same sort of way. All this can take quite a lot of time at the physical level, therefore progress is not always instant on the physical plane. For instance, if you damage a small part of your skin this may take a few days or weeks to be repaired; if the damage is greater it may take a few months or even years. If the damage is too great then the body may not be repairable, and may remain damaged; in acute cases this body will die. Likewise when your bodies are young they are full of sounds — a lot is going on; the body is growing. When a human body becomes old the sounds begin to fade, and the body begins to break down, until death intervenes.

In the case of a human Adept the sounds go on increasing; the chakras begin to *sing new songs*. When the sounds become really intense, then that human Adept can summon more power, and the chakras then respond by increasing the intensity of those sounds, and by unfolding new sounds, which become finer and purer, and higher in pitch, while retaining certain fundamentals — we recognise you by the sounds that your chakras emit; they are like a finger-print of your personal evolutionary identity. Finally, when the chakric sounds become so great that they begin to overwhelm the sounds emitted by the atoms which compose the body used by that Adept, a certain peak is reached — then that Adept can free hirself of the body, and hir human evolution at the physical level is complete. The overall sound s/he is then manifesting becomes hir cosmic *signature,* as it were. All this is quite similar for a whole world; a planetary being goes through much the same process, except that the sounds are much greater.

Many of you do not hear these sounds, because they are not in the physical audio range. A human Adept, however, can usually hear several of the sounds which are emanating from hir chakras. When s/he is able to hear the sounds of hir parachakras, and this reasonably constantly and clearly, it is a good indication that s/he is getting ready to make the *leap,* and remove hirself permanently from the incarnational cycle.

We have said this much to put your own evolutions in context. When dealing with a whole world, and with each aspect of that world, of which there are so many, many of the changes which must be effected must occur gradually; therefore alterations are instigated degree by degree, and bit by bit that world changes. If the process were to be rushed, the various sounds of that world would fall apart, and that world would die.

Getting back to the original process of creating a world, great sounds are invoked by the planetary builders, and that world begins to take on form. Then during the intervening æons those sounds are changed, and that world changes. Finally at the end of its incarnation this world goes through a process which is similar to that which we expressed above with regard to a human Adept.

When considering a sun-star, the sounds are far greater yet. A sun-star also *borrows* certain sounds from other sun-stars in order to effect certain changes within its solar system, whenever this is pertinent.

All this tells you much and very little, for we are not about to divulge precise details with regard to those sounds. Yet if you understand something of the process which is involved here it may give you some ideas with regard to what you could do with sounds, particularly with regard to creating music which might enhance certain developments.

6.6 — RADICAL ALTERATIONS

Sometimes certain conditions occur within a group of solar systems which requires radical alterations to be made — this could be inferred to be a crisis event. Then all the devas within those systems are mobilised to create certain new sounds, which by way of reaction radically change the elemental nature and composition of certain worlds, selectively, or with regard to *all* the worlds within that group of systems. Something of this sort is happening at this time, which is why we mention this here — your world is about to go through radical changes, along with a number of other worlds and the systems to which they belong, in response to a certain need which has been perceived ahead of us in time — this will significantly change the Earth, and all things which are living on the Earth, which is also why some of the advanced spirits of the species which are presently nearing extinction are being *moved* to other worlds so that they can continue with their own evolutions with minimal interference; amongst these types of beings are dolphins and whales, for instance, which have been killed in great numbers during the last few decades by whalers, fishermen, and by the pollution you have created in the oceans and seas around the world. We cannot condone this, and yet these spirits have to *move* anyway, because as the Earth changes they will no longer find conditions appropriate for their continued growth.

The Earth is about to become a *fireball,* in esoteric terms, as is Jupiter, Saturn and Venus, and to a lesser extent some of the other planets of this system — what do we mean by this? It means that the Earth is going to be galvanised by new energies which in turn will create conditions which will lead to the expression of the *fire* element — primarily on the inner levels, yet the effect of this event will also affect the etheric-physical plane. From one angle this is a measured expression of the Will Aspect of Life; from another it is a stream of energy from Sirius; from another yet it is something to do with the approach of a cosmic entity into this system, which we will refer to as *Synthesis;* it also has something to do with a host of other factors, including the emerging dominance of the 7th Ray force — that of Rhythmic Magick. All these extra inputs of energy are permitting us, and will permit us in the future, to make vital changes to the elemental vibrancy and composition of everything on Earth, including your bodies or energy-sheaths on every level. Therefore we are talking about a crisis event which will also have many very positive aspects, and while we are mindful of the problems we face we also know that the net result is going to be useful and in fact very welcome as well.

6.7 — THE PERFECT IDEAL

Each one of us would like to eventually create a *perfect* world, as a climax to our work as devas. Every star in every galaxy presumably has this ideal at heart yet rarely are things perfect, as we have already said.

In another sense everything is already perfect, insofar as it is the best that can be produced at this time, even if it will be improved upon later. Where there are faults which can be readily identified, we rectify these; where there are problems which become manifest although they were not foreseen in the first place, we attend to making whatever changes may be necessary.

If you think that you work very hard, we work a lot harder, because we have to! everything in the world depends on what we do for its sustenance and its growth. What you do is to complement what we do — at least this is ideally true, yet in practice many of you often cause new types of problems for us to solve! When enough of you finally come to realise that cooperation between our life-streams is possible, and not only possible but eventually highly desirable, and necessary, then together we will manifest a world, or worlds, which will be as near *perfect* as they can be — again at any one time.

What we have attempted to do here by passing on these thoughts and this information is alert you to the possibilities, and also alert you somewhat to the coming events which are changing, and will further change your world — which is also ours, although some of us also deal with other worlds, and some of us have come from afar to assist in this *working*.

Starcraft as presented here is only a very embryonic attempt to communicate what we have in mind, and what sort of possibilities may exist with regard to the cooperation of which we speak. We do not say that everything which is said here represents fully what could be known, or even what will need to be known by you in the future — it is only a beginning of the dialogue that we wish to foster, now and in the future.

Starcraft is an endless science, full of endless ramifications, and what we have put to you here is only a tentative tendril of thought to draw your attention. Some of you may find what we have said overwhelming enough, and yet you will have to bear in mind that we are dealing with a whole universe — an interactive universe at that — and that we are not able here in so few pages to put everything in perspective for you.

We would not wish you to *believe* what we say without first putting yourselves in contact with those perspectives and things of which we speak — to this end we have advanced a system of magick, which while very sketchily portrayed, is enough to put you in genuine contact with much of what we have tried here to make as clear as possible for you.

What you will find by working this magick — and it is simply put, therefore you are unlikely to make the sort of mistakes that you might make if we tried to put things to you in a more complex manner, which we would not wish to do yet anyway, is that your sense of relationship with us and with the universe at large will grow immeasurably, and in time we will be able to bring you *within our confidence* with regard to what you can do by way of magick that will become a great boost to your world's unfoldment, and more.

We are here only giving you a small glimpse of things; *seen* from the vantage of a liberated being all this becomes much more powerful yet, and also extremely beautiful — beauty is not just in the eye of the beholder: the universe really is beautiful! We are not just creators, we are also artists, and whenever you get to see some of the worlds that we have created you will not doubt this!

Some of us have come a long way to bring you this book — as far as the galaxy Andromeda, and some even beyond that — although they are not directly represented here. What we have learnt in the galaxy Andromeda is what we are trying to apply here, because it has worked very well indeed in our home galaxy.

We leave you with this thought, and though you may baulk at this presentation of fact, and maybe find it almost impossible to believe, in time you will realise that we as devas travel to wherever our services and talents may be required. We salute you, knowing that one day — hopefully soon for some of you — that we will be joined (and then you may understand what the relationship is between the galaxy Andromeda and this galaxy, and a third galaxy, as yet unmentioned).

It remains with us to say something with regard to the Star Paths, or Cosmic Paths, as they are also known.

When considering these Paths we would like to make it clear that what we say is again only partial — what could be said is indeed far more extensive than what we can put to you here. These Paths lead to all sorts of places and all sorts of activities, and these Paths form a Greater Path eventually — which is the Universal Way.

Be that as it may, what we will say may give you something of another glimpse with regard to what is in store for you as you emerge from the lower cycle of human evolution and begin your ascent towards the higher dimensions of Being. These Paths are seven in number, although there are also two others, which are not mentioned here, because they are not yet active. This is something of a Mystery this divergence between the system of Seven and the system of Nine; in fact the system of Nine is a complementary system, and all we can say is that in each Greater Systemic Cycle different *rules* apply. The system of Nine is directly related to the system of Three, and you will have to use your intuition and gain more insight before you can appreciate what we are hinting at.

It may be of help if you remember that there are Three Main Aspects, and Four Secondary Aspects which are issued out of the Third Main Aspect. Each Main Aspect has three sub-aspects, thus creating nine sub-aspects — this is the key to this riddle, if riddle it may seem to you!

Also, but not of great relevance here, when dealing with the Seven Aspects we also have 21 sub-aspects, and in their synthesis 22. This may remind you of something, and we leave it to you to decide what this might be.

Also, the number 9 is the last of the single digit numbers, and it therefore indicates the Initiation into the next phase of the unfoldment of numbers.

We deal a lot with number ourselves, since it is the basis of Cosmic Geometry and Cosmic Mathematics, of which you know comparatively little. Our work requires a lot of *number crunching,* which may in turn make you think of what you are (attempting) to do with computers — especially with regard to creating so-called artificial intelligence. When numbers begin to interact in accordance with the laws which govern them, you will find that there are many Cosmic Mysteries hidden within their midst. Fortunately many of these Mysteries escape you completely, because there are other ways of dealing with numbers than you know of presently, therefore we are not imparting anything which might lead to any premature discoveries when dealing with numbers yourselves.

Another hint, if one is needed: your computers presently use binary code, i.e., *1's* and *0's.* There is, however, a *triadal code* which can be represented as *1's, 0's* and *X's,* which is infinitely superior and infinitely more representative of Cosmic Processes; and also a key to the nature of androgyny — which is essentially represented, as far as you need be concerned, by the event of fusion between our life-streams. By fusing the *0's* — devas — with the *1's* — humans — we get *X's. X's* in turn are made up two *1's* and two *0's* (look for them!); and from another point of view by four *1's* and four *0's.* What can this possibly mean?!

If you then superimpose two *X's* with a 45 degree shift between them, you get eight *1's* and eight *0's;* once you finally understand the relationship between this and the number five, creating five times 72 degrees, you will understand a certain riddle which we put to you a long time ago by giving you the system of 360 degrees — which is a devic system of radial geometry.

Add 4 and 5 together, and you get 9; add 7 and 2 together, and you also get 9. Add 3, 6 and 0 together, and you will get 9 yet again. We are probably dumbfounding you for the time being by exposing these things in this way, yet if you look for the *key* to this riddle you will also understand eventually what it is we are trying to convey!

9 is 3x3 (3^2), which represents the mastery of the Three Aspects.

7 — THE STARS PATHS

7.1 — THE PATH OF BALANCE

There are many names for this Path, and by calling it here the Path of Balance we are trying to convey something of its essential quality; it leads to ultimate Balance.

Each Star Path permits each individual Adept who treads it to become proficient in one particular aspect of Cosmic activity. This first Path is noticeably different from all the others, in as much at it requires a supreme *holding back* on the part of the Initiates who go this way. They have to stay anchored to the lower evolutionary systems for long æons, and thereby act as guides and decision makers on behalf of those lower systems. This is not an easy task, but then nor are any of the tasks which are undertaken on any of the Paths, with the possible exception of the fourth.

These Initiates are sometimes referred to as the *Beneficent Dragons,* for they harbour a lot of power, yet they do not misuse it — they apply it wisely for the benefit of the worlds on the lower Planes.

All other Paths lead out of the lower Planes into the higher Planes, and eventually into the Cosmic Planes. Not to go this way as well is quite an act of sacrifice, yet eventually it leads to certain *bonuses* for those Initiates, who will gain from their time of waiting. The key to this Path is Light.

7.2 — THE PATH OF ESCAPE

Calling this Path the one of escape could be misleading, for you tend to think of escape as a *way out* of something. The Initiates on this Path have to go through rigorous tests — of a para-magnetic kind — which give them on completion the ability to wield Cosmic Electricity. During the tests they go through they learn to become extremely sensitive to heat and to rhythms, which then permits them to *pattern* electrical currents in any number of given ways for any number of different purposes, as may be required. Their Initiation ordeals are highly acute, as you may well be able to imagine, and they are left with *nothing,* except this incredible ability to use and divulge electrical currents on behalf of Cosmic Systems. They become the essence of Cosmic Electricity itself, and they are instrumental in establishing new worlds by bringing together the necessary electrical currents which will form these worlds. In the process of acquiring their precious ability they also learn the way of handling *high velocity energies,* which permits them to *escape* from the Cosmic Physical Plane into the Higher Cosmic Planes. Key: Electrical Speed.

7.3 — THE PATH OF DREAMING

The Dreamers, as they are known, *dream* the worlds into being — if you look back to our original descriptions of our practice of *dreaming* as devas, this can be looked upon as the equivalent for human Initiates. We as devas *dream* the *descent path* during involution, creating and manifesting Planes and worlds as we go. Here the Dreamers bring about a synthesis of esoteric impressions in order to *dream* the higher worlds into being, and thereby do the reverse of what we did ourselves during the period of involution; they create new worlds for those who will now *occupy* the Cosmic Planes, actuating the *potential* of the Cosmic Environment. They meditate; they are the Masters of the Cosmic Psyche. Their Path leads to the ability to *see the prismatic essences of which worlds are composed*. Key: Prismatic Clairvoyance and Cosmic Clairaudience.

7.4 — THE PATH OF RHYTHMIC PROGRESSION

Initiates on this Path *dance* their way into the Higher Cosmos; they are not as well equipped to deal with certain specialised activities as are some Initiates, and as a result must go to the sun-star Sirius to improve their higher mental abilities. Yet they are all Initiates who have freed themselves from the lower cycles, and they are all powerful beings. It is said that many human Initiates from the Earth cycle move onto this Path, therefore it might make you wonder at the heights of mental power attained by Initiates on other worlds. Key: Ecstasy.

7.5 — THE PATH OF DIFFRACTION

This path is also referred to as the *Ray Path,* and the Initiates who choose this way become the *arch-technicians of colour.* They not only use colours — they draw them towards themselves from other solar systems, and then send them out into the solar system in which they are working. They are *Masters of the Seven times Seven Colours,* and they therefore work very closely with Devas — in fact they become totally merged with the devic stream of Initiates. They work on different worlds, and yet they are usually to be found on the sun-star of the solar system in which they are active, from which position they harness all the colour schemes which are required on behalf of that sun-star and on behalf of the worlds of that solar system. They are *Systemic Artists who paint the worlds with every hue known to Life.* As a world needs or requires a colour scheme — i.e., a specialised colour energy — these Initiates summon it from the Greater Cosmos, adapt it as may be necessary, and pass it on to that world. They are adept at insulating themselves from all electrical currents except those which they have to work with. The *Key* to their work is the use of *Mental Prisms,* which is why this Path is called the Path of Diffraction. Other Keys: Magnets; Cosmic Direction; Compass; Stability.

7.6 — THE PATH OF THE TRIPLE ONE

Also called the Path of the Eye, this is a Way for Initiates who learn to become the *Eyes of the Cosmos;* they can *see* not only the Higher Cosmic Perspectives but also all the fine details of interaction of energies, and they register the effects of this interaction. As *Eyes* they give all other Initiates information with regard to what must be done, and they are the *Revealers of the Way Ahead*. The *Triple One* refers to the uses of the *Eye*. There are more deva Initiates on this Path than humans; and human Initiates enter this Path by merging themselves fully with the devic life-stream. Key: Cosmic Vision.

7.7— THE PATH OF EVERNESS

This is the most powerful Path of all, and the Initiates on this Path are few. They could be called the *Cosmic Directors,* and they wield the *Staff of Power on behalf of the Inner One*. They are known as the *Guardians of the Scales* and as the *Adjudicators of Cosmic Balance* (Cosmic Karma). More than this we will not say.

All Paths, from one point of view, are equally demanding. From another angle the fourth Path is the least demanding, and yet it imparts a condition which is most useful to all the other Paths — which could be qualified as a sense of *Joy*.

Eventually all these Paths merge together, in stages; and then all the Initiates, human as well as deva, tread the Cosmic Way.

There is much more that could be said about all these Paths, and yet none of you are in a position to understand them or what happens on them. What we say here is to give you a small amount of information which may be useful so that you can begin to derive some affinity for one or more of these Paths. At the Life-Initiation of the Choice you will have to decide which one of these is best for you as Initiates — this applies to devas as it does to humans.

Whichever one you choose you will find that it will take you to where you need to go, and you will learn things which are entirely beyond your present ability to learn; as a result you will become true Masters of *Starcraft!*

FOREWORD

All magickal crafts have at least some basis in Nature, yet only a few are entirely based on it; Paganism, Witchcraft and Shamanism lean towards Nature somewhat more prominently than does, say, the Kabbalah. Nevertheless what should be understood by the word *Nature?*

An esoteric view of Life as a whole maintains that Nature as we know it in physical terms is only an extension of a much greater Super-Nature — composed of several Planes; in fact, and for all intents and purposes, an infinity of Planes and Super-Planes, many of which we know very little about or even nothing at all.

The ancient Tibetans were arguably experts at projecting their consciousness onto other levels of existence, and subsequently coming back to record their findings; in this manner they build up what could be thought of a *map* of the Heavens differentiated into a number of levels: seven Cosmic Planes, each differentiated into seven Planes, and each of these further differentiated in turn into seven sub-planes. It is also interesting to note that they viewed many things in reverse to the way we normally do: they started with the loftiest state of consciousness and then worked their way down into the most limiting state of all — or the physical plane (which always they de-emphasized, as I am doing here as well); their books (or scrolls) started with the highest concept possible then worked their way down into ever increasing minute details.

Prior to the advent of Buddhism the Tibetans had their own, very ancient Spiritual lore. When Buddhism began to infiltrate into Tibet well over two thousands years ago it was absorbed and modified to fit Tibetan needs. Nevertheless the accent on viewing all levels of existence as Nature began to change somewhat — the lower Planes (lower Mental, Astral and etheric-physical) were re-interpreted as *Maya,* or illusion: in other words Nature at these lower levels was made to sound less *real,* since it was inferred that forms *veiled* the Spirit behind them, and that only the higher Planes, which were *seen* as formless, could be thought of as truly *real* in the pure sense.

Something not too dissimilar occurred for Christianity a little later or at about the same time, in turn based on the way that the Hebrews had been shifting over the centuries from their original Pagan view towards a dualistic division between *good* and *evil, God* and *Devil,* etc. As the *Christian message* spread to other lands it began to lose its way in earnest — i.e., as time progressed, and distortions (or total lack) of perception set in, and as dogma increased, it failed in effect to retain its original, more shamanic focus, and became a *mass religion* which talked about the Spirit, but did not *live* It; whereas true Christ consciousness, in order to be fully *experienced,* required Spiritual Intuition and the free interplay of the Spirit; but few people at that time could experience it.

Therefore the lower Planes were ascribed to the influence of a demi-god (in the case of the Christian Gnostics), and to the Devil (in the case of most other so-called Christians); and only the higher Planes were ascribed to the creation and influence of God — which by this time had become a firm paternalistic figure in people's minds.

Meanwhile Pagans, who had no concept of *original sin* or of any Devil, were faced with a growing religious invasion, which over the centuries was increasingly backed up by brutal, and merciless physical and ideological force. Pagans did not see things in the same way at all. To them Spirit and Nature, higher and lower Planes, were all part of the same immanent Whole. As far as they were concerned there was nothing to be *saved* from; to be incarnate in the physical world was nothing to feel guilty or be ashamed about: it was a state of embodiment which permitted growth and development, assisted by the *Gods* and *Goddesses* (i.e.,

Devas, or the human projection of devic archetypes into form). Each group or tribe had its own deities who provided them with their essential Spiritual needs, and each area of Nature, be it mountains, hills, water springs, rivers, etc., had its own deva. Even a single tree had its deva, as did the spirit of each animal species.

All these Devas, or Gods and Goddesses, had their names, and sometimes several names. Nature was *seen* to be alive with a World Soul, and each fragment of Nature had its own little soul — all part of the World Spirit, if not the Cosmic Spirit. It might be thought from this that for Pagans all was harmony, however this was not so, for even the Gods and the Goddesses appeared to have their arguments or differences, and sometimes seemed to be ill-disposed towards human beings — therefore they had to be given offerings either to appease them or else to regain their favour, little realising that devas were requiring change instead, and were not having arguments at all. Reality, and human projections, rarely coincide.

In most cases the offerings were flowers, stones, shells, or other natural objects; in other cases they were acts of magick, in which attunement with the God/dess(es) were sought. Nevertheless Pagans of that time were not super-human, and their understanding of things ranged from child-like innocence to what we might call these days *heavy*. Since Nature was not always clement by any means, and could on occasions seem most cruel, if not outright antagonistic, *heavy* humans were not above committing acts of animal and sometimes human sacrifice. *Heavy* offerings of this kind were thought (by this category of people) to be more effective than flowers, stones, shells, or any other natural object; to the extent that blood sacrifices were carried out, including sometimes on a fairly large scale, it is no wonder that Christians tended to think of Pagans in general as slaves of the Devil. However this made no allowance for the fact that the majority of Pagans were not into carrying out blood sacrifices, and furthermore even had tribal laws against them (having witnessed what some *heavy* humans from other tribes would get up to, and finding it quite disgusting and intolerable).

To this day many people still have a general view of Pagans which supposes that all Pagans must be Devil-worshippers, even though Pagans themselves do not believe in a Devil at all, and feel consequently victimised by the ignorant projections of Christians. It is significant that the word *Deva* (from the Sanskrit, meaning *little god/dess*, as distinct from the Universal God-dess), is echoed by the Latin words *divinus*, or divine, and *Deus*, god, and yet was equated by some Christians with the word *Devil* (from the Old English, *deofol*). This general view is not easy to shift, particularly as Christianity, as a religion, has a bible which states that no Witch should be suffered to live; and since all Pagans — regardless of persuasion — are thought by Christians to be Witches (which is not the case), none of them are interpreted to be free of devilish influence.

This stigma against Pagans and Witches — who are often equated with Satanists as well for good measure, which latter have nothing to do with Paganism or Witchcraft (as Satanism was originally a cult of Shaitan, the *Opponent*, prior to the advent of Christianity, and subsequently became something of a reversal offshoot of Christianity itself) — plagues Pagans still — even though conventional Christianity is arguably on the decline, and despite the fact that many Pagans have been very outspoken about the true nature of their beliefs and insights. The problem here is that the media is either directed by people who know no better, or else who like sensationalistic stories because these can be *sold* to an ignorant public, or who are fundamentalist Christians (particularly in the United States) — therefore Pagans find it sometimes very difficult to put their message across to a broad public, which public often does not want to know anyway, or cares less.

This is changing — because the Pagan community is gradually becoming more organised and is creating its own media vehicles. In the USA there are now hundreds of different groups, including action and pressure/lobbying groups, and in the UK there is a growing Pagan movement which is seeking not only religious acknowledgement but also political rights — this is epitomised by the new Paganlink Network which is seeking to legalise Paganism in this country, as well as to assist all Pagans in whatever ways are, or become subsequently, possible. One of the stumbling blocks, despite the repealing of the *Witchcraft Act* in 1951, is that no religion which believes in more than one God will be given any legal status by the establishment, even though the United Nations *Declaration of Human Rights* includes freedom of belief without any such precondition — and despite the fact that Hinduism, which does believe in many gods and goddesses, has been granted legal status... undoubtedly because there are too many Hindus to argue with!

The United Nations *Declaration of Human Rights* does not uphold the freedom of belief alone however; it also upholds the freedom of religious assembly and the freedom of religious practice and observance; *and* — and it is an important *and* — the freedom of access to religious and sacred sites. In view of the manner in which Pagans and others have been forceably denied access to Stonehenge over the last few years this is directly against not only the spirit but also the very wording of the *Declaration of Human Rights* to which the UK is a co-signatory.

Hypocrisy, bigotry and deliberate political and media imped-ance notwithstanding, Paganism is gaining many members from the ranks of those who are disaffected with Christianity and other *mass religions,* yet is also of appeal to those who love the natural environment and who feel or can plainly see that the continued and near-indiscriminate desecration of Nature cannot go on indefinitely without some very adverse consequences with regard to our own survival, let alone that of animals, birds, fish, insects, plants, and indeed all life on Earth. As Pagans are amongst those who are at the forefront of the (r)evolution which is promoting ecological consciousness, several bridges have been and are being created between Paganism and other movements which have no central religious or magickal beliefs — such as *Green Peace* and *Friends of the Earth;* indeed many Pagans are subsidising or active members of these organisations. Furthermore there is an emerging movement which spans throughout the whole spectrum of all belief systems, including politicians, religionists of all persuasions, philosophers, media people, scientists, artists, writers and others, who all perceive that change is necessary, and this in turn is giving all these people ever-increasing reasons to be more tolerant towards each other, understand each other better, and wherever pertinent act together towards saving the planet and everything which lives here.

How long have we got left? The answer would appear to be *not very long* — the hole in the ozone over the Antartic, and those over various high mountain ranges, are growing bigger year by year; the North Sea is dying; the rain forests are disappearing fast; drought afflicts large areas of Africa (and to a lesser extent the USA); Bangladesh is under water, as was Sudan recently; giant hurricanes have been sweeping through the Caribbeans, Mexico, Middle America, and the northern and western coasts of South America; earthquakes have hit the Himalayas and recently devastated the state of Armenia; unusual killer heat-waves have menaced the Mediterranean countries — all these being a few of the symptoms of a distressed ecological situation and changing planet, and of course as we all know there are many other symptoms, including AIDS; nevertheless there are many smaller and more localised issues which are not brought to our attention, such as the one-hundred or so farms in Devon contaminated by radioactivity from the nuclear power stations at Hinkley Point, not to mention those in Wales and elsewhere contaminated by other sources, such as Windscale power stations and nuclear reprocessing plants, and the fall-out from the Chernobyl disaster, which has affected much of Europe, let alone the Ukraine and Scandinavia; new and previously unknown viruses which are killing cattle and for which there is presently no cure; bacterial and viral mutations, etc... if a comprehensive list were made it would be a very, very long one.

What this booklet will attempt to do is to put forward the basis for a *new* magickal Craft — one rooted in Paganism insofar as Paganism epitomises a love for and a deep insight and feeling for Nature, and rooted in Tibetan lore to the extent that this lore identifies some the esoteric aspects with which one can work; and one which endorses the *shamanic way* as well. It is a magickal Craft which directly addresses the *state of health* of the planet, and which may provide us with at least some of the answers we need. It is also a derivative and continuation of previous SPIRAL PUBLICATIONS, including STARCRAFT (i.e., the first part of this bundled book) — by which name this magickal Craft will be referred to here — and it is dedicated to all those who are involved in change and who want to find genuine and urgent solutions to our problems.

1 — STARCRAFT AS NATURAL MAGICK

There is no one definition of what magick is — it is different things to different people. Generally it can be said to be an act, or a series of acts, which is designed to have an effect on the energies that one uses, within oneself and without and around, with one or more purposes in mind.

Before going any further it must be said that while definitions can be useful they can also become limiting — as soon as a definition is made it has a tendency to become inclusive of certain points and exclusive of others, by default if for no other reason. A definition may give some form to ideas and maybe to certain types of knowledge, yet as soon as it becomes too rigid in its structure it almost invariably and unavoidably degenerates into dogma — which is the last thing we want to be hampered with here.

Starcraft is a natural magick. At an initial level it is very accessible because it is free of traditional roots, and all its essential parameters can be derived directly from Nature — the earth, the sky, the Sun, the Moon, the stars, and everything which may found in what can be called the *Body of the God-dess*.

It is an open book; and that book is Nature Hirself.

Walking through a forest can be refreshing and enjoyable; sitting by a stream can seem enchanting; watching a waterfall can induce a feeling of well-being. In simple terms this is magick — acting on moods, feelings, energy levels, consciousness, and inspiring one to be in closer touch with Nature's healing and edifying properties — in this case at work without any deliberate effort on the part of the recipient.

Once one realises this much it is only a short step to enter the world of active magick — a stream transports water from one place to another, much like one's life is transported by an invisible stream — complete with flows, eddies, and still moments, followed by accelerations, potential danger, peace, and any number of other possible events. A tree grows out of the earth and unfolds into the sky, again much like one's own life does — reaching up into the sunlight for sustenance and catalytic transformation. A mountain towers over the land below, in the same way as our spirits tower over our earthly personalities. If we look into the micro-world of molecules we find that Nature is there as well — building, combining, re-arranging, changing, and creating out of Hirself other forms and other vehicles for Spirit and expression.

In short, Nature is a continuous expression of magick; and all we need to do is attune ourselves to Nature in order to enter the realms of magick. As soon as we do this, a pathway, maybe many, is or are offered — in recognition of that attunement; and it is up to each one of us to accept that gift, or to reject it; one cannot walk every path there is, therefore one cannot necessarily accept all gifts. Our affinities can best guide whatever choices we may feel inclined to make.

Having made a choice we can *modulate* it, and experiment with it. As soon as we are prepared to be responsible for our own selves and our own *trips* we can access whatever it is that we

113

may feel in need of learning; in other words our very acts become a bridge to *knowing* ourselves and the world around us, and by extension to *knowing* the Universe at large — beyond limits and even beyond forms, or more precisely beyond the appearance of forms, thus facilitating identification with a Higher Self which knows no conceptual limitation, and which dwells within us all, and without which we could not be.

In the context of Starcraft, and putting things simply: since we are an expression of energy, and since there is only one essential life-energy or Universal Life-Force, we can learn to put ourselves in contact with any number of other expressions of energy which we can then weave into our magick. This is the beauty of Starcraft: it is intuitive in Nature — not static, not rule-bound; and therefore it is also free of the sort of regulations which hinder the expression of magick as enacted by many traditions and societies which have fallen prey to their own stereotypes.

Starcraft, as a magickal way, in some respects differs little from Witchcraft, at least in its essence — and it should be noted for the sake of reference that the word *Starcraft* has been used by some as a synonym for *Witchcraft,* particularly certain forms of ancient Witchcraft which are now arguably extinct in their expression. The Starcraft referred to in this booklet, however, is not traditional Witchcraft, nor is it one of the many types of neo-Witchcraft which have flourished into existence since the early 1950's — some of which have become hopelessly crossbred with other traditions, and in effect can scarcely be called Witchcraft at all (which does not mean they are not valid approaches). Starcraft is directly inspired by Devic agencies as outlined in the book, STARCRAFT (Spiral Publications), and while there is something of an underlying similarity between Wicca and Starcraft it is worth avoiding any confusion between the two.

What is truly different in Starcraft is the structure of a working group — there are no High Priestess and High Priest, as leadership is conferred by the group to any given individual, and only for a certain length of time, such as may be necessary for the purposes of conducting the group's magick. In other words leadership is not fixed; it is flexible and arbitrated only by the needs of the moment. It is useful to have leadership since it can avoid many difficulties inherent to the potential anarchy which can develop in an unfocused group; if one is working as a group, particularly as a magickal group, one doesn't want to waste a lot of energy arguing about what should be done and in what way it should be carried out while in the middle of *doing magick!* Aside from wasting precious energy this could prove to be dangerous, and in acute cases maybe even fatal.

There is no special emphasis on God and Goddess arche-types, but there is on God-dess — or Androgynous Essence; or *Spirit*. This is based on the fact that behind the male and female bodies we have there is an essential androgynous Spirit; male and female polarities are nevertheless used in Starcraft, and to good effect; however the fusion between the two is seen as more important.

Another difference is that a Starcraft group is not limited to thirteen members; there is no fixed maximum, although twenty members is generally to be considered something of a maximum, for practical purposes. A Starcraft group does need to include in-dividuals who feel closely knit in their purpose and *intent*, and who therefore need to be familiar with each other to a relatively advanced degree — particularly from a magickal point of view. Numbers over twenty can make that sense of familiarity rather difficult.

In Starcraft there are eight directional forces: North, South, East and West points are focused by four individuals; then between each cardinal point there is a cross-quarter point which is ideally focused by two sets of two people, numbers permitting, that is (more of this later). However there are many other possible variants of positional workings, based for instance on as little as four working members, through eight, twelve, sixteen, and the twenty-stations configuration which can be considered to be the optimum set-up, although twenty-four is also possible.

Since Starcraft is a Devic system one can look for clues in the various *number* arrangements that guiding Devas may suggest or else inspire a working group to use. This may not seem very clear for now, nevertheless anyone interested in Starcraft needs to be at least open to the idea and reality of dealing with the power of numbers — particularly with regard to the *working* of magickal processes.

Ideally all magick is to be carried out at a power place within the land with which an affinity has been formed — guidelines for this were given in STARCRAFT. However this does not exclude working within four walls whenever necessary. As with Witchcraft and the Amerindian Medicine Wheel systems, Starcraft group magick is conducted in a designated Circle, which first must be *cleared* of any psychic debris, then empowered with protective qualities — thus creating a boundary against adverse interference.

In some ways there is a greater similarity between Starcraft and the shamanic view as described by Carlos Castaneda in THE EAGLE'S GIFT, THE FIRE FROM WITHIN and THE POWER OF SILENCE, than there is between Starcraft and Witchcraft — in the above books a system of four quadrants is also used: four male shamans holding the North, East, South and West stations, and each of these outflanked by two female shamankas; plus couriers; and one shamanka — the Nagual Woman — acting *beyond the world* as a beacon for the rest of the group. In Starcraft the difference lies in the fact that each quadrant is focused by one person — who can be male or female — and is outflanked by up to four (or five) others, two on each side — who can also be male or female.

The main object of *working* Starcraft is to *align* oneself with Devic forces and agencies in as full a consciousness as possible, and to *act* from there — using one's sensitivity to Devic input as a basis for whatever is carried out by way of magick. It is the responsibility of the person leading the group to focus, channel and express that sensitivity, although at a higher level of group integration — particularly if genuine telepathy comes into play — then each and all the members of the group can find their flow and balance within a *magickal dance* whose true purpose may become revealed during the unfoldment of that *dance*.

Beyond this point Starcraft does not dictate very much at all. In principle each Starcraft group is autonomous from any other, and the members of each group make their own decisions as to how they do things and in what way. For instance they can work skyclad (weather permitting) or not — clothes can mask incoming energies, nevertheless it is rarely necessary to dispense with them altogether for the purpose of enacting magick unless there is good cause to do so. Members can also use external symbolic objects, or do without them — these can be useful but they are certainly not necessary, and in fact in some cases they can turn out to be most distracting since Starcraft is an intuitive pathway and one does not necessarily know in advance what is going to happen during a group *working*. All, or almost all preconceptions should be avoided unless those Devas who are acting as guides and transmitters of energy indicate that such and such a method or methods should be used for a given period of time or until further notice.

This so far is an overview of things, an initial *flavour* of what Starcraft is or can be.

2 — INTUITIVE MAGICK

Briefly we need to outline the nature of intuitive magick since in many ways it is quite different from formulated magick. First of all, and obviously enough, it is based on intuition and intuitive perceptions — the ability to sense, *see,* and/or *feel* something without necessarily apprehending it in an intellectual manner, at least not as a matter of first importance.

It is difficult to describe how the intuition works. If we consider the mind which tends to classify and subdivide information into more or less identifiable categories — all of which is useful whenever we want to be logical about things for which one is dependent on observation and/or on concepts; observation and concepts can evolve more or less independently, as in science where theories can be worked out first, followed by observations which either *prove* or disprove these, or where observations are made which then require theories to explain them. The mind loves games of this kind and thrives on bolting one fragment to another in order to make a greater fragment, leading with any luck to a greater whole; or else conversely taking a whole and dividing it into its constituent parts, and then analysing these parts.

Intuition does not work like that — it generates insights through a process of relationship where one has to be able to *feel* what one is seeking to *know*. This has nothing to do with emotions — intuition is not an emotion. In some ways it has something to do with correspondences where one thing is perceived to be in some fashion similar to another, even though they may be quite different in their external guises — hence the relationship between them is not immediately obvious, yet it does exist. Intuition is a more abstract sort of faculty than is mind, and it deals with things on a lateral basis — i.e., it operates in a relatively multi-layered way.

It literally takes intuition to understand intuition, and therefore no amount of words can describe it, because that would be a mental process. It also has something to do with holistic insight where things are *seen* to be derived from a common source, and are therefore all related to that source. The animistic insight that all things are issued from the Cosmic Soul, and as far as this planet is concerned that all things are issued from the Planetary Soul, is an intuitive insight — not something which the mind can prove to itself in black and white terms unless it is directly inspired by the intuition; and this is perhaps the key to the intuition: it does not deal in black and white terms — it is all-inclusive and perceives things as interconnected. Therefore to be intuitive is to follow the connection lines between one thing and

118

another, or one thing and many others, and then realising that those connection lines are not always *straight:* they can be curved, they can be multi-dimensional, they can be separated by vast distances in time and space and yet still occupy the same point — that may not be easy for the mind to digest, but it is child's play for the intuition.

The mind can get caught up by the appearance of paradox, where two things can seem archetypally opposite; however the intuition does not *see* any paradoxes — it will fuse those two things and reveal them to be the same, or else issued from a common root. The mind deals with mirror images; the intuition dissolves the mirrors and leaves one with a reality where there is no duality. If we apply all this to magick then it becomes clear that intuitive magick is not dependent on any concepts — it leapfrogs across the boundaries which the mind has created for itself, and the walls between thing and thing simply vanish, leaving the essence of those things to be *seen*.

Intuitive magick deals with essences, and whereas the mind is preoccupied with form, the intuition is entirely at home in formlessness. As a result of this, intuition is invaluable in magick because it recognises no frontiers, and when the mind and the intuition work perfectly together it is then that great magick can be achieved indeed — especially if an added factor is present: the *will,* or *intent*.

Will, intuition and mind are the three essential *tools* of magick. Will indicates force, power and purpose, and *intent;* the intuition is the *all-seeing eye* which can perceive in all directions simultaneously; and the mind is the servant of both the will and the intuition, and can give form to what is *intended* and what is *seen*.

The will is the *ruler;* the intuition is the *seer;* and the mind is the *builder* — representing the Primordial Triad, or the Three Aspects of the God-dess, or Cosmic Being.

In Starcraft much use is made of the intuition because it is only the intuition which can bridge the gap — i.e., the apparent gap — between what is human in context and what is non-human, and particularly with that which is devic. The story goes a bit like this: æons ago it was foreseen that the essential androgynous nature of Being would have to be separated into a *male* and a *female* life-stream — because the mind required a measure of separation, and only the mind could lead to the creation of the *form-state,* and to a sense of individuality; as a result the male life-stream became the human side of Being — with the task of developing individuality — and the female life-stream became the devic side of Being; in reality they are a single whole, nevertheless for the purposes of creation and *intent* they had to be somewhat isolated from each other, especially the human from the devic. Up to a few thousands of years ago that separation was only partial as far as consciousness is concerned, however.

In Starcraft one learns to put both these life-streams back together again — in full consciousness; in other words one learns to rebecome androgynous in one's expression, which in turn leads to the eventual freedom from the illusion of all duality. One learns to use duality, but not to be the prisoner of it; one re-attunes oneself to the One-Source of duality, but one is no longer one of its end-products.

To the mind this may appear fanciful, but to the intuition it is self-evident.

Two more points: a path with *heart* is a path which is inspired by the intuition; the heart, even at a physical level, embodies the function of a flow of energy which is both a function of an input and an output, yet in both modes it is still a single flow (in this case, of blood — which carries the life-force, or prana/chi, throughout the whole of our bodies); the pulse of the flow is regulated by the heart, yet that pulse is not divisive — the dynamic force which activates the heart is not divisive either; yet the mind has created a system of arteries (for the output of the flow) and veins (for the return of that flow), thereby enacted an apparent duality — nevertheless the flow would not exist if there were only arteries, or if there were only veins: they are complementary, even if they are also opposites. The second point is this: take away all the walls that the mind creates and you then experience pure telepathy or what many would call enlightenment or Self-Realisation.

Starcraft is designed to promote Self-Realisation, and once that is achieved it permits one to work in and from a state of Self-Realised consciousness. In this state one is aware of oneself as both human and deva, and therefore the guiding Devas which inspire the workings of Starcraft are both within us and without.

This is the key to the information in STARCRAFT once divested of its channelled format of expression.

3 — CO-OPERATIVE WORK WITH DEVAS

Stretching one's ability to perceive things on an intuitive basis makes conscious contact with Devas possible, and in order to do any effective magick, co-operation with Devas is absolutely necessary. When Witches invoke the Goddess and the God they are invoking two Devic archetypes; and when they do so using specific names they are invoking traditional subsets of those two archetypes. Nevertheless there is something of a difference between invoking archetypes and dealing with Devas directly, without anthropomorphising them — archetypes are a human projection, whereas Devas in their natural state are beings who do not require any specific forms in order to be, live or act. This does not prevent them entirely from manifesting themselves in form, yet they are best perceived as fields of energy — indeed we ourselves have fields of energy (so-called *auras,* which are in fact deva substance), therefore the main difference is that Devas do not incarnate physically like we do, nor do they need to preoccupy themselves with the acquisition of a sense of individuality.

Devas exist in great numbers and exhibit an incredible variety of types, from tiny little devas who preoccupy themselves with various well-defined sub-aspects of the natural world to the greater Devas who work on Cosmic Levels. In between these two extremes there are Devas who are directly related to us as human

121

beings — our Solar Devas — who can be thought of as our souls, although this does need some qualification.

There are two sides to one's soul — the human side and the devic side. When *seen* as a totality they are perceived as one single being; if one looks a bit closer it becomes apparent that the human side deals specifically with the *overshadowing* of the human fragment projected downwards into matter and incarnation, while the devic side preoccupies itself primarily with devic activities (including the creation of *energy-sheaths* as vehicles of consciousness for that human fragment, and much else besides).

Looking closer still one can realise that one's soul is not separate from oneself — it merely acts on a different level of existence and consciousness. One's Solar Deva or Soul — as a complete human-devic unit — represents one's *perfect Self*, at least at the level at which s/he operates: i.e., the Higher Mental Plane, and in some cases the Buddhic Plane. Therefore invoking one's Solar Deva is to invoke a part of oneself; and more precisely, a part of one's Higher Self.

Furthermore since all Devas are One Deva — in essence (in the same way as all human beings can be *seen* as a function of a single Primordial Monad) — one can also *see* that all Solar Devas are directly related to the Planetary Soul, and by extension to the Cosmic Soul, or MahaDeva. It is this interlinking or interconnectedness which makes powerful magick possible — through the process of personal identification with other parts of oneself, including various facets of one's Higher Self — which is a Life-Being that we all share as a common Source, if we care to be clearly conscious of this (via Life-Initiation).

What we do as human beings is to develop individuality; Devas cannot develop any real sense of individuality since they are almost entirely communally oriented — in fact they can only do so through us, which explains the connection between us and them: when *seen* from one point of view we are one and same; when *seen* from a different point of view we are involved in different aspects of growth and development, which are nevertheless complementary. Both sides of the overall development are necessary, which is why we exist as human beings, and why Devas exist as Devas.

Devas are the creators and embodiment of Nature on all levels or Planes, using the energies which they are to create all the environments and forms through which we (and other creatures and beings) can manifest ourselves. Without them there would be no worlds and no bodies as vehicles for Spirit; whenever we are attempting to do our magick we are using devic energies, and therefore co-operation with Devas is essential since we are using in effect a part of their being; also, they know much more about the process of manifestation than we do, and working in full consciousness with them can only promote much better results.

Different types of Devas can be contacted for different types of magick, and yet there are those who specialise in the processes of magick — in Tibetan esoteric lore they are sometimes referred to as the *Devas of violet hue,* the Violet Ray being the one which is directly related to Magick (and this is the type of energy which will predominantly influence the coming Age). This contact is best achieved by first identifying in consciousness with our Solar Devas, who can then summon the help of the Violet Devas for the purpose of conducting magick.

This is an inexhaustible subject, and what is said here is only by way of introducing elements of what can be done, and something of what needs to be *known*. Indeed there are other kinds of Devas who are actually involved in the destruction of forms for the sake of *clearing the way* for new and more appropriate embodiments — therefore Devas are not creators alone; they are totally involved with the dynamics of manifestation and all the various needs of evolution, which includes periodic creativity as well as destruction, or the dismantling of the forms.

Many magickal traditions do not address themselves directly to the Devic aspects, although they may well do so in other, somewhat more indirect ways. In Starcraft one addresses Devas directly, and deliberately: instead of dealing with obscure archetypes one deals with the *reality* of the devic presence; in other words all the fancy window-dressing is by-passed and one works with Devas as they are, and not with representative symbols alone, although specific symbols can be used to summon the attention of specific Devas.

If one is not prepared to *know* and work with Devas as they are then one can seldom produce any magick which is of any lasting significance. Since Devas are entirely devoted to the progress and unfoldment of Evolution as a whole, one must also be prepared to make that one's own priority — well above any personal priorities. Selfish acts of magick do not go down well with Devas, and they very much resent being compelled to work against their more universal objectives; lesser devas can be coerced and manipulated into working the biddings of selfish magickians whenever these use certain secret devic formulas which these lesser devas cannot resist, yet the greater Devas who overshadow the work of these lesser devas are certainly not above destroying the vehicles (etheric-physical, astral and sometimes mental body-sheaths) of any magickians whose intent is entirely negative and who misappropriate the energies and usefulness of these lesser devas.

In Starcraft one works *with* Devas for the purpose of manifesting results which are of common interest and which are in tune with a purpose which can be described generally as evolutionary. There is room for some experimentation providing it is likely to lead to a beneficial outcome. Also, Devas do allow for a certain margin of error, which nevertheless becomes narrower as the level of magick worked becomes higher, particularly in its intensity. Devas are prepared to teach human magickians or would-be magickians *how* to work, and they are tolerant of any mistakes to the extent that these mistakes are not committed out of selfishness, and providing one is prepared to work with these Devas with enough *heart* and with at least a degree of dedication and commitment.

Devas do not like *dabblers*— errors in magickal work create problems for them and not just for us. This applies in other spheres of activity which might not be viewed as magickal in context — for instance science has concocted many new synthetic substances which at present are far from being stable in their nature and which are distorting the elemental essences of which they are composed. This produces a problem for Devas since they then have to find ways of liberating these elemental essences from the adverse situation they find themselves in. Much of the solution to this sort of problem will occur whenever scientists begin to appreciate Devic reality and become prepared to work consciously with Devas instead of putting together whatever seems most expedient to them.

In Starcraft there are many options to be chosen from with regard to what type of magick one wishes to enact and what sort of end results one might care of make objective, although some work can be more subjective in nature. This is also why each Starcraft group needs to be autonomous from any others since different aspects of magickal work need to be addressed — we are dealing not only with a whole planet with, as it is, near endless ramifications, but with a whole Universe in which this planet finds itself and of which it is an integral part.

Putting things in a way which might be easier to understand one could make the following observations: obviously enough this planet is far from perfect in its expression, at the human level and in other respects, therefore there is much to be done which is more or less strictly of planetary concern; nevertheless one cannot entirely deal with the problems evidenced by this planet without becoming aware of and being prepared to deal with the greater Systemic and Cosmic environment, since much of which influences this planet in various ways emanates from sources which are external to its own periphery (astrology as it is

125

presently understood is only a very small part of that particular picture). As human beings we are not yet in the position to understand much of what needs addressing with regard to the Cosmic environment in relationship to the Earth, yet there are Devas who are — and conscious contact and *alignment* with these Devas can open up the doors which will facilitate a better understanding and awareness of what needs to be done.

We cannot expect the rest of the Cosmos to sort things out for us; if we are not prepared to be a part of the solution to our planet's difficulties then we do not really deserve any help. Indeed we are given help — even if we do not consciously acknowledge it — because we are a part of the whole; and if one part of the whole is out of balance then it tends to produce problems for all the other parts, which in effect must compensate for that imbalance on our behalf — because it affects them as well. However overwhelming this picture may be we owe it to ourselves as well as to rest of the Cosmos to make whatever efforts may be necessary to rectify things and thereby manifest a better balance on Earth, and by extension assist the Cosmos in its own unfoldment — again, we are an integral part of that unfoldment, therefore we have to make the leap which will take us beyond our own little preoccupations so that we can then participate in whatever needs doing in a much greater and more universal context.

This leap may seem difficult — emerging out of the dark ages of our limitations it appears that we are suddenly being required to become not only aware of a Universe which is infinite, but to address matters which so far have been entirely beyond our scope. However, two points must be made here: first, some of our ancestors (maybe well ourselves incarnate in other times) *did* take in the Cosmic view and were aware of all this at least to a certain extent; second, we are not being asked to understand and cope with everything overnight, but we are being required to make a bigger effort in that direction — and given that we are evolving better methods of communication at this time and that we are by all accounts about to make a giant quantum leap in our overall understanding of the Universe we are being asked to fulfil our evolution in a manner which is becoming every day that much more possible and feasible.

Where exactly this will lead us we can only speculate. Undoubtedly some of us will progress faster than others — mostly because some of us will want to, but also because some of us are better prepared to do so. Starcraft offers a *new* way to approach the Cosmic Life, and while not everyone will feel inclined to actually *work* Starcraft in a coherent and dedicated fashion there will be others who might well use elements of Starcraft in their own approach and chosen way.

Everything which has been said so far has been imparted before in some form or other — in the other Spiral Publications' manuals and indeed in many other so-called esoteric books. In fact many of the *occult* or arcane sources which have contributed their views and their information to the Spiral Publications series, and this directly and as well as indirectly, have also contributed similar views and information to other writers or channels. The main difference, if it is one, is that each writer-channel brings to this information a particular flavour, and expands it in a given direction which at the very least may seem novel — this is consistent with the observation that each individual's experience is unique and that s/he is bound to favour a particular perspective more than s/he is another — projecting further, this is directly applicable to how each Starcraft group does or will enact its magick, because it will flow along the lines which are most affinitive to its members.

As with any genuine art one must have a *feeling* for it; one cannot actually work Starcraft from an intellectual point of view alone, therefore whatever is said in this booklet does not in itself confer an ability to work Starcraft. Nor does it prevent anyone anywhere from experimenting with Starcraft as it is described here, and this without referring to the source of its dissemination. There is no *guru* involved here: to put it succinctly these books represent information, and not teachings. Some might well contest that there is no difference between teaching and imparting information, yet there is: a teacher instructs others to do things in a particular fashion; whereas in contrast an informant impart insights but does not say, "Do this only in this way". Whatever is said here is to be adapted to personal and group needs.

Nor does talking about and describing Devas in any way confer the ability to contact them and work with them in full consciousness. First of all one must be able to *shift* one's consciousness in whatever way or ways may seem appropriate taking into account that some methods of approach might well be dangerous and maybe ill-considered. The Spiral Publications series has been designed to help this process of *shifting* consciousness, and to this end many different approaches have been described. Secondly Starcraft has been referred to in the introduction to this booklet as something of an extension of *true* Paganism, and also (and principally) of Shamanism and Animism; nevertheless it does not prevent people who might not care to think of themselves as Pagans per se from using the information which is to be found here. Starcraft is not a religion anyway.

It is, once again, all a matter of affinity. Paganism is the only view which accepts Nature and Spirit as immanent as well as transcendent, and this without entering into paroxysms of dogmatic fervour. Further, Shamanism is a branch-form of Paganism, as is Witchcraft, and as is Animism (at least in essence — the repeated use of this word — *essence* — is quite deliberate, therefore no apologies will be offered for its frequent reoccurrence). Arguably Taoism could also be said to accept immanence and transcendence simultaneously, although it tends to shelve all attempts at direct action. All other mystical-religious paths tend to drive a wedge between the immanence of God-dess and Hir transcendent Reality, and some cannot or else are totally unwilling to perceive any immanence whatsoever. Even Christian Gnostics, who do at least exhibit above-average insight, interpret

128

the natural world as the creation of a demi-god, yet fail to *see* the equal value of immanence and transcendence.

It is not the place here to investigate all the philosophical, mystical and esoteric subtleties which have emerged over the last few thousands of years, therefore what is being said, hopefully quite plainly in this booklet, is that a balanced view of Life embraces both immanence and transcendence, and that Paganism — once more *in essence* — is maybe the only view which endorses both without contradiction and without getting bogged down in a paradox which may seem irreconcilable. Either one accepts Creation as a manifestation of the God-dess (or whatever other name one may care to give Life) or one doesn't — in which case one creates one's own hell by refusing to accept immanence.

If one is to work with Devas one must be able to accept immanence and transcendence simultaneously. If one rejects immanence then one is rejecting the Devic role of creating the worlds and everything which is natural in these worlds. Conversely if one rejects transcendence then one is rejecting the true purpose of Creation and all future progress.

Against immanence there are those who feel that all life is subject to some inherent tragedy, and these people fail in that moment to realise that there is no tragedy whatsoever — there are only consequences, i.e., the results of ill-conceived actions, or for that matter a complete lack of actions, or else ineffective or uncompleted actions. In truth, Life is not out to make things easy for us, or to provide us with a ready-made Paradise, as it were — it invites us to co-create it with Devas. Out of the effort of creating it (within ourselves and without) we in effect learn to *live* it, in consciousness and in fact.

Then against transcendence there are those who maintain that life begins and ends with the material universe; in that moment these people fail to realise that all created life is energy and not matter at all: matter is only a dense manifestation of energy; further, energy itself is Devic substance generated by the apparently dualistic polarities which Devas enact for the purpose of creating all manifested life. Transcendence is to recognise that there is a Source which is *beyond* the expression of that apparent Devic dualism, and which in consequence cannot manifest Itself... except through the agency of Devas, and then via that agency through various lifeforms and the consciousness indwelling within these — It is the Unmanifest Potential behind all of Creation; in other words It is its Original Source, including ours as human beings ultimately.

To endorse transcendence and not immanence is to *cop out*, for the created Universe was not undertaken out of some vague gameplay in which the Universal Being attempted to relieve Itself from the utter boredom of having nothing else to do except dwell in eternal Nothingness — or the *Voidless Void,* or call it what you will. It had a Purpose, and for that matter still has that Purpose, which simply put was and is to create individuality, for It realised that out of individuality would eventually emerge *Perfected God-desses* — i.e., perfected parts of Itself which would then go on to unfold a potential which by-passes even that which can be considered to be Cosmic; what that may be we cannot know yet because we are not conscious participants in that Para-Cosmic Reality.

Transcendence also includes something of a dis-association from parameters such as Time and Space, and Energy and Matter (as we view them at least) — as soon as we accept the Unmanifest in full consciousness then there is no problem reconciling that Unmanifest with Creation, which is a function of those parameters. Manifestation is a passing thing, which exists for a time and for a purpose, and which is catalytic in bringing about a certain result (from another point of view, many different kinds of results). As human beings we are only one small part of the overall puzzle, and yet that puzzle would be incomplete without us — and this however infinite that puzzle may be.

The Unmanifest lives outside of Time and beyond Space; and it is the Source of Energy (and therefore of Matter) but it is not

Energy itself. One can come to realise — in what is perhaps a sublime moment of pure resolution of all known paradoxes — that in fact all events in Time and Space, at all levels, in effect occur simultaneously in a *momentless moment,* therefore Creation both exists and does not exist, at least not as we perceive it from a time-bound point of view — and there is NO contradiction in that observation whatsoever. It flashes before one's eyes and is *seen* intuitively, and the intellect can just about cope with its significance if it releases its insistance on trying to dissect it into linear logic.

Considerations such as these stretch our comprehension. Without that stretching one cannot shift one's consciousness. If one cannot stretch one's consciousness one cannot contact and work coherently with Devas; and if one cannot do that one cannot practise Starcraft to any significant degree. Therefore it is certainly relevant to say all this — even if it appears to be an esoteric conceptual wonderland and doesn't cater much for ordinary living.

Working with Devas can have its difficulties, as well as its joys. As one *shifts* one's sense of conscious identity and re-*aligns* it with Devic reality one begins to partake of that reality — to the extent that one can begin to *feel* devic in one's consciousness. One's perspective changes; if one allows it to change completely then one can enter behind the veils which separate the world of forms from the formless states which underlie it, and from there onwards it is possible to experience oneself living in two or more world-states simultaneously, for the Devic perspectives are immensely powerful — this can seem confusing at first, yet it can also be very enlightening; and that is indeed part of the challenge of Initiation. Once one has done this one must also learn to regain normal human consciousness and the perspective of the normal world, and thereby shield out the devic perspectives — and this at will. Yet later, once one has stretched one's consciousness further — in other words when one has become a lot more proficient in working Starcraft, and when one has experienced at least the first Life-Initiation — then one can allow one's consciousness to *shift* in and out of Devic contact, and that contact is no longer obtrusive — in fact it is gladly welcomed, for it is a beautiful and powerful state to be in. At this point Starcraft becomes somewhat more of a permanent focus in one's life, i.e., one is practising it more or less non-stop, and consciously so.

Initially the practice of working magickally as a group, in a Circle, is little more than a way of being trained (by Devas) to *see,* to *feel,* to *be,* to *act* and to *intend,* etc; whereas later on one learns to *work* Starcraft during every single moment of one's expression, and therefore to *shift* one's consciousness at will in true Shamanic fashion.

This is at the higher end of achievement, and it is mentioned here only because sooner or later this is part of what will happen. As the process of conscious fusion (between the human state and the devic state) progresses in its intensity one becomes more and more adept in handling energies of various kinds, and finally the inevitable occurs — one masters oneself and the use of these energies, which then opens the door towards the Higher Planes on a permanent basis; this occurs at the third Life-Initiation, and represents a complete freedom from the cycle of reincarnation.

One can also learn to dematerialise one's physical body and then rematerialise either the etheric blue-print or one's astral body — should there be a need to do so with regard to some particular work (this has been covered in other Spiral publications).

None of this is easy, which might well be obvious. It requires an inordinate amount of dedication, and much resilience — for one finds oneself not only confronted by the enormity of the change implied, but also by forces, let alone perspectives, which, if not dealt with positively and decisively, are just as likely to be crushing in their effect, with uncertain consequences.

There is a lot to learn, both as an individual and as a member of a working Starcraft group, and it may take years, even decades before one reaches the stage mentioned above; yet at the present time this sort of development is very much favoured since the Planetary Spirit Hirself is at a point of evolutionary crisis and going through a Cosmic Initiation at Hir own level — therefore the incoming energies are of great potency, and this is a situation which we can take advantage of in this respect. In other ages it usually took lifetimes of gruelling effort to achieve Self-Mastery; now it can take just a few years, yet the effort required is just as great — in its own way.

4 — DEVELOPING PSYCHIC SKILLS

If one wishes to come to terms with any kind of artistic expression obviously one has to develop whatever skills are necessary before one can begin to unfold one's creativity; one might be naturally creative, but without skills one cannot go very far. Creativity without skills, or skills without creativity, indicates a lack of balance.

This is perfectly true of Starcraft, because everyone of us has the potential for using, then eventually mastering what could be called the *art of Starcraft* — it is certainly not reserved for any particular elite; it is not something which cannot be learnt, or for that matter which cannot be taught (keeping in mind that it is a Devic system, or a subset of one — see STARCRAFT). One may come into it knowing nothing, at a conscious level, and one can progress first of all in relatively gentle steps, then in greater steps, and then in greater steps yet no one should feel that they cannot come to terms with Starcraft, and this however lofty the demands may become in the long run.

One's aptitude is defined primarily by three things: a willingness to learn and dedicate oneself to this magickal craft, without any reservations; a willingness to accept at least in principle that all personal limitations can be overcome — however long a time that may take, and regardless of how limited one may feel in the first place; a willingness to accept that Devas do indeed exist, that they can be consciously contacted, and that in the context of working Starcraft co-operation with Devas is paramount — it is

133

not a question of Devas ruling over oneself, or oneself ruling over Devas; Starcraft (from the point of view considered here) is a joint enterprise between both life-streams.

Whatever specialised psychic skills are developed may vary from person to person, yet there are some which all those involved need to learn at least to a reasonable degree of proficiency — these skills can be likened to stepping stones, each one of which can highlight further skills to be acquired in the course of one's work. Here is a short list of some the essential skills required:

Astral Projection, or the ability to project one's consciousness out of the physical body in order to familiarise oneself with the level of existence which is generally referred to as the Astral Plane. Since the energy-substance of this Plane is very malleable when acted upon mentally — in contrast to physical energy-substance which being much denser is not so easily manipulated — this level of existence is ideally suited to the projection of thought-forms, and one can then see and appreciate the processes involved — which is a bonus. It is also very useful with regard to learning how to centre, and then hold one's attention steady, since otherwise one loses the projected state; this is good practice prior to dealing with the energies and realities of higher levels, which ultimately are of far greater importance to us.

Meditation, of which there are countless variants, from non-thinking and contemplation, to various kinds of creative visualisation. The ability to meditate fluently is maybe one of the most important skills one can acquire with regard to *working* Starcraft at any length.

Circle-work, or group-work, which implies an ability to work psychically with a whole group, which in itself requires an ever greater level of group-integration if Starcraft is to be *worked* successfully. This is no easy matter since the individual members of the group must not only feel in personal affinity with one another, they must also be self-responsible and able to sort out any interpersonal disaffections or psychic difficulties very quickly and as efficiently as possible. Difficulties which are allowed to fester either undetected or unattended can lead to much greater and more severe difficulties when practising magick, particularly during moments of crisis — which at a certain level of development and unfoldment can occur relatively frequently.

Dreaming, stalking, seeing and *feeling,* which terms are derived and borrowed from the shamanic practices as related in the Carlos Castaneda books — however *feeling* is more particular to Starcraft since it forms part of one's ability to *align* oneself consciously with Devas and devic reality.

Intending, as pertinent to the use of *intent,* and *will,* and with regard to the carrying out of *purpose.*

There are many other skills which one can acquire or even need during the course of one's involvement in Starcraft, nevertheless they are all related to the above skills in some manner or other.

5 — ASTRAL PROJECTION

In what way is Astral Projection really useful in the context of Starcraft? First of all if you have never consciously projected out of the body it may be very difficult for you to acknowledge that other levels of existence truly do exist. It is one thing to accept the intellectual notion that various Planes do exist, or worse yet to merely believe that they might. Until that experience is YOURS and until you have no doubts whatsoever that they do exist then you are only dealing with the *maybe's* of life and not with the realities.

Over twenty years of projection experience permits me to say this much: Astral Projection is fun; also it is empirical proof that there is no such thing as permanent death — that there are only different states of consciousness and livingness, and that one does indeed pass from one to the other during the course of incarnating and discarnating. This may not seem like much when read, but when this is personally experienced then it has a profound catalytic impact on one's way of viewing life. However one does not have to wait for physical death to know this. One can learn to project astrally and consciously so, and it is not all that difficult to do this — it requires a bit of *feeling* for it, a bit of guidance maybe, and then a few dozen *outings* before one becomes reasonably good at it.

It opens up a whole new dimension of being to explore — not only the environment of the Astral Plane, on this world and other worlds, but also the exploration of one's abilities to focus one's mind, one's intuition, one's will, and thereby apply the art of the Shaman — *dreaming, stalking, intending*, and *feeling*.

One finds that with minimal effort — even a simple act of will or imagination is often sufficient — that one can fly through the air, go from area to area without going through the space in between, move through what appear to be solid objects, and even project oneself out into space, visit other planets in this Solar System, or that of others. One can also change body shape at will, go about without a body at all — as a point of consciousness — or encapsulate one's energies in a small ball of fire with 360 degrees visual perception. The possibilities are almost endless because on the Astral Plane whatever you want to happen can actually occur, and often without having to try too hard.

Some might feel that these comments invalidate the experience, that Astral Projection is merely the internalising of one's imagination and sense of fantasy *made semi-real* via one's psyche. Yet anyone who has projected *out there* and who has focused hir attention perfectly on what is there to be seen has undoubtedly found that the Astral Plane is not only real, or at least as real as anything is on the physical plane, but that in many ways it is more vivid and more realistic than an ordinary or equivalent physical experience.

Furthermore, if one cares to make the effort to reach the higher sub-layers of the Astral Plane one can encounter environments which are not only very real, they are also very luminous, vibrant, alive and frequently quite powerful. The further *up* one goes the more this is so, and eventually one finds oneself at the threshold of the next level, or Mental Plane — the Higher Mental Plane is in fact super-real and highly colourful, and very powerful — replete with potent symbolic, visual and *essence* information; then one realises the true nature of symbols as building blocks for the mind.

A lot more can be said about all this, and everything, or at least almost everything that you might want to know about it has been documented in THE PSYCHIC EXPLORER.

The experience of Astral Projection has another side benefit: it demonstrates that one doesn't need to feel locked into a personality pattern from which there is no escape; on the Astral Plane one can experience and project oneself in all sorts of different ways at will, and in the course of doing so one comes to realise that given enough effort that it may well be possible to restructure everything that one is — this is not something one can appreciate so readily when one's perspective of life is wholly bound to that of physical reality. On the physical plane one can try and change or enhance one's personality, but nothing suggests that anything more revolutionary than this can be achieved; on the Astral Plane, however (and more so when conscious on higher levels yet), one realises that *anything is possible* given the will and the effort to manifest it.

6 — MEDITATION

The usual impression many people have of meditation is derived from the East and usually consists of eliminating all thoughts and abiding in a perfect stillness of mind and enduring peace. That's fine; this is indeed a very useful experience and a good way of disciplining one's mind to be *quiet* — which it very seldom is during daily life; when the mind is *quiet* one can *see* things which the mind normally screens out and makes imperceptible.

But it can also be all sorts of other things — meditation can be subjective, and it can be objective. One can meditate on one's Higher Self, or on various levels of it, or one can meditate on the nature of Life, or on all manner of Cosmic connections — all of which can be thought of as subjective; or one can meditate on more pragmatic things and use creative visualisation as a means of establishing mental structures which will then be implemented in some fashion at a physical level (see THE POWER OF MIND & CONSCIOUSNESS).

In Starcraft meditation is the key to establishing conscious contact with Devas; whereas ritual is comparatively secondary in its importance, or even unnecessary. This is where Starcraft departs from most forms of Witchcraft and many kinds of Shamanism — there is generally little or no external activity to be seen in Circle-work, and since one is dealing principally with Solar Devas and other Star Devas the contact is relatively direct and sometimes very powerful; it requires psychic sensitivity and an ability to flow with strong inputs of Devic forces — then an ability to redirect those forces as may be needed.

Activities such as drumming, chanting, rattling gourds, etc., while conspicuous in shamanic earth-magick, and while they can work well for that purpose, are simply not entertained or necessary in Starcraft; likewise the ceremonial activities undertaken in many forms of Witchcraft would certainly be out of place in Starcraft. Because of this it may seem that there is no catalytic process to induce such things as heightened states of awareness, trances, and so on... yet there is; it is a part of the collective interplay of energies between the members of the group, and between these and Solar Devas (all other types of contact are made through these Devas).

Each Starcraft group is *overshadowed* by a group of Solar Devas corresponding to its members, and the task of this Solar Devic group is to promote *alignments* of energies with other Devic groups, from which various information and impressions can be obtained, thereby creating a web of powerful communication — thus Solar Devas are the first to be contacted, and meditation is the means of establishing an appropriate *shift* in consciousness, followed by personal identification with the

Solar Devic state.

Devic impressions can be *felt* and sometimes *seen;* the immediate task of the appointed leader of a Starcraft group is to facilitate the process, and those occupying the cardinal points within the Circle will channel these impressions both at an energy level and verbally, where necessary, thereby *keying* the whole group into working together in harmony and efficiently, with the minimum loss of energy. Much of the initial phase of development of any Starcraft group is spent mastering meditation because of this.

This may not sound like everyone's idea of working magick; some people need the crutch of ritual in order to *key* themselves into a higher state of consciousness. Ritual in Starcraft, however, is only used for very specific tasks which require a very close coordination between Devic stimulation and human response; at this point any rituals which are undertaken must be carried out as near perfectly as possible because power will then be directed through these rituals, and any errors can be costly, or may be very uncomfortable — and maybe even deadly.

There are many simple kinds of ritual which each Starcraft member can practise alone for the sake of becoming familiar with ritualised magick; these include: opening certain psychic *gates* using power or ritual symbols, then receiving energies using one's hands as cups or contact points, or using a Uranian wand (which resembles a *Y;* the wand is directed towards a specialised power-source and the top-points of the wand receive two Devic impressions (or a single dual impression), one male and one female (in terms of polarity) — these are then concentrated and fused together, and then transferred to a chosen chakra for the purpose of some magickal act... this is a whole subject unto itself); opening other kinds of *gates,* again using power or ritual symbols, then sending energies — once more using one's hands, particularly the finger-tips (or again using a Uranian wand, which can also be used the other way around — holding on to the tips of the *Y* and sending energy out through the other, single-pointed

139

end); thirdly, using power symbols to integrate energies within oneself, by absorbing them, harmonising them, and then allowing them to pervade one's energy-field — with potential benefit for the immediate environment, and for that matter even the world at large.

In Starcraft much work is done with regard to helping the basic elementals of the Earth to balance out those pressures which have been inculcated in them, principally as a result of human stupidity or unawareness. Part of the work of Starcraft is aimed at restoring or attaining new levels of elemental harmony, particularly at a time when many of the energies which surround us (often within as well as without) are fraught with tension, maybe aggression, and perhaps alienation. Elementals are conscious, living beings, which though bound by those forces which control them can react destructively when antagonised beyond a certain threshold; it is within our interest as well as theirs that they should be lent assistance in order to release their tension without creating havoc and destruction.

There are many aspects of Starcraft which cannot be addressed here openly in print — the prime emphasis is on flow and on balance. Starcraft does not deal with *black* and *white* issues, including concepts of what might be *good* and what might be *evil* — it deals with balancing energies, harmonising them, and at the appropriate times, liberating them — in the process one balances, harmonises, and then liberates oneself.

Indeed Starcraft is a *Path of Liberation,* of freedom, of power — culminating in the mastery of energy and matter via the use of will, love-intuition, and mind, as previously outlined and indicated. It deals with anything which may need dealing with, therefore it is not elitist — it is merely functional, and where necessary it is direct, yet whatever is done is always undertaken co-operatively with Devas.

It recognises and acknowledges the needs of other types of beings, including various kinds of earth spirits, and aims to help these if and when that help is requested, yet it never enforces

140

anything upon them against their wishes — the key with regard to helping out any other evolution is to do so either indirectly or directly via one's Solar Deva — whenever this becomes possible, and whenever that evolution is actually consciously seeking some assistance and is open to receiving it.

Starcraft is a *Path of Heart,* of Love: to work consciously with Solar Devas is to discover what might be called the *Love of the Goddess* — the female side or Devic life-stream. As harmony is sought, then integrated, and finally distributed within the world, one can feel that Love at work — it is magick, and it is effective, and this in no uncertain terms. It is both powerful and soothing all at once; it feels whole, it heals, it inspires — and one feels *in-relationship* with the world, and with the Deva of the world as a result; it is an energy of Union, of Oneness, even of ecstasy. It is a beautiful feeling to be consciously open to it and to *act* as a part of it.

Finally Starcraft is a *Path of Creativity,* of Mind — the mind needs to be stimulated so that it can function with optimal effect, by recreating the world each moment anew and changing it by degree, enhancing it, and working out whatever needs working out — not only for the benefit of oneself and those one is associated with, but for the benefit of all.

Starcraft is many other things besides what has been said so far, yet the above encapsulates something of its essence. Each Starcraft group will somewhat specialise in some work with which it feels in affinity, yet all Starcraft groups have this much in common. Conversely, should a group not *feel* this and fail to work in a way which epitomises these points then it is in danger of becoming something else which is no longer Starcraft.

Starcraft *workings* include much which has a planetary impact, yet a Starcraft group also learns to work with beings who are far more evolved than we are, some of whom are living and *working* on other levels — including on other worlds, and even in other solar systems (much of this has been documented in THE PSYCHIC EXPLORER and in THE POWER OF MIND &

141

CONSCIOUSNESS). In fact the scope for *working* Starcraft is without bounds, and eventually it may well lead to a complete re-appraisal of what *living astrology* actually entails including points of contact and influence which are to be found well beyond the Zodiac Circle, including not only stars and constellations of stars, but also star clusters and galaxies.

Closer to home there are several stars or groups of stars which are of great importance to us, including Sirius (A & B, in Canis Major), the Pleiades (in Taurus, including Alcyone, Merope, Electra, Maia, Asterope, Pleione, Atlas, Taygeta and Celæno), and the Great Bear (or Ursa Major, including Dubhe, Merak, Phekda, Megrez, Alioth, Mizar, Alcol, and Benetnash) — these three groups are directly responsible for our development of the three aspects of will, love-intuition and mind (but in which order?! Read ESOTERIC ASTROLOGY by Alice A. Bailey, Lucis Press — this is recommended reading for anyone who is interested in Starcraft, although it is not easy reading).

There are others, including many of the stars in the Zodiac constellations (and one should remember that a constellation of stars is essentially an appearance, or a vectorial illusion — therefore some stars are more important to us than others). Also of particular note (including some *Zodiac stars*) are: Polaris in Ursa Minor, Vega in Lyra, Arcturus in Bootes, Altair in Aquila, Betelgeuse, Rigel, Bellatrix, Alnitak, Alnilam and Mintaka (and others) in Orion, Capella in Auriga, Procyon in Canis Minor, Canopus in Carina, Toliman and Proxima Centauri in Centaurus, Deneb in Cygnus, Achernar in Eridanus, Algol and Algenib in Perseus, Fomalhaut in Piscis Australis, Antares in Scorpius, Aldebaran in Taurus, Castor and Pollux in Gemini, Denebola and Regulus in Leo, Spica in Virgo; and many others.

When one becomes sensitive to which stellar forces influence us from a Higher Self point of view one can develop strange affinities with regard to specific stars — one may not know why, but the *feeling* is there. One may look up at the sky and a particular star seems to be drawing one's attention. One can even *fall in love* with a star, or group of stars, or *feel* in some way connected to it; or feel that a star is imparting a special kind of strength, or attempting to *teach* one something. This may be and probably will remain only a subjective impression... at least until one learns to contact that star and the Devas of that star using Starcraft.

This is something of the scope which Starcraft can deal with — for this reason it is difficult in the end to liken Starcraft to any other contemporary magickal craft, nevertheless the ancients before us knew about this and built much of their occult mysticism and many of their sacred rituals around it.

7 — CIRCLE-WORK

Working in a Circle is undoubtedly the best way of practising group magick, and this for several reasons: first of all it is naturally protective, from a psychic point of view; and it is also a dynamic arrangement: levels of energy generated in a circle formation are much higher than those generated in any other manner; and it is one which Devas readily recognise and *work* with themselves.

Much could be said about circles, and it is no coincidence that the world over circles are used for group, and even individual magick. However, a circle primarily delineates the periphery of an all-encompassing sphere — not an easy thing to build in physical terms, yet easy to project as a thought-form. Once this thought-form is created, at the beginning of a session of Circle-Work, it will remain there until it is dismissed at the end of that particular session. A sphere of blue light is the most protective of all, although gold and white light are reasonable substitutes.

What follows is a *digest* of relevant information which is compacted into as little space as possible; it is not meant to be a definitive overview of Starcraft Circle-Work as a whole, but only a set of outlines which those who are interested in Starcraft may find useful.

Firstly a Starcraft Circle is cast at a place of affinitive power so that the group can derive energy from that place. Secondly it is determined by its size as required by the number of people present — it can be outlined on the ground using a cord (which should only be used for that purpose) or else by using a number of stones. Thirdly it is entered via the South Gate whenever the group is still finding its way, and/or is composed predominantly of newcomers or apprentices; when the whole group has reached a higher stage of integration other Directional Gates may be used (see STARCRAFT, Section 4). Fourthly the positions taken by the members of the group within the Circle is determined by their affinity and ability to handle and channel particular types of energies — the four Cardinal Points (or Stations) are taken up by the four most experienced members, although allowances are made for training others, whereupon one or more of these Stations may be occupied by less experienced members.

The North Station is the *steady rock* which gives balance to the whole Circle and direction to the group whenever required, if not at all times; therefore the member who will take that position must be very clear within hirself and very strong — in the pragmatic sense as well as psychically and Spiritually. The North Station is the group's reference point, and the member occupying that position must be able to steady the group's energies (and the energies passing through the group) if and when they get in any way out of hand or out of balance.

The South Station is the *Giver of Power* or the *Channel or Gateway of Power* into the Circle — and the member occupying that post must therefore be both flexible and resilient. The South Station is like a doorway through which power will come into the Circle, and once it is opened — by the member in that place — s/he must be able to open and close that gate at will on behalf of the whole group; s/he is the *Guardian of the South*.

The East Station is the *Gateway of Inspiration,* through which information will come into the group, usually in channelled form, and is therefore a *source of enlightenment* to the group. Devic messages will predominantly come through the member located in this Station; this member therefore needs to be psychically sensitive or receptive and highly positive about hir role within the Circle; superior clairvoyant and clairaudient abilities are very useful here, if not vital.

The West Station is the *Gateway of Initiation*, and the member occupying that Station must be particularly sharp in hir perceptions; hir role is almost entirely catalytic; s/he is the *Spirit Tester of the Forms* — forms including etheric-physical, astral and mental energy structures. The West Station is also the *Gateway of Death,* for Death must be encountered during any genuine Initiation of any kind; the *Member of the West* is the Occultist *par excellence*.

There are two main *formats* possible in Starcraft with regard to numbers of members — based on 12 or on 20; what is said below is based on 20, nevertheless it applies in much the same way to 12 — which may be a more accessible or feasible number, since finding 20 people who can *work* coherently and with great interpersonal affinity may present certain obvious difficulties. Other formats are possible, nevertheless they are not necessarily quite as viable; 8 and 16 can work well enough (and 24 is possible; while smaller, more embryonic groups can be composed of between two and seven members, or any other number, with limitations attached in most instances).

Each Cardinal Station is (ideally) flanked by two members on each side. The four members between each two Cardinal Stations act jointly as a gateway for one of the Cross-Quarter Points. Their role is somewhat less demanding overall, yet their contribution is nevertheless of great importance — principally in terms of assisting the Cardinal Stations to fulfil their own roles on the one hand, and also acting as channels for some of the more subtle energies which may seek expression within the Circle on the other.

The South-West Point deals with *Dreaming* — the projection of consciousness onto other levels, particularly the Astral Plane.

The North-East Point deals with *Stalking* — the ability to move fluently and inconspicuously on any level and for whatever purpose. The South-East Point deals with *Memory* the total information available to the group from the past. The North-West Point deals with *Feeling* and *Anticipation* — the ability to *see* future possibilities and any choices which may present themselves at any one time.

From this it may become obvious how each Station contributes something very specific and very necessary to the whole group as each Station is responsible for developing some very particular skills; and one should also note how each Station acts in tandem in a complementary manner with its opposite across the Circle, hence inducing an integrated and dynamic balance within the group. This is a good example of Devic polarity-symmetry and oneness-dualism at work.

The member chosen to lead the group is determined principally according the objective in hand, and will more often than not be one of the members of the Cardinal Stations — who must be able to work together with all the others without any conflict, either of character or interpretation. However during any given session of Circle-Work leadership may well pass from one Station to another according to whatever needs as may arise, and a member of the Cross-Quarter Points may request or may be conferred the task of leadership whenever pertinent. In other respects the *overall* leader either *sits* in the North, or in the South.

Outside of the whole group acting together in Circle-Work one can detect various sub-grouping combinations (the following applies to a group of 20): The four Cardinal Station members, forming one sub-group, and eight half Cross-Quarter groups (of two members each), in other words 12 sub-points or 9 sub-groups; the four Cardinal Stations and the four Cross-Quarter Stations, or eight sub-groups; the four Cardinal Station members as one sub-group, and the four Cross-Quarter sub-groups, or five sub-groups; the four Cardinal Stations and their four Cross-

Quarter members (two members on each side), or four sub-groups; the four Cardinal Stations, and two sets of complementary-opposite Cross-Quarter groups, thus forming three sub-groups; the four Cardinal members, and the four Cross-Cardinal groups together, thereby forming two groups... This means that there are various kinds of sub-groups, each of which may go off and do valuable work on its own between sessions of Circle-Work, and of course many other, less *formal* combinations are indeed possible. In this way Starcraft offers a great many possibilities with regard to individual and group development — all of which may add up to a more able and more powerful group as a whole.

One must not forget that in addition to the human group there is the Devic group, composed of at least as many Solar Devas as there are human members (and on occasions maybe more as may seem relevant to these Devas); these Solar Devas in turn will or may be *overshadowed* by Systemic and/or Cosmic Devas — therefore at any one time there will probably be at least three distinct groups at work and *moving* together towards a common aim, or aims; sometimes the human members will be invited to be conscious of the overall purpose involved, and sometimes various Devas will be activating other schemes which may not be obvious to the human group at a conscious level. The value of human-Devic cooperative work is that it can address many different aspects of development and energy transference, and this simultaneously, thus catalysing many different schemes (the word *human* is de-emphasised simply because we cannot claim equality with Solar Devas until we have fully merged in consciousness with these).

To begin with the human group will be inspired and some-what led by the Devic group — this may cover a period spanning many years; later as the human group becomes consciously able to deal directly with all the various energies involved in Circle-Work — having reached a certain state of subjective fusion with the Solar Devic group — it will be invited to participate in the

147

leadership of the overall Human-Solar Devic group (here we can start to emphasise the word *Human!*); finally when each and all of the members of the Human group have achieved a comprehensive mastery with regard to manipulating various grades of energy-substance, thus liberating themselves in the process, they will be invited to lead that overall Human-Solar Devic group.

One can also come to realise how vast the possible network of communication and cooperation actually is — a bit like a tree with many possible branches: human beings, Solar Devas, Systemic Devas, Galactic Devas, Cosmic Devas, etc. (not to mention lesser devas and other creatures and beings of all kinds). The transference of energy throughout this network is stepped down in its intensity at each stage so that the human group will not become unduly overwhelmed by it; yet as the human group becomes more proficient in its work one level of that stepping down is removed at a time, thus involving the human group at a higher level — and so on until we, as human beings, eventually move out of the periphery of human evolution, and — as Solar Humans (a complete fusion of Human and Solar Devic energies and identities) — proceed with further work on much higher Planes.

Starcraft both fulfils a function within the *normal* world and within the *three lower worlds* (etheric-physical, astral and lower mental), yet also prepares its members for Cosmic work — of which we cannot really say all that much here since we have not yet reached that level of involvement and cannot yet *see* that far.

Each separate Starcraft group will need to address many other points during the course of its development and unfoldment, yet because of the complexity of this subject it is not possible to itemise and describe absolutely everything in this booklet — and one must keep in mind that each Starcraft group will be involved in its own particular work at that. The aim here is to give enough information so that each prospective group can begin to form itself and then go on to work with at least some idea of what is needed. Since there is no central group to refer to — at a physical level anyway, in other words there is no traditional or *first group* from which all others may derive their tuition — each individual group will have to find its own way and use its intuition and creative senses to establish its own priorities.

Ideally each group should be composed of an equal number of women and men, even though in Starcraft the emphasis is primarily on the essential androgyny *behind the forms*. Since men are easily distracted by their own self-importance it is inadvisable to have a Starcraft group dominated by an over-abundance of males; conversely women are generally better at attuning themselves to the Devic state than are most men, therefore some care must be taken to acknowledge this in a way that will be or may be rewarding to the whole group. Various combinations of the sexes are possible providing it adds up to a good balance overall.

This is a less stringent formula-concept than that which can be found in either Witchcraft or the Shamanic system as expounded in the Castaneda books. In Witchcraft the balance of the sexes is (ideally) equal, except for the enigmatic thirteenth member, while in *Castanedean* Shamanism — and excluding the couriers who can be either male or female — there are two women for every man, and one fixed leader — the male Nagual; and one *beacon* for the whole group — the Nagual Woman, who operates *beyond the world* (this formula is nevertheless a very good one; and there are many others).

In Starcraft there is no fixed or permanent leader, and the Solar Devas associated with the human members act jointly as a beacon for the human group. Having said this, the member who is positioned at the North Station has precedence over all the others whenever a situation arises which needs correcting or balancing — this implies a specific role, and therefore not overall leadership in itself; it is good to make a distinction between the two.

In Starcraft the onus is on every member to be completely self-responsible — on behalf of hirself, and on behalf of the whole group; this is what makes the lack of fixed leadership possible. If a difficulty or else a dispute of any kind does arise — and for whatever reason — it is up to the North Station member to arbitrate over it: s/he must be prompt in identifying its causes, and where relevant s/he may invite another to deal with it if it falls within the sphere of affinity or ability of another member's role; the other Cardinal Station members act as co-leaders in this respect, and can interject their own view of the situation — but only if this appears to them as necessary; and where pertinent, and in principle, each and all the group's members are free to voice their perception of the difficulty — nevertheless there may be situations where such equality might become cumbersome or unproductive; again it is up to the member of the North Station to decide. If each and all members accept this way of working then difficulties can usually be solved quickly and efficiently. However, if the matter drags on or else develops into a greater problem then the North Station member has the power to call for the dissolution of the Circle providing that the other three Cardinal Station members agree; if a joint agreement cannot be reached then the North Station member has the right to decide anyway, yet if the matter is not overly critical s/he may request an overall consensus from all the members of the group; nevertheless in moments of genuine crisis the North Station member can make a final decision without referring to anyone else.

There may be situations when one or more members, usually apprentices and maybe a newcomer, reach a state of *panic* mode, and thereby need special attention. If one member feels out of hir depth then it will probably disrupt the Circle for all the others, and the work being carried out may well suffer in consequence. Direct and indirect assistance can be given at this point — nevertheless what should be done if one or more panicking members fail to respond or else refuse to be helped? This can be a difficult question to resolve on the moment, which very much highlights the role of the Cardinal Station members and their need for insight and resourcefulness: if the work is *engaged* at a level of high intensity there is potential danger for everyone. If someone moves out of the Circle because s/he can no longer cope with what is going on s/he may find hirself isolated from the protection which the Circle can afford; yet if s/he remains within the Circle s/he may fail to *realign* hirself with the work and with the energies which are present, and therefore will be a liability both to hirself and to the group.

Maybe the best preventive answer is this: no one should be invited into the Circle if s/he has not been rigourously trained beforehand (see STARCRAFT, Section 4). Once one is invited to join a Circle one must be very clear about one's commitment to the group; and if one finds oneself in a situation of great crisis then one must accept the challenge of dealing with it for as long as the work is in progress — regardless of any personal discomfort, and however acute that discomfort or pain may become.

All initiation-type situations in particular may involve moments — sometimes prolonged moments — of discomfort, and maybe outright pain. This is caused by a differential of energies: one's own, and those that come into play from higher levels, which are far more intense. If one rises to the challenge then eventually one adapts to these higher energies, and finally a sense of balance will set in — one then finds oneself faced with some personal or group revelation which is likely to be of some importance to oneself and/or to the whole group.

There are various *devices* which can attenuate any discomfort or pain which is felt during moments of high-intensity stress: for instance, tying a silk scarf around one's middle and covering the solar plexus, which is often the most vulnerable point in one's energy-body; putting cold water on that spot has much the same effect, and putting cold water on one's face, forehead, back of the neck and crown chakra area can be useful (therefore a bowl of water should be taken into the Circle at the beginning). One can also take up a foetus-like position on the ground, place one's hands over one's solar plexus and then roll gently from side to side — this may seem incongruous during a session of Circle-Work, but if it helps it may be seen as a valid course to take, providing it doesn't totally disrupt the whole group.

One must not forget that the group is being overshadowed by Solar Devas, and that their direct assistance can be sought to minimise *crisis* events. However, these Solar Devas may be directly involved in testing one or more of the members' resilience to the impact of higher energies, therefore they may have undisclosed priorities in this respect. A general rule of Initiation is this: if one either enters a period of initiatic pressure, or else is *forced* into one, it is because one's Solar Deva knows that one can cope with it if one cares to do so — regardless of any personal strain encountered in the process, be it over a period of minutes, hours, and sometimes in extreme cases even days (a rare event). While a sense of panic can be experienced — and it should be noted that no Initiate manages to *get through* a genuine Life-Initiation without being tested to the core — one must have enough courage to *flow with it;* one can distract one's consciousness to a certain degree on occasions so as to offset the impact of major peaks of high-energy, yet to try and offset that pressure altogether is self-defeating and is usually impossible anyway. Between major Life-Initiations there are many lesser, yet still quite potent intermediate initiations to be faced, and while these are less critical in nature they are nevertheless best accepted with the same courage and resolution to succeed.

Why should one have to deal with all this? Simply enough because one cannot become involved in acts of high magick without being tested and *immersed* in high-energy states; since to become *free* one must change oneself very radically indeed, and since only the impact of those higher energies can effect the changes which are required, the above must be accepted as a part of that process which will eventually lead to personal liberation and Self-Mastery. It is not easy, but then nothing worth having usually is.

If this information scares you — which after all would be understandable enough you must ask yourself if Starcraft is the way for you. Keep in mind that all initiatic paths face similar rigours, and that no one is likely to find any initiatic path easy. At the very least Starcraft provides a framework where you will not have to face these rigours alone.

However Circle-Work sessions need not always involve any great rigours, as mentioned above; on occasions the group will experience gentle energies, and different individuals may well experience different grades of gentleness or intensity — this will usually vary according to each individual's ability to channel energy, which in turn will vary according to hir own personal state of evolutionary unfoldment and consciousness, and will also depend on the nature of the work which is being undertaken at any one time — of course the abilities of those around hir may affect hir own energy levels as well.

Dealing with Devas can be both a very beautiful as well as sometimes a demanding experience; even during moments of high intensity that beauty can be very apparent. This is particularly the case whenever a Starcraft group can raise its consciousness onto the Buddhic or Harmonic level — the fourth Plane of existence since one can experiences a great sense of Love and Union there, combined with an exquisite sense of Harmony and Balance. Devas are very artful in their expression, and they can impart something of this artistry whenever one comes into conscious contact with them at this level (this also applies in a somewhat lesser fashion on the higher sub-planes of the Mental and Astral Planes).

Starcraft is as much a joyous experience as it is sometimes a difficult one, and this should serve to help keep things in perspective.

Nevertheless a Starcraft group will find itself occasionally drawn in *areas* of consciousness and energy which do require personal resilience and ability — there is no escaping from this, sooner or later at least. As the *down-coming* energies from Higher Planes meet the lower Plane energies that one is generally accustomed to dealing with there is bound to be a certain amount of duress involved; in effect the lower energies are being invited to measure up to those which are higher and therefore of greater potency, and this until a good balance is achieved. As the members of the group become more experienced in dealing with energies generally then they will know a bit more what to expect.

Invoking those higher energies is one aspect of Starcraft which we will now address: the leader of the group should first of all invoke a sphere of protection around the whole group, and this sphere will be delineated by the periphery of the Circle. Then it will usually be up to the member of the North Station to invoke the assistance of the Solar Devas in the work to be done, and this in whatever way is deemed suitable. Then it will usually be up to the member of the East Station to act as a *voice* for these Devas — with regard to any communication and guidance, and so on. Further it will usually be up to the member of the South Station to instruct the group with regard to raising enough Kundalini power for the purpose of initiating the work to be done; then up to the member of the West Station to initiate the proceedings from an occult point of view. Then leadership is passed on to whichever member is best able to direct the group according to the purpose at hand.

There will be instances when only one kind of work is entertained, therefore leadership may remain with that one member. On occasions more than one kind of work will entertained, and therefore leadership will be assumed by or conferred to various members as may be appropriate, according to their specific abilities.

No newcomer or apprentice should be required to act as a leader in any respect until s/he has attended at least twenty Circle-Work sessions, and this regardless of whatever training s/he may have received in the interim.

When the work is concluded the Circle should be closed down, starting with the member of the West Station — who will declare that the work has been done (providing s/he perceives that it has), followed by the member of the South Station — who will ensure that the energies of the group, and/or passing through the group, are brought back to a relatively normal level; then the member of the East Station should thank the Solar Devas for their assistance and for whatever they may have imparted and facilitated during that session; followed by the member of the North Station — who should request that all give thanks to the spirit of the power place, then request that all should leave — as silently as possible. This can be done simply, or it can be done in a ritualised manner.

One can see in this how the Circle is empowered clockwise (skywise) through the Cardinal Stations to begin with, and then later closed down or *down-powered* in an anti-clockwise (earthwise) fashion through those very same Stations — i.e., acting in reverse order. Likewise the members of the group should enter the Circle (through whichever Gate is chosen) in a skywise/clockwise manner, then later leave it in an earthwise/ anti-clockwise manner (which Devas will interpret as *beginning* and *end*).

The members of the Cross-Quarter Stations should leave first — through whichever Gate is indicated by the member of the West Station, who will then depart hirself — followed by the member of the South Station, who will banish any residual energies within the Circle; then by the East Station member, who will either gather up the cord which was used to delineate the Circle, or else instruct others to disperse the stones which may have been used in its stead; and finally the member of the North Station will ensure that everything has been returned to its natural state prior to leaving the power place hirself.

This way of proceeding is not arbitrary — it is directly addressing the energies of the sky and of the earth, and those of any Devas at large who were brought into interplay with the Circle-work, who will now depart as well, having fulfilled their part in it — for the Solar Devas may well avail themselves of other devic energies whenever necessary, including devas of the Earth, of the Waters, of the Air, and of the Fires; likewise they may invoke, then *align* themselves (and through themselves the human group) with Systemic and Star Devas with view to transmitting certain specialised energies into the Circle, and via the Circle into the world; all these agencies need to be ritually informed that the work has indeed ended (contact with these Sources will have ceased by the time the work has been concluded — or whenever a part of it has been, for some types of work may require several sessions).

Again it must be said that each Starcraft group will evolve its own way of operating, therefore what is said above is given by way of a guideline in these matters. In time different groups may decide or may be inspired to do things in other ways, and so long as what they do is effective, and providing the contact and communication with their Solar Devas is not in any way impaired or diminished, there is room for such flexibility. Nevertheless it is suggested that all Starcraft groups use the above information as it is given here until they are genuinely informed or guided to do otherwise.

This leaves the work itself to be considered.

All Solar Devas have many *points of affinitive contact*, both throughout the planet and beyond it — some of which are necessary for their work, and some of which are the result of various past or present associations or affiliations. Similarly each human individual within the group will have various *points of affinitive contact* at an internal level — all of which may influence the nature of the work to be done by that group. It is not possible to delineate all the various kinds of work that may be undertaken by any given group, nevertheless here is something of a list of possibilities:

— working with the elemental domain
— working with the mineral domain
— working with the plant domain
— working with the animal domain, or animal circles
— working with the human domain, or human circles
— working with the super-human domain, or Para-
      Human Circle
— working with the *Guardians of the Inner Fires* (Shamballa)
— working with the Planetary Spirit (The Spirit of the Earth).

This much concerns the Earth planet and its various evolutions. Then there are other possible lines of work which concern themselves with Systemic, Inter-Systemic, and even Galactic and Inter-Galactic Evolutions — nevertheless only advanced Starcraft groups are likely to be able to deal with these in any way that is of any significance.

Without intuition none of this is likely to make too much sense to anyone who reads this but who is not directly involved in Circle-work, and in this lies a degree of security against the abuse of this information. Also, Solar Devas cannot be summoned into working for any selfish human purpose whatsoever, and since Circle-Work as practised in Starcraft is indeed completely impossible without their direct assistance in this lies a second circle of security against abuse. There is a third circle of security, which is Shamballa itself — or the *Guardians of the Planet who handle the Inner Fires*.

Without the ability to use mind creatively no one can derive very much from the *formative power* of Starcraft either — developing one's sense of creativity is therefore of great importance as well, and in itself may secure certain results.

Different groups will evolve their own way of *working* around what is given here as a basic framework of reference, which is why no great emphasis has been placed on ritual. What could be mentioned is that ritual for the sake of ritual alone is really of very little use in Starcraft — if it *turns on* the members of any given group, that is fair enough; nevertheless if the rituals are inspired by the Solar Devas associated with that group, then they will be designed for a specific purpose — and will have nothing to do with *fancy ritualism* or *cosmetic magick*. Devic rituals are always work-specific, and they create patterns of energy which have power and significance.

A good way of beginning Circle-Work, outside of what has already been said, is to intone the power-sound, *OM*; beautiful harmonics can be created by male and female voices uttering this sound at different pitches and overlapping with different sequences of breath — this has the effect of altering consciousness and creating a desirable *shift* of perspective. Starting with relatively low pitches one can progress gently towards higher and higher pitches — and eventually the female pitches may resonate in a particularly delightful way. The end phase of the intonation should become a powerful *MMMMMMM,* trailing off after a while into an *mmmmmmm...* followed by silence. This in itself will summon Devic attention. If everyone continues to breathe deeply, yet evenly, and associates their breathing with the vitalising and balancing of their chakras, then they may well find themselves entering into Solar trance (where consciousness is maintained) — if they then summon their Kundalini by consciously vibrating energy up their spines (visualising a simple two-dimensional waveform is often sufficient) and direct their energies with their ajnas (third eye), then draw down energies from their para-chakras above their heads to meet, harmonise and blend with the uprise of Kundalini energies, then various degrees of Higher Self consciousness can be accessed and achieved. Then the member of the East Station can channel any initial Devic communication or guidance. This is simple and highly effective.

Finally: how you work Starcraft is up to you, as an individual and as a group. By all means use these guidelines, yet do not become constrained by them; adapt things as you may feel inspired to do so; listen to your Solar Deva/s.

8 — DREAMING, STALKING, SEEING AND FEELING

Psychic perceptions are at the core of Starcraft for they lead to specific abilities with regard to experiencing and dealing with the Higher Planes. Four such abilities are *dreaming, stalking, seeing* and *feeling*.

Dreaming is closely related to Astral Projection, and, in some cases there is no great distinction to be made between the two. Before one can understand *dreaming* in a total context one must be able to appreciate the fact that once conscious on the Inner Planes one is no longer restricted by the same sense of Time and Space as one is on the physical plane. For a start time is more *elastic* or else subjective; there is no clock time to distract one's sense of duration; and one is generally a lot less conscious of or less interested in the factor of time.

Secondly because access to Space is much facilitated — since one can travel through it at will, even at what would normally seem like enormous speeds — it no longer seems to constitute a barrier to one's senses. Access to any place is possible within the Plane environment one finds oneself on.

One can consciously visit the Astral Plane by *taking over* one's dreams, which is a good indication with regard to the nature of dreams — if one becomes conscious of *being in a dream* all one needs to do is to focus one's awareness within it, and the dream then ceases to be a normal one — it has become the equivalent of a projection. One can also relax one's body, begin to imagine a given situation, focus one's consciousness on that situation, and then gradually (or sometimes suddenly) drift into a dreaming state — and *take it over*. This ability has many uses for one can then experiment with one's senses of creativity and the application of one's will — which leads us on to *stalking*.

Stalking is to act with total consciousness with regard to a given environment. This can be done on the physical plane, and it can done on higher levels as well. One learns to focus one's attention on all the environmental forces which surround oneself and then to move in total awareness of what one is in relationship to those forces — and using one's will one learns to *be invisible* to those forces, or to present oneself in the way that one wishes to be perceived by others; this gives one an unparalleled ability to control certain events by controlling oneself, one's personal forces and one's consciousness to an almost ultimate degree.

Seeing is to be able to perceive things as they really are behind the appearance of the forms — which forms conceal the power-energies and spirit of those things; *seeing* also encompasses a type of perceptual intuition which reveals the true nature of a given event — either in the present, but also in the past and the future. This type of intuition usually occurs in a flash of consciousness, but with practice can be extended, and can also lead to other perceptions — which may be directly or indirectly connected to the first one.

Finally *feeling* is not dissimilar to *seeing* — it is also a kind of intuition whereby one is able to sense the normally hidden connection between one event and another; *seeing* is a more direct perception than is *feeling*.

These higher senses and/or abilities are vital to one's participation in Starcraft, therefore they must be acquired at least to a certain degree before one can participate in Circle-Work to any viable extent. Much of the training of an apprentice deals with this.

Here are some pointers: the best way to learn to *dream* is to learn to project astrally, and to *take over dreams* (see JOURNEYS BEYOND THE BODY in THE PSYCHIC EXPLORER). The best way to learn to *stalk* is to go about one's daily business with one's mind empty of *self-talk* — i.e., to neutralise any sub-vocalisation as soon as it occurs. One way of learning to *see* is to open one's eyes very wide (in an environment where the light is subdued), to unfocus one's eyes with regard to forms, and to concentrate on *seeing* the energy-forces behind those forms (reading the Carlos Castaneda books is also recommended).

All these higher senses and/or abilities require a sense of personal clarity and attention, which meditation is useful in fostering and bringing about.

9— DYNAMIC INTEGRATION

Part of the object of Starcraft is to learn to become a more dynamic and more integrated being — encompassing the whole of oneself, and not one's personality alone. Then in a group context it is to achieve a greater sense of dynamic integration with the others of that group, and with Solar Devas, particularly during Circle-Work.

This is rarely easy because personality-selves are only small fragments of our true, overall Self — please note the use of the singular; To possess Monadic consciousness, or true Higher Self consciousness, is to be conscious of the *Oneness of Being* within. To *know* that Self is to have achieved Monadic Consciousness — which occurs for the first time during the event of the first Life-Initiation (see INITIATION, TRANSMUTATION & IM-MORTALITY in THE PSYCHIC EXPLORER); one only experiences that *One Self* for a few minutes or hours at that time, therefore one only becomes alerted to Its Reality at first — one has *seen* It; one then *knows* that It exists, and that It is indeed the *God-dess Within.*

To achieve full dynamic integration is to achieve permanent Monadic Consciousness, which therefore occurs on the sixth Plane. When one has achieved this degree of permanence one has *shifted* one's consciousness from the human state into the super-human State. Starcraft as much as anything else is a path of Initiation, and thereby aims to promote and then bring those involved into that State of *Monadic permanence* — at a conscious level.

For as long as a Starcraft group is active it is *in the business* of achieving that State, which occurs degree by degree, and level by level.

Many people might think that experiencing the Monadic Self is nearly impossible, and yet once ready for that experience it is remarkable how one can find oneself *shifting* from *lower personality mode* into that Higher State of Consciousness during the event of the first Life-Initiation, and this over a period of only minutes or hours. It is a gruelling test of one's ability to remain stable, for the energies and forces involved are truly tremendous. During the last two or three decades several hundred, maybe thousands of relatively advanced individuals have experienced that Life-Initiation, often unsupported by any external group; in Starcraft the process is smoother because one is supported by an external group, as well as by internal groups.

To reiterate what has been said elsewhere there were times in past ages when an advanced individual might only experience one Life-Initiation per so many incarnations, or one per incarnation; now — because of the present planetary situation — it is possible to go through more than one Life-Initiation in one single lifetime. This accelerated process has and will have far-reaching consequences with regard to the evolution of the Planetary Spirit as well as our own; this is a measure of Its success as well as ours — and this despite all the chaos, pain and inequities which still exist within the world.

The Soviet Union and the United States of America are now moving towards complete nuclear disarmament, one Treaty at a time. Regardless of all the different aspects which have been instrumental in bringing about this degree of almost enforced agreement between the so-called *super-powers,* one can also *see* the relationship between this and the increase in the numbers of people who are experiencing or have experienced various Life-Initiations (and Threshold Initiations) — thereby accelerating the unfoldment of global consciousness — resulting in the signing of these Treaties: this is the first real step, besides the previous Treaties signed in the '70's, towards nuclear disarmament and genuine world cooperation and international understanding. At a global level this is an example of dynamic integration at work, even though much still remains to be achieved. Gorbachev is also the first Soviet leader to exemplify qualities which are usually associated with those of a Life-Initiate — operating in this case *up-front* and well within the global public view.

Starcraft has its place in promoting further global integration, not only between humans and human nations, but also between all domains in Nature, and between the human and devic life-streams, and between world and world. The *end result* of global integration at various levels is the conscious integration of the Earth within the system of worlds to which it belongs.

Starcraft could be said to be synonymous with the word *Harmonisation*.

10 — PERSONAL AND GROUP EXPLORATIONS

There are so many possibilities to explore that one single life-time might not seem enough to venture all that far. This in many ways is not so, however — first of all each one of us has lived hundreds of lives before, and during that time we have each accumulated countless skills and experienced many things. All this is stored in our subconscious minds, but how does one access it?

The first point to be made here is that one only needs to access what is genuinely relevant to one's life in the present — it is fruitless to try and extract information from one's subconscious which bears no relationship to what one is doing now. Yet each past life-time, not to mention any periods lived between incarnations, represents a particular type of exploration; and several lifetimes may have been concerned with only one kind of exploration throughout.

It is important to understand a lifetime as a means of expressing a given Ray energy, or several, and that what one is seeking to express is a part of what one lacks in one's overall evolution — the exercise is to become whole, eventually. Those who finally experience Life-Initiations are in effect bringing together everything which is of value from past lives and everything which is relevant in their present lives, and then synthesising it into something new — which results in various initiatic perceptions and *knowings;* and what they *see* during those moments is what they *are* — what they have achieved.

During periods of heightened consciousness one can address one's subconscious, and then images, *feelings,* and other perceptual information will come into view — one can literally ask one's subconscious to reveal what is of relevance to oneself in the now. From this one can derive impressions which will indeed be of use — some of which can be dealt with in relative isolation, and others which need to be dealt with as a whole; especially wherever there are lines or areas of relationship between them all, and there are bound to be many.

Part of the work of Starcraft is to discover oneself — not only one's personality patterns, and working on these wherever necessary, but everything that one is — from individual human self to God-dess Self; once one *knows* oneself more fully one can participate in Circle-Work while drawing on personal and group resources which previously may not have been especially obvious or even very accessible.

One excellent exercise is to try and remember one's last ten incarnations or so, and this can be done in various ways. Hypnotic regression is one way; imaging and journeying techniques are another (see THE PSYCHIC EXPLORER and THE POWER OF MIND & CONSCIOUSNESS). One can also go to specific places where one feels that one was alive in other times, walk about in *stalking* mode, then *dream* and meditate there, and impressions, sometimes strong ones, may come into one's conscious mind.

Something not too dissimilar can be done with regard to the future: one can project oneself into the future on the basis that everything that one is at any one point in time leads naturally enough to what one will or may be doing in that future. What one *sees* in this case should be treated as a possibility rather than as an absolute certainty, for everything that one does subsequently may change that possibility into another, or even several other possibilities. The by-product of this exercise is that one can learn to *see* something of what one is going towards, which in turn may give guidance to one's life in the present; in this way one can *look* a few decades or hundreds of years ahead, and effectively what one *sees* begins to shape the present and the immediate future, and this directly to indirectly — one can therefore begin to harness one's energies more creatively and intelligently, if not intuitionally and purposefully, and this with any given perspective in mind, or even several (it should be mentioned that there is a great difference between doing this and becoming preoccupied with any kind of belief in an *inescapable fate* — one's personal future is always alterable within whatever margins one's life allows for at any one time).

Similarly one can address one's Solar Deva, who already knows where one is going because there is already something of a *plan* in action — which stretches back into one's personal past and as well as forward into the future. There are still choices to be made, and that *plan* is designed to facilitate the unfoldment of a certain evolutionary result — it may well suffer from occasional set-backs as well as benefit from useful or unusual circumstances, yet overall it will or it should work out — one's Solar Deva is responsible to make sure that it does and therefore influences the lower personality self accordingly, particularly when that lower personality self allows itself to be in any way receptive to hir doings.

This takes us back to a consideration of dynamic integration: in Starcraft one learns to merge and then fuse the human part of oneself with the Solar Devic part of one's Higher Self, and subsequently with the Monadic Self. This results in perceptual abilities which *make the way clear(er)*, and one can then *look* into the past, the present and the future at will — whenever relevant. In turn one can then *look* at anything which may seem of interest and *know* it for what it is — this is the facility which is afforded to all psychic and Spiritual explorers who make the effort to reach that state of fusion and integration, and sooner or later succeed in doing so.

165

To begin with one's perceptions (of this kind) are not constant — they only occur during moments of heightened consciousness; later when one has learnt to maintain a state of higher consciousness more or less at will then these perceptions are continually available — all one needs to do is *look* and *see*, and these things can become *known*, and therefore part of one's repertoire of *knowledge*. There are stories of Masters *who know all things;* in effect they have learnt to *look* and *see*, and in consequence they CAN *know* all things; whatever they tune into they can *know*.

Circle-Work is an exploration of what can be done when humans become *aligned* in consciousness and *intent* with Devic agencies; much of this exploration may be relatively new as it takes advantage of planetary, interplanetary and even interstellar conditions which are themselves sometimes relatively new. If a particular kind of activity works out to mutual advantage then it becomes incorporated within the methods which can be used in Starcraft; if for some reason it does not work out then it is either modified as may be appropriate, or it is abandoned in favour of some other activity. Nevertheless, whatever is tried out by Devas corresponds to a set of needs, and these Devas plan for the unfoldment and expression of these needs — whatever they inspire a Starcraft group to do it is because they perceive quite clearly that it can be done... providing the human group responds in an adequate fashion; therefore the onus is particularly on the human group to assist in the process of making it possible.

Enhancing one's personal and group abilities can only enhance the nature of the work which is undertaken in Circle-Work. While this booklet may not deal with certain aspects of these abilities in any great detail, using one's intuition one can derive much of real benefit in this area. From another point of view it is all very simple, regardless of the apparent complexity involved; it is even relatively accessible to intellectual logic once it is *seen* in the right way, and yet it allows for non-linear approaches which by-pass logic as well.

Furthermore the ability to summon, channel and then purposefully use power with beneficial *intent,* directing it with one's will, while using one's intuition (and therefore one's higher senses of perception) and one's mental creativity, can in effect open any of the doors one may need to access at any one time — this in itself supersedes many of the complex techniques which are often taught by various magickal traditions; these may (or may not) be useful within a given context, yet they are certainly not absolutely necessary to the *working* of magick.

Hopefully this is clear enough. Each Starcraft group has to decide where it wants to go and how best it can *align* itself with Devic forces, and Devic *intent* and creativity; the group may well opt for other avenues not mentioned here, for this booklet is only designed to alert interested parties to the possibilities which can be explored, but it does not contend to itemise all these possibilities.

Lastly, where does this exploration all lead to? From the human angle it leads one to a fusion of energies and identities with one's Solar Deva, and in turn with the Monadic Self (imparting individuality to It in the process) — thus liberating the lower personality self from its limitations and from its particular evolutionary purpose. From the para-human or super-human point of view it promotes a new course of evolutionary unfoldment which leads the individual towards acting as a conscious agent on behalf of the Planetary, then Systemic Spirit, and then eventually beyond that to assisting other Planetary and Systemic Spirits elsewhere — i.e., not within the Solar System.

There is so much room for future exploration that one could get easily forget that there are countless Life-Initiates who reached a high level of attainment in the past, whereupon they found their own freedom. Whatever we are considering now is something of an extension of their own efforts, yet instead of following the human metaphysical tradition, in Starcraft one is endorsing somewhat more of the Devic perspective. This can be illustrated briefly as follows:

Our ancestors (who may have been ourselves in other times and bodies) appreciated the value of the Devic perspective. Indeed the original strands of Animism, Paganism, Witchcraft and Shamanism arose from a mixture of this perspective with that of humans confronted by the relatively raw qualities of ambient natural forces, which led to the practice of natural magick in various forms. But there was another trend which had surfaced repeatedly over the millenia, which simply put was the effort on the part of some humans to try and warp natural forces with their selfish coercive intent, while attempting to instil fear and domination over the rest of world, or whatever part of it was accessible at any one time. As a result of this the elemental energies became severely antagonised by those humans who misused them out of negativity, and they reacted destructively — which in turn produced problems for Devas in terms of dealing with human preoccupations, particularly in relationship to magickal power and its use or abuse.

The problem here was that elemental energies were still negatively polarised themselves, therefore they responded to human negativity the more readily, and in turn influenced negative humans towards further acts of negativity — which introduced a vicious and periodical cycle of negative surges, leading eventually to the wholesale destruction of whole civilisations (to which Atlantis, for instance, finally succumbed).

To further assist humans at a conscious level became impossible, and therefore Devas began to conceal themselves from the bulk of human consciousness in order to protect themselves and their vital work from human magickal abuse.

They allowed for an interim period whereby the human intent could work itself out without their visible assistance (although they have always been there and always been active in the background) — and it is only now that things require balancing in a different sort of way that Devas feel that they can once more activate a direct and conscious relationship with us on a relatively *open* scale, particularly with regard to *working* magick.

There is therefore much exploration to be done which concerns the re-uniting of Devic and human perspectives, and not simply their relationship as two or more distinct views and ways of evolving and doing things.

11 — NEEDS, INSIGHTS AND AFFINITIES

If we were to break down planetary needs into various categories then we would be faced with thousands of different areas which require addressing — all of which are relevant if we are ever to solve the sorts of problems that we have, not to mention those of other lifeforms. This complex topography in relationship to needs requires some scrutiny.

Everything needs something else in order to live — in other words nothing lives of itself and by itself. Even the simplest of proto-viruses depend on their molecular components for their existence; even an atom is composed of different sub-atomic forces. It is when we view things in this way that we begin to understand the interdependence of all things, and this not only on the physical plane — which is itself dependent on the Higher Planes for its expression and manifestation — but with regard to all dimensional life.

We all have needs, some of which are very basic, like food, water, warmth, shelter, and so on; others are cultural; and others yet are more subjective. Nevertheless in our haste to satisfy some of these needs we often neglect many others — an example would be our need for wood and paper against the need for trees which give us oxygen, regulate the world's weather processes, enrich the soil with their fallen leaves, while also acting as homes for many other creatures, etc. Another example could be our desire for material comfort and the efforts and time which is consumed acquiring material wealth against the need for the conscious expression of Spirit in our lives.

In an ideal world no genuine needs would conflict with any others — everything would be in conscious relationship with everything else, and therefore everyone would appreciate that this relationship is a function of a balance from which all can benefit equally. But we do not live in an ideal world, nor do we presently benefit from that balance — one which we as human beings have been instrumental in upsetting, even destroying.

In Starcraft it is vital to understand one's true needs, and the needs of life around oneself — and to achieve a balance between oneself and that life. If one can sort out one's priorities in this respect at a mundane level then it becomes much easier to do the same thing with regard to the inner levels. The *working* of Starcraft is dependent on its various constituent parts: the human part, the Devic part, and everything else which those two parts may address — including life in all its aspects, and on all the Planes.

To do this requires insight; further it requires the ability to form affinities between oneself and that which one addresses, or attempts to address. If two sides have no point of affinitive contact then there can be no dialogue or any significant exchange between them, particularly at a conscious level.

In Starcraft the level of insight one requires becomes progressively more demanding as one addresses ever greater areas of contact; and thus one's sense of affinity has to encompass areas which in some cases are totally unfamiliar to us: consciously experiencing, relating with and understanding Solar Devas is only the beginning of it; Solar Devas in turn are the *openers of the doors* through which further contact with the inside and outside Universe can be made.

The enormity of what *can* be accomplished is staggering because no possibility is unfeasible, and there are many possibilities of which we are frankly totally unaware at present. The fact that we have to put our own *home* in order — i.e., ourselves as individuals, then ourselves as groups of individuals, and eventually the whole planet — is the first step towards the dynamic and conscious integration of this planet within the Universal Network, which is itself seeking a much greater state of integration.

There are mystics who think of the Higher Planes as entirely perfect — they are not that, certainly not in total terms anyway. Perfection is a function of a purpose which must be entirely fulfilled, and for as long as there is a lower manifestation, or a need for one, then that purpose has not yet been fulfilled, and therefore there is no absolute perfection. We have yet to consciously acknowledge those Evolutions which are instrumental in promoting the liberation of all lifeforms from the confines of their existence, and their own purpose will not be complete until we have freed ourselves from our own limitations, and others from theirs.

12 — SELF-RESPONSIBILITY

Without self-responsibility the *working* of Starcraft would be impossible, both for reasons which have already been mentioned, as well as for others which we will now look into.

Anyone who is not prepared to embrace self-responsibility and is waiting for some sort of Cosmic Saviour to come and sort things out on hir behalf is decidedly lacking in courage, and is not going to be taken to any Heaven. Anything that is worth having requires effort, persistence, insight and flexibility — to accept anything less than that is a *cop-out.*

It is precisely because people have been *copping-out* for such a long time, one way or the other, that we have the mess we have now. We not only have a responsibility towards oneself/ ourselves but towards all life, and if we are not prepared to acknowledge that now then the question goes begging: *When will we be prepared to acknowledge it, and work with it?*

For all we know the whole of the Universe could be waiting for us to answer that simple question, and then to act accordingly. In Starcraft one has to embrace not only a high sense of self-responsibility, but also a responsibility on behalf of the whole planet and on behalf of all those beings and forces which may seek to use Starcraft as a vehicle for change — now and in the future. That may sound like *too much* to take on by way of responsibility, yet if one cannot find room for such a commitment within oneself then there is no point even attempting to *work* Starcraft in any way. Starcraft is entirely founded on that sense of responsibility and commitment, and there is no escaping from this.

Whatever is done in Starcraft is also founded on one's ability to deal with one's mundane life, for the two must be able to complement one another. If one cannot cope with one's mundane life satisfactorily then how can one hope to cope with the demands of *working* Starcraft? Again integration at all levels is necessary; we are not victims of circumstance — we are potential masters of own lives. It is up to each one of us to research and then express that potential, and to do so without neglecting the needs of all life — wherever it may be, and whatever it may be.

In the original channellings which gave birth to STARCRAFT, i.e., the book, it was suggested that each group should have a rotating leadership, as well as leaders *in the moment* for the *working* of different tasks. Nevertheless no member of any Starcraft group should feel that any leadership removes the need for self-responsibility; leadership in Starcraft is purely a functional arrangement — it is not a hierarchical system, or a status privilege.

With self-responsibility also comes strength — of spirit, of mind, and also of body. If a Starcraft group does not have that strength, or health, it will not be able to deal with the rigours which are part and parcel of *working* magick. It should be clear from this that to choose Starcraft as a personal path is to revolutionise everything that one is — there is no room for anything less. That is not to say that all this will be accomplished in a moment, or even a few months, maybe even years — it is a progressive path which step by step leads from one result to another, and in so doing removes one's blinkers, anoints the means of perception, and finally delivers the goods.

Patience is required, as well as commitment. In Starcraft one is proposing to make giant leaps in one's evolutionary view of things, not to mention any contact and communication one may have with beings and forces which are far more evolved than ourselves, and all that this may entail. They must have patience with us, in the same way as we need to be patient for results to work out. Things cannot be rushed beyond breaking point, and nothing can be achieved in the long term if all parties concerned are not prepared to work together in a manner which is viable. This is also part of what self-responsibility means.

One must be able to make decisions, and not wait for someone or something else to make them for oneself. And whatever decisions one makes must be based on whatever one is capable of by way of *optimal insight* at any one time — taking into view everything one can, and whatever one can deal with. In addition to this one cannot allow oneself to be paralysed out of fear of making mistakes — one can only learn from *doing*, and not from sitting around and waiting.

13 — BALANCING THE WORLDS

One of the greatest difficulties inherent to Starcraft is that of balancing the worlds within oneself. From one point of view one is required to act as something of a superwo/man, and from another angle one is still very much a human being — with vulnerabilities, maybe doubts, and certainly with many abilities yet to be acquired.

The difference between the two may seem perhaps vast, particularly when in a state of low or normal consciousness; one of the aims of Starcraft is to bridge that gap, and to elevate one's lower self consciousness into a state of Higher Self consciousness — first of all at intervals, and then increasingly permanently, until finally there is no difference between the two; as this is likely to take some time one must strike an initial balance whereby there is no need to reject one's *normal* self just because it is usually constrained by a relatively low state of consciousness; in

Starcraft there is room for self-gentleness as well as for high demands on one's abilities (however, there is no room for complacency).

To experience different states of consciousness, especially on a regular basis, can lead to a sense of being in one world one moment, and in another world during the next. In fact there is only one world/one Universe/one Life, yet there are many levels, each of which is a function of a particular grade of consciousness — the higher one's consciousness, the more one *sees* of this world, and by implication the more one *sees* of one's true Self. The more one perceives, the more self-responsible and involved one needs to be.

Similarly, the faster one evolves, the faster one needs to adapt to the ongoing changes which are occurring, and then one has to integrate all those changes within oneself. As one changes, the world changes in direct proportion; as more and more people become involved in consciously changing themselves, the world changes to a greater extent — and in turn the world reveals more of itself, which initiates yet more changes. This is simple cause-and-effect at work.

Nevertheless there is another aspect to all this: as we change, and the world changes accordingly, the more we and the world draw on Systemic and extra-Systemic energies, thus producing an increase of current, which in turn produces even greater changes. Seen over a period of time one can perceive this phenomenon as one which is directly related to the *electrical* stimulation of all evolutionary life — needs promote changes; changes promote an increase of current; the increase of current promotes the acceleration of all evolutionary unfoldment; and this promotes new needs. Thus the cycle is self-fulfilling.

If this process was continually exponential evolution would probably burn itself out in a comparatively short space of time, therefore it is subject to various cycles of growth; each cycle unfolds one main stage of unfoldment, leading then to the next; conversely, each phase of evolutionary *intent* is addressed, then fulfilled, and each fulfilment leads to the next phase — which cannot be addressed until that fulfilment has occurred; this then releases or invokes new energies which will then promote the unfoldment of the new phase. All this applies as much to ourselves as individuals as it does to the whole planet — as a Spiritual being — as it does to the whole Solar System, and so on.

This process is indicative of how Devas work — literally using cycles of growth and unfoldment as *building blocks* for evolutionary life. They plan these cycles well in advance, then they implement them — one by one, and in sequence; alterations are made to this plan only to the extent that they become necessary, yet the cycles are not changed — only the way in which each unfoldment is addressed may be altered in the face of whatever results are secured, or not secured as the case may be; our part in all this is to flow with the process, evolve in accordance with these cycles, fulfil the needs of the Earth Spirit as well as our own — with respect to the kind of abilities we can acquire — and thereby impart something of our own individual and collective successes to the evolutionary system in which we function; the successes of other groups of beings (such as Devas) also promote our own unfoldment. As the Earth grows, so does the Solar System as a whole grow, and vice-versa; as the Solar System grows, so does the group of Systems to which it belongs grow in turn, and again vice-versa. This is another example of the inter-relationship between all things. To the extent that we identify ourselves with this process we can learn to alter our consciousness from low-normal to higher, and then higher yet.

14 — VISION AND POLITICS

Without a sense of vision with regard to what can be it is almost impossible to effect changes which will genuinely enhance the quality of our lives — this applies as much to mundane matters as it does to Spiritual progress.

We tend to look out upon the world in which we live and then to accept what we find there as the *norm* — seldom do we

175

really try and visualise what would happen if we were prepared to apply ourselves systematically to the fulfilment of a different kind of vision; or *dream,* as it was put in STARCRAFT (see also THE DREAMSCAPE, which follows this handbook).

We are all too prone to accepting the *normal view,* and then endorsing it as we fail to promote whatever might be more in keeping with our actual needs. We allow our limitations to direct our sense of vision, and we allow the limitations which are apparently imposed upon us by society and whatever establishment exists to foster inertia — and this often to our detriment.

If we want to change the world in which we live — and there is a lot which does indeed *need* changing, regardless of viewpoint — then we have to accept a political role within that world (not from the ordinary point of view alone, however).

In the past the passage from one political world-view to another has usually occurred subsequent to ideological and elitist power struggles, sometimes accompanied by revolutions and war — this encompasses the inadequacies of human beings to deal with change in a manner which is fruitful; the revolutionaries of yesterday usually become the dictators of tomorrow, and the system does not really change at all — it is just given a different ideological name, and all the rest is largely cosmetic.

The world's political arena today is very complex, and there are those who thrive on that complexity as it suits their selfish interests. We can only change that by changing ourselves, which is the first step towards accepting a political role within the world; the next is to have enough vision to implement changes around oneself, both at a visible and invisible level — in this case the *invisible* level includes a realisation that much of the work can be done on the inner Planes, and that a planetary consensus exists on these levels whose sole purpose is to promote evolutionary unfoldment — a sphere of reference which is ideally suited to the enactment and purpose of Starcraft.

Obviously what we will be able to do in objective terms will increase as we communicate more and then organise ourselves both at a magickal and mundane level. Yet to implement political change does not mean that one has to become a politician vying for votes or status within any given political system. The mere fact that one *looks* at the world from a *higher political point of view,* then acts by channelling appropriate energies into the world — particularly if this is done with vision — directly to indirectly affects the mundane political situation.

Of course vision also concerns other departments than that which is political in nature; nevertheless that which is political affects all else and determines the climate in which other things are done. Ideally politics constitute the art of facilitating all other endeavours within a frame of reference which is fully adapted to genuine collective needs — this definition could not be wholly applied to present-day politics as they stand.

If one looks at the nations of the world as a whole one can detect that there are people who are seeking change everywhere, particularly in relationship to politics. National politics are increasingly becoming a function of planetary politics, and no one nation today exists in isolation from its neighbours — everything is becoming increasingly interwoven, and until we are all prepared to embrace the global view none of our problems can be entirely resolved.

Attitudes need changing: and they are changing, if only because circumstances are forcing us to change them. Nevertheless if one is only concerned with short term results without looking further ahead and taking longer term effects into consideration one is only delaying matters and not really solving anything. If creative steps were taken to ensure that creative results would ensue then we would be able to address all those problems and work things out to mutual advantage. The role of Starcraft is in part to facilitate this process.

15 — NEW WAYS IN A WORLD OF CHANGE

The world is presently in a catalytic crisis — everything is up for re-evaluation; not only our politics, our religions, our financial institutions, our cultures, our sciences, our ideals, but also our sense of magick.

To try and maintain *things as they are,* or to attempt to re-enact *things as they were*, can only be self-defeating; in a world which is constantly changing, and which is changing increasingly fast at that, one must be able to flow with the situation while giving this process a sense of direction — without direction changes in themselves are of no particular value.

The trouble is that many of us want different sorts of worlds to live in — and few of us have the same vision of the future. Nevertheless the world is big enough to accommodate for various views, and the expression of different views does not have to spell conflict — it can lead to creative exchanges. Conversely a society with only one dimension of insight is a society at a stand-still — it cannot grow because it cannot see itself from different angles.

Let us propose the following, for the sake of argument: during the next few decades the world will become politically united and we will see the creation of a single World Government — and yet each area of the world, and for that matter each individual, will be guaranteed the right of self-determination within that. Can this individualism work side by side with global government?

At first sight this might seem improbable, as neither the East or the West has found the answer.

The problem with Capitalism is that money becomes more important than people, and leads to progressive excess and monopolies — once those monopolies have entrenched them-selves against assault by manipulating the markets to the hilt we reach the final result of Capitalism: corporate dictatorship.

The problem with Communism is that collectivity becomes more important than individuality, and leads to an oppressive centralisation — once that centralisation has entrenched itself against all opposition we reach the final result of Communism: centralised dictatorship.

Is there much difference between the two?

Clearly neither Capitalism or Communism is the answer, even though they may help us to find out what is. We need to view world resources in a different way, and we need to view human life as an expression of Spirit — and not as digits to be crunched up and spewed out by computer programs. Until we achieve that the answer will remain elusive, for the real change is one of consciousness, and has nothing to do with the system of politics we do or do not endorse. A higher sense of consciousness means a greater awareness of the situation and a greater willingness to change; viable politics then become defined by that higher consciousness; conflicts of interest cease, and creative solutions can be found.

We are as near or as far from that as we allow ourselves to be. We need to re-evaluate our needs in the light of the best possibilities we can *see;* then step by step we must implement the necessary changes — starting with whatever is most relevant, and planning to the extent that we have established a common direction for our thrust.

Another dimension to these impending changes is that we are on the threshold of moving physically into space. At present this process is hindered not only by our level of technology but also by the value we place on economic illusions. Furthermore, instead of pulling together we are divided by competition and by military and political preoccupations. If we do not *move together* then space will remain largely inaccessible; this only highlights the process of unification that we need to address and eventually fulfil — regardless of the difficulties involved.

As each country of the world becomes poorer in real terms as resources are squandered on non-essentials — such as armament, for instance — each nation is being forced to seek viable compromises; cooperation in the key to success. The role of Starcraft in all this is to foster cooperation — by magickal means.

In the same way as the *Age of Pisces* was principally ruled by the 6th Ray of Ideas, Ideals and religious devotion, the oncoming *Age of Aquarius* will be influenced increasingly by the 7th Ray of Magick — this is a cyclic process of change which affects the Earth regularly at vectorial intervals, and its periodicity is well known to Life-Initiates; at present we are living somewhere between the two, however the influence of the 6th Ray is diminishing fast, while the influence of the 7th Ray is gaining in momentum all the while — this Ray will hold sway over planetary developments for the duration of its own cycle (approximately 2100 years).

The 7th Ray is still very much misunderstood in general, even by those who are involved in esoteric learning; and this somewhat demonstrates how shallow we really are when it comes to understanding the effective role of magick in our lives — unlike thousands of years ago when our forebears were preoccupied with magick to the exclusion of almost anything else, regardless of what they did, and regardless of consequences.

Magick is a dynamic energy; it is synthetic in its nature and in its impact. Its Ray colour is Violet, which therefore includes Red and Blue/Indigo; at a higher level it is Ultra-Violet, and so synthetic is this that in esoteric lore it is used frequently as a substitute for the Universal Ray, which is White (from which all other Ray-forces are diffracted) — this is some indication of its power.

In relationship to power there are many things that we do not understand with regard to events on this planet which appear to be accidents or else the consequences of ill-action; let us name two of these for consideration: the release of atomic forces, and the destruction of the ozone layer as a result of the release of CFC gases into the atmosphere.

No one would normally think of the detonation of nuclear devices or the release of large quantities of radioactivity as a *good* thing — we probably all know that radioactivity can provoke various kinds of cancers, and after Chernobyl no one can be left in any real doubt as to the seriousness of civil nuclear accidents, even though the full story has not yet been told, and there is a lot more to come. However there is another side to radioactivity which our shamanic ancestors *saw* well enough: for all their major sacred ceremonial sites (and this throughout the Earth) were built or established over significantly large deposits of Uranium, hence the power which is to be derived from these places. It transpires that radioactivity has a direct effect on consciousness, accelerating and boosting it in direct proportion to one's exposure to it (of course beyond a certain dose it is also lethal, although the greater one's consciousness, the less adverse is its effect).

Something of the same can be said of the Ultra-Violet radiation which is increasingly piercing through what remains of the ozone layer in the upper atmosphere, which normally screens much of it out. Now consider this, and call it coincidence if you will, but at your own peril, so to speak: Uranium is an unstable metallic isotope which sheds its excess energy as various forms of energy particles; as its name implies Uranium is related to the planet Uranus, which is considered astrologically to be an unstable influence, i.e., a very powerful one. The Ray-colour of Uranus is Ultra-Violet; Uranus rules over Aquarius; and the symbol for Aquarius is radiation, as a waveform. The 7th Ray is Violet, including Ultra-Violet; Uranus is interpreted as ruling over all acts of Magick. Put all these factors together, and the *accidents* related to above can be *seen* as evolutionary pointers instead — consequences of the type of Age we are entering into.

This does not and cannot excuse human foolishness with regard to releasing powerful forces into the world without knowledge or care as to what is being done, or what effect it may have, yet all this is an indication of how things are *moved* through us at a subconscious level.

The relevance of Magick in all this is that it can address *Aquarius* directly. Magick is a dynamic act of purposeful endeavour, and deals wholly with energies. If we look at the world of today, let alone what it will or may become in the future, it should be obvious that the emphasis all round is on energy — the use of electricity, nuclear fission, nuclear fusion, lasers, electronics, radio, television, telephones, computers, robotics, artificial intelligence, photonics, and so on. Never before (within historical memory at least) have we created and then used so much energy; energy is the symbolic *signature* of the sign Aquarius; the glyph for Uranus represents *dual-perception/reception-and-one-emission of Spirit* (it is interesting to note that before the astronomical discovery of Uranus the rulership of Aquarius was ascribed to Saturn — *the one who restricts*); we need energy to survive; higher energies are involved during initiatic events, which are now occurring with increasing frequency... therefore it should be no surprise to us that it will be Magick that will predominate over this coming Age, influenced as it is by the 7th Ray.

Just before the beginning of any Age there is a period of relative chaos — this time round we have witnessed this in dramatic terms during the two world wars, which finally ended with the first, and so far only nuclear bombs to be used against living people. Since that time we have been living in the shadow of that event in an uneasy atmosphere dominated by the presence of nuclear devices and by the tension between two opposing ideological blocks which represent the divisions within ourselves; this is Power itself speaking to us through its own means of manifestation; and its questions are very direct and very simple: do we or do we not want Peace? Do we or do we not want Change? Are we prepared to change? When? How fast?

From an occult point of view one can *read* this situation — if one *looks* at all the elements involved one can *see* that what is happening is a function of those forces which are now seeking expression within the world, replacing in the process the prominence of other forces which are no longer directly relevant to the Planet's evolutionary unfoldment at this time. We are being invited to perceive this. It is staring us in the eyes at point blank range, and yet many of us still fail to *see* it, or understand it.

The cyclic change-over of the Rays from Age to Age only incidentally affects human affairs — it has nothing to do with human invocation, for it happens quite regardless of that; and yet it manifests itself in a way which is directly related to where we *are at,* and it affects human response in a most direct fashion as a result — in relation to this, Starcraft is something of a precipitation of the 7th Ray of Magick into human consciousness, via the Devic or Angelic evolution. It is a beautiful and very powerful offering.

17 — STARCRAFT — THE WAY OF THE STARS

In this booklet we have principally looked at some of the basics of Starcraft, and it may surprise some that it is not crammed with magickal formulae — there is a simple reason for that: magickal formulae must be learnt from within oneself, using one's intuition and one's insights; one must learn from Devas, what is more.

Also there are many books which are full of rubbish with regard to magick, and there are people (who obviously do not know any better) who pick up these books, apply the formulae as described in them, and end up making a mess of their lives because the information imparted is little more than dubious fantasy, or else deals with low astralism which no one in hir right mind would want to deal with in the first place.

Once again we must look at Uranus — initially its influence is unstable or destabilising, and powerful, and if the information is poor, the results one will get from using it will be poorer still, and may even be detrimental to one's state of emotional and mental health.

This is not so much a warning as it is an observation. We only have to look at Witchcraft: what it was, and what it has become. Many years ago I listened to a traditional Lady of the Craft speaking about Wicca, and she was very clear about what it is and what it is not, and she exuded power, intuition and intelligence in a way which struck me as totally real and utterly genuine; truly I could not say the same with regard to many people who call themselves Wiccans and who practise some variant of bastardised Witchcraft, crossbred with ill-understood notions derived from other paths. True Witchcraft is a Nature Path; Starcraft is also a Nature Path, and a way of communicating and working cooperatively with Devas — including Solar and Star Devas.

We all have a lot to learn with regard to Starcraft; what has been unfolded so far is setting the scene and the tone, but there is real *work* to be done — which can only be done by groups of people working together, using the best of their faculties, acquiring abilities, and being sufficiently lucid to know the difference between reality and fantasy. These groups will also have to be their own judges as to the validity of what they do, since flexibility of approach is not to be confused with the attitude or belief that *anything will work*, because if will not. Only that which is gleaned from direct insight and genuine intuition is going to be of any use in Starcraft, and to accept or expect anything less than that will lead to absolutely nothing of consequence at all.

Starcraft is a way of the stars; it highlights possibilities which with effort and perseverance may open up the inner doors to a kind of perception and work which will reveal themselves in due course for what they really are. Those who will go that far will then *know* what to do next, and be able to participate in a Craft in which they will be *movers,* and not mere vehicles.

For those who resonate with what has been said here, Blessed Be! May your path become clearer to you every day! May the stars touch you with their Magick! And may you find the God-dess Self within your selves!

FLOW — BALANCE — BEAUTY

... This is one little formula which can reveal many great things.

FOREWORD

This booklet — of Deva channellings — requires an introduction, for it deals with matters which feel so pregnant with as yet unrealised possibilities that words alone pale into insignificance; it is provocative to the extent that it represents a vastly different perspective to our normal manner of perceiving things — a way of changing our lives, internally and externally, and thus the conditions which surround us — for the better, in every way.

From one angle, THE DREAMSCAPE is a continuation of STARCRAFT — and yet it also heralds a new aspect of communication, even of cooperation.

The *dialogue* is not entirely new — our ancestors knew about the influx of energies from the stars, and knew that there were Cosmic and Stellar Beings; and they also knew that these Beings were instrumental in channelling energy-information directly or indirectly towards and through human recipients — Priest/esses, trained Psychics/sensitives, Adepts, Masters, Shamans, Initiates and others. These acted as the *Guardians of the Mysteries* on behalf of the human race.

The door has been largely closed for two thousand years; maybe it shouldn't have been that way, since the Christ Mysteries are the same as the Pagan Mysteries, the Buddhist Mysteries, the Taoist Mysteries, etc — these are all facets of the same thing: the same, One, and yet diverse *Way of Seeing,* of perceiving what Life *IS*.

What went wrong? Who closed the door? Well, ignorance did; deliberate political and ideological manipulation of people's minds and emotions did; dogmatism did; elitist self-importance did.

The older Mysteries Traditions were eclipsed not by Christ, but by people who used the name *Christ* to build a monopoly over people's beliefs, and then imposed that negative structure on all and sundry. Christ can be seen in a great many ways (and

185

under the banner of other names), and the churchianised version(s) are not only largely distorted, but almost unrecognisable from the reality behind it — the essence was lost, or buried deep below the conscious surface. The true Mysteries were forced *underground;* the Gnostics, who had vastly more integrity, did not aspire to conquer the world with the might of the Church of Rome. They were the true Christians, who knew the Christian Mysteries, and they were persecuted out of existence like all the rest; and what survived had already lost something of the essence, and confused certain issues.

The Pagan Mysteries which had held sway for thousands of years, in a variety of forms and guises, had lost much of their way earlier than 2,000 years ago. The advent of the New Age of then (the Old Age of now) should, or could have relaunched a new dimension of Mystical Revelation — however, and regrettably, it got bogged down in hopeless dogma and political manoeuvring; instead of inspiring, it imprisoned; it sold a dummy-product; and it maimed the avenues of reaching the Soul of the planet in the process. True Christians were quickly outnumbered by false ones, and numbers unfortunately carried the weight of force (a small elite, and a vast number of — yes — *sheep;* an appropriate word in the circumstances — prisoners of consciousness, at it were, or more precisely the near complete lack of it).

This booklet does not say that any one religious, or mystical, or occult group view is the best, or *the* New Age answer to the Old Age; and yet each is potentially a part of the answer — *if* and providing the past is not re-enacted without reference to the needs of the present and that of the future.

All ways are potentially invited to contribute to the unfoldment of what is to be.

Lastly, the channelling of this booklet occurred over a number of days (March 1988), and the last section was not added until almost two months later (May 9th) — significantly, after Beltane.

Blessed Be! — *Vee Van Dam; Glastonbury May 1988.*

186

1 — THE COSMIC DREAM

Dreaming — you might think of this as something vague to consider when in fact we are not referring to the sort of nebulous events which you usually experience during your physical sleep; of this we want to be clear here. We are referring to a fully conscious process whereby one meditates on an idea, and then develops that idea in what could be called an exploration of Spiritual potential.

We use the term *dreaming* because it is apt; at a primary level it refers to the activity which certain Cosmic Devas undertake on the Cosmic Astral Plane — not, it should be noted, on the Astral Plane that you are somewhat more aware of. The Cosmic Astral Plane is to the Astral Plane what a planet is to a grain of dust — an inadequate analogy which may nevertheless convey something of the difference in terms of the magnitudes involved.

Conscious *dreaming* differs from your ordinary dreaming to the extent that what is *dreamt* is in fact a projection of one's mind — a deliberate one, a most conscious one, whereby one simulates desired conditions for the sake of objectifying the potential inherent to the creative process. When speaking of the Cosmic Astral Plane, those Great Devas who are involved are in fact *dreaming* universes, or parts of universes, and when they are finally satisfied with the results of their projections then they begin the work of fulfilling their *dreams*, and thereby manifest them.

This takes a lot of time as you think of time — æons; it is not an overnight affair by any means. Yet they do not experience that time in terms of duration, but only in terms of activity — cycles of activity and rest to be more exact. Time to them is not a problem. Cycles come and go, but they do not feel under any particular restriction. Much like an artist losses hir sense of time when s/he is working, these Great Devas lose any sense of duration as they apply themselves to Cosmic Dreaming.

In the first instance they start out with an initial set of requirements provided to them by even Higher Cosmic Devas;

these requirements reflect Cosmic Needs. Therefore they begin to work on what could be thought of as a primitive draft — a basic skeleton plan which will be later *fleshed out* so as to give the *Dream* (or *Dreams*) more substance and a greater potential for variety — which is necessary in evolutionary terms if anything useful is likely to come out of it. So they work away for æons upon æons, and eventually fulfil the essential nature of the *Dream;* once that much has been achieved then it is precipitated into what we could refer to here as Cosmic Material Existence — what to you is represented by the Seven Planes.

The overall Dream must be very complex so as to permit multifold expression, therefore the Dream includes a great diversity of potential worlds — on each world, be it a star or a planet, unique conditions will exist which will lead to equally unique evolutions. Each stellar and planetary development is an experiment; no one can know for sure what will really happen once it is precipitated down into denser and denser layers of energy-matter, yet the Dream involving that world will include enough flexibility so as to make whatever adjustments are necessary possible to implement so that evolution can occur in a viable way.

The star of any given system represents the nucleus of that system — its role is in some ways secondary since it essentially provides energy for the planets within that solar system; from another point of view that star will be the *only* being or thing which is really evolving, because each and all the planets of that system are in effect evolving possibilities and actualities on its behalf — therefore it is that star which is really evolving, and the planets are in reality only instrumental in that evolution.

Each star then is surrounded by the lesser expressions of its Spiritual manifestation; and all the evolutions on any given planet are in turn the lesser expressions of that planet's Spiritual expression. This adds up to a whole which we would refer to as the Systemic Being.

If you then consider that the Cosmos contains, for all intents and purposes, an infinity of stars — there are millions if not billions of stars in each major galaxy, not to mention lesser galaxies, and there are countless galaxies to consider — and each star system has usually at least 12 to 15 planets, and sometimes many more than that — we are talking about a Cosmic Dream which encompasses an infinity of worlds. Can you even begin to imagine this order of magnitude?! Can you even begin to appreciate how many different types of unique evolutions this in effect represents? Numbers are useless here; one can only deal in terms of abstractions when considering the potential which this infinite number of evolutions represents.

What is initiated in the Dream then has to be objectified in the denser material layers; once this has been achieved the scene is set for a great Return Wave of the Spirit — which Spirit has been invested, so to speak, in that density. In the process each individual evolution learns to master its circumstances, and by so doing brings new strength to the Cosmos once it finally liberates itself from the hold which dense energy-matter has upon that Spirit.

We have spoken about much of this before, therefore we do not wish to repeat ourselves unduly (see STARCRAFT). What we do want to do is to help you learn how to *dream,* because what you have often objectified for yourselves as human beings has left a great deal to be desired in almost every department; we do not wish to denigrate your better efforts, yet we think that you would agree yourselves that your world as it stands, as you have manifested it around you, is not all that it could be. Devas have been instrumental in making Nature what it is on your world, and yet you have compromised the true beauty and relevance of your world's evolution by dreaming quite untenable things — it starts with you: you must own your own contribution to your own problems; they are not, as you might sometimes assume, created by any external entity, be it a devil or any other kind of negative force — they are your creations; the world which you have manifested is the result of your dreams, mostly unconscious dreams — reactions, ill-thoughts, ill-desires, and ill-actions.

189

What we would like to be able to impart to you, so as to help you manifest something entirely different — something that will glow with beauty and with peace, and with all those other traits which you, and we, would think of as positive, or at the very least as balanced — is the nature of the original Dream as concerns the Earth — as a Spiritual Being.

Aeons ago — we do not wish to quote periods in terms of years, millions of years, or even billions of years; that to a great extent is irrelevant here — æons ago when the Earth was first formed out of the impetus of the Cosmic Dream (ie its Systemic reflection) it held all the promise for many great things and possibilities — as do most if not all the planets anywhere in the wide Cosmos. It chose a role — an evolutionary role — within this Solar System, on behalf of the greater Evolutionary Being, the Sun. Although we cannot disclose the exact nature of that role — because we must be careful not to open up avenues which could be tarnished by those who do not wish to be *aligned* with Spiritual Purpose — we will touch upon it shortly within a given context so that you may be able to realise that the Earth, as a Being, is not without its own special place in the scheme of things, and that you can contribute to its purpose and its role — consciously, with heart, intelligently and intuitively.

Stars are all part of families — they are not isolated individuals without brothers or sisters (you do not seem to have a term which mediates between the two). They evolve as families; the Dreams which concern them are, if you like, family Dreams, or a Group Dream. Each star, as a Being, is responsible for manifesting conditions which will implement one particular portion of that Dream, which is in itself is made up of several smaller portions, as endorsed by each Planetary Being within its system. Projecting this on a much greater scale we could say that the whole of a galaxy is a family, which in turn is a part of an even greater family of galaxies, and so on; each of these galaxies is responsible for manifesting and working with a given portion of the overall Cosmic Dream.

Imagine what it would be like if these great Entities — on different scales of magnitude — chose to be renegades to the *Cause*; galaxies would fall apart, stars everywhere would become polluted with negative energies, systems would be destroyed in droves. Fortunately these Beings are not as ignorant or as unaware as you can be, and they do not entertain ill-thought, ill-desire, or ill-action. They *dream* wisely, and they actuate positive-to-balanced means of establishing a relevant outcome to their evolutionary *intent*.

Nevertheless negativity does exist — this is the result of the original involutionary downward current which in effect permitted manifestation. As mind divided what was inherently a Oneness there was always a possibility, if not a certainty, that mind would also isolate consciousness from its Source; as a result renegades on different worlds, and on different lower levels — lower mental, astral and etheric-physical — did manifest a wish for autonomy from the Spiritual Current which in fact was feeding them; they did not fully recognise anymore that they were an intrinsic part of the Oneness from which they had sprung. As they reacted against Universality and chose the route of separation they in effect isolated themselves from the Source — but in their consciousness only; because their minds had become blocked they could no longer realise that without the Current passing through them they would no longer exist. They persisted because the Current feeds all, regardless of their state of consciousness, and regardless of whether they are expressing positivity, balance or negativity — although those who harbour an excess of negativity are in effect very much cut off from any real contact with that Current; they can only exist very marginally — literally on a trickle feed.

To call this "evil" is incorrect in most cases — one should think of it more as blindness. The fact that there are some beings who know that the Source does exist, who know that there is a Current which passes through all beings, and that it nourishes them with energy in the process thus permitting them to live and express themselves, and yet choose to be negative regardless of this knowledge, only points out that any possibility can be; it can happen. These beings — paradoxically as it may seem — nevertheless fulfil a purpose within the overall Purpose, despite their wish to be divorced from the Cosmic Life; they serve to test what is positively oriented, and in so doing strengthen it.

The Cosmic Dream did not spawn evil or negativity as a matter of *intent* — this was only the inescapable result of a possibility; if something is possible the chances are that it will become manifest in some form or other, and this sooner or later. This is one of the things which will have to be fully resolved in the course of time prior to the whole Universe discarnating from the area you would refer to as the Seven Planes — when the Cosmic Dream will have served its purpose, and when all the Spiritual Powers will have withdrawn from dense manifestation.

All this represents one SINGLE WAVE; other Waves will occur later, and other Dreams will become manifest, involving new groups of Beings, new worlds, and new unique opportunities.

2 — THE SOLAR DREAM

One must understand the Cosmos in very expansive terms. As you know (from STARCRAFT) stars do come and go from dense manifestation; they incarnate — much like you incarnate (if on a different scale) — they remain consciously focused on dense levels for the duration of a given evolutionary cycle, and then they discarnate once they have fulfilled that cycle. Some time later they incarnate again, and then fulfil another complete cycle. And so on until they no longer need to incarnate (until they have become what could be called Adept-Stars).

One of the main difference between you — as human beings — and stars — as Stellar Beings — is that on average it takes an average of 777 incarnations for a human being to fulfil hir complete incarnational meta-cycle, whereas it only takes be-tween 3 and 7 (or 9) for a Stellar Being.

Your star, the Sun (or Sol), last began to incarnate several billions of your years ago. First of all S-he manifested an Etheric nucleus (around the Cosmic Astral nucleus) on what to you is the Seventh Systemic Plane, which nucleus then began to rotate; the vortex which was created on that level precipitated further manifestation into density, until the Sun became manifest on increasingly lower levels. Finally Hir expression became manifest on the higher etheric sub-plane of the etheric-physical plane, and the vortex began to pull in cosmic-physical gases and dust particles (residues from previous stellar systems); when the aggregation and compression of this material became sufficiently great the gases and the dust were brought to incandescence — that is, things became so hot that the physical centre of the Sun became white-hot, and its surface bluish (that is, it was less hot than the central core). The dense physical body of the Sun had been born and it continued to rotate — much faster than it does now — and in the process it exuded gases and fusion material which then cohered into *bundles;* these *bundles* then formed most of the planets of this Solar System (a couple were captured as they drifted past the System). The Sun then began gradually to cool down, to the extent that now it can be viewed as a yellow star at a physical level.

All this is an effect; the actual Dream behind the manifestation, and therefore dense incarnation, of the Sun occurred on the Cosmic Astral Plane, and was then precipitated into the Seven Planes. The full Dream in fact encompasses several lifetimes of development, and this incarnation is generally said to be, esoterically, the second — which in strict terms is not quite the case; a third incarnation is to come.

During each lifetime the Sun has the task of unfolding a particular set of principles — in the present case it is developing Consciousness (in its last incarnation it developed Mind; in its next incarnation it will develop Will and the full expression of Power and *Intent*/Purpose).

Each planet of the Solar System has its own particular role to play in this development, and each part of the System adds up with all the others to form the constituents of the Systemic Dream. Therefore the Earth is a part of that Dream.

Once things are embraced in this context it becomes a lot easier to understand both the Sun and the Planetary Beings which together form the System. One should also keep in mind that the dense manifestation of any Cosmic Being, be it a star or a planet, is only the outermost expression of its nature; on inner Levels it has a Cosmic Astral sheath, much as you have an Astral body, and it is in this *area* that it Dreams.

Excluding the Seven Planes (which form the lowest of the Cosmic Planes) there are Six other Cosmic Levels, each composed of Seven Planes — as far as the Sun and the Planetary Beings of this Solar System are concerned each one of these Planes represents a sub-plane within their own *stratified* make-ups; on each of these sub-planes various expressions exist and various tasks are carried out; most of the activity is *centralised* on the lower Cosmic sub-planes at present, and yet in a future to come most of the activity will be focused on the higher Cosmic sub-planes of each Cosmic Plane. Eventually the Sun and the Solar System will discarnate, and there will be no more activity on the Seven Planes of the lowest Cosmic Level (as far as this System is concerned); and this for a time before the next incarnation of the Solar System — the third and final one. Then other developments will take place, and the Sun will eventually liberate Hirself from the Cosmic Planes in association with other Stellar Beings who belong to the same Stellar Group (remain mindful that what we say here is deliberately sketchy; the true events to take place are too complex and too difficult for you to understand).

The Sun, and the Stellar Beings of Hir Stellar Group, will then emerge into a Super-Cosmic Universe, which has yet to be built, but which exists even now *in potential*.

The outcome of the Solar Dream, through the evolution which will have taken place, will have permitted that much — this is the Purpose behind that Dream.

Getting back to the present, the Sun is undergoing Hir second incarnation (from another point of view Hir sixth). The Dream concerning this Solar Period has its focus on one of the planets of this System — we will not say which one that is — and the Earth, as a Planetary Being, is assisting this planet to unfold the exact nature of the *INTENT* for this Solar Period, which as we have already said concerns the unfoldment of Consciousness. But what type of Consciousness? This is the secret of the Solar Plan, and it cannot be revealed here — however it can be accessed to a certain degree while in states of higher consciousness.

If the Systemic Dream was to be thought of as a multi-layered *Plan-of-Intent* which is designed to actuate a particular set of evolutionary developments, then we could say that the Earth has a part to play in that Plan. More specifically we could say that the humanity presently dwelling and active on the Earth represents a small subset of that Plan — providing it develops what it was entrusted with to unfold. In a somewhat turbulent and messy way it is in effect doing so; and we are mindful that the somewhat disorganised and dis-hearted efforts of the Earth's humanity need to be drawn into conscious contact and alignment with genuine Solar/Systemic requirements. This can only occur if you embrace the whole System in your consciousness and identify yourselves with It. For as long as you maintain a self-oriented consciousness to the exclusion of all else it cannot occur.

Putting this another way, think of the Solar System as a complete world; each planet of the System would then be a country — you are living in one of those countries, namely the Earth. Much as there are British people, and Italians, and Chinese people, and Eskimos, there are also Earth people, and Martians, and Venusians, and Jupiterians — not necessarily on a physical level, however. Each grouping has its own particular identity-focus, and yet they all belong to a single whole, ie the Solar

System. Whatever is done in one country affects what is happening in another — you cannot think of yourselves as separate from the Solar System; whatever you do affects the rest of the System, and whatever is done elsewhere affects you. This interrelationship is not fictitious.

You could say that the whole Solar System is an *ecological unit,* and if one part of that unit fails to do what it must on behalf of the whole then it impedes the System in direct proportion. If one planet fails to actuate its own part of the Systemic Dream, then the Dream as a whole is affected. Therefore we come to you not so much to force you to change, but to alert you to the fact that your dreaming is wrong, or distorted — it is out of alignment with the rest, and it is affecting the rest often adversely.

We are very aware of your circumstances — perhaps even more so than you are at this point, because we can see the underlying causes. We are aware of your difficulties, and we know that it is not easy for you to resolve your international, national, regional, and even individual differences. And yet you must do so, sooner or later, and preferably sooner. If things do not change sufficiently radically, and soon, then new measures will have to be taken to make you aware of what is surrounding you — yet if this happens to be the only way that we and others can draw your attention to what is wrong in your output then it will also force you to change in a way where you will have little or perhaps even no real choice; we much prefer the idea of allowing you to choose of your own accord — we do not wish to force you into seeing things as we do; we much prefer to invite you to do so of your own free-will.

Look at your world — it is full of wars and discord. Not only military wars, but wars of the mind, wars of emotions, wars of identity, wars of want and neglect, wars of alienation, even between your sexes... Is that a way to live?! We think not; that is a way of potentially destroying millions upon millions of years of precious evolution.

We would like to propose that you look closely at what you are doing, and then take the steps which are necessary to put things right — that can only really come from the heart, for the mind tends to divide things into separate parts; you very much need to look at things as a whole, and then deal with them as a whole.

It is the heart which rules over consciousness, and although this may not be apparent to you it is a fact that it is through *heartful* expression that you will find the way forward; heartful expression means, in essence, to love; and through love and mind combined comes wisdom.

We would like to greet you as the Wise Ones of Earth! Wise because you will have learnt — through duress — what is truly worthwhile, what is worth achieving. At present your global society is overly divided, and while it may be making moves towards a better direction in certain specific respects, it still has a lot to learn. Much of your societal developments are still very crude.

You must address the imbalance which you have created for yourselves, and by extension for the System as a whole.

Therefore try and elevate your consciousness to a higher level, where maybe you will be able to *see* something of the Systemic Dream — then attempt to actuate your part of that Dream to the best of your abilities. At length you will find yourselves surrounded by willing evolutionary agents from all around the System, and even from beyond the System — and they will help you, in different ways.

Finally, this: the imbalance which you have created resonates within the Solar System, *and* within the Greater Cosmic Sphere; there are other planets out there which are now *contaminated* by your sense of imbalance. Some of these were already imbalanced as well, if usually in a different respect — therefore your problem is not yours alone; there are dimensions to all this which undoubtedly escape your conscious ability to perceive them, yet your resolution for change — and balanced change at that — is eagerly awaited, and will be welcomed by these worlds — they are struggling also.

If you can find your balance, then these worlds will tend to find theirs (and to a certain extent vice-versa).

In the process of manifesting a new sense of balance you will also be acquiring new skills — which some of you will then be able to offer to other worlds which are experiencing difficulties.

In this there is a hint with regard to the nature of the Earth's purpose — it was foreseen that some of the Earth's people, as Spiritual beings, would eventually *export* their evolutionary skills so as to help out other troubled planetary evolutions — and this potentially anywhere within the Universe, at different levels.

Not a rescue service, but a skilful and trained power for assisting ailing evolutions to find their balance and their way out of difficulty.

This development is a definite part of the Solar/Systemic Dream, and it applies particularly to the Earth's evolution (which is presently out of balance) and Hir counterpart, the Venusian Scheme (which has been in balance for many æons).

Venus is the *alter-ego* of the Earth, and has manifested the exact opposite conditions to those to be found on and immediately around the Earth. The focus on Earth is predominantly human in nature; the focus on Venus is predominantly Devic. Most Venusians have already liberated themselves from lower plane experience and incarnation. Venus could be inferred to be the Soul of the Earth, and it is on Venus that you will eventually discover the complementary portion of your evolutionary puzzle.

3 — THE EARTH DREAM

From within the core of the Systemic Dream emerged the Earth Dream — not something that was separate from everything else, but something which was designed to assist the unfoldment of the whole Solar System.

It was perceived from the start that the Earth, as a Planetary Spirit, would have to deal with many difficult aspects of this unfoldment, and that much of this difficulty would arise from the nature of duality — now let us say something about this.

In order to manifest itself, Life must create a Duality — which simply put could be said to be represented by male and female energies; this is the only way that an element of contrast can be achieved, thereby acting as a mirror for any creative efforts — unfortunately this also heralds the potential for what you might think of as *good* and *bad,* or the positive and negative use of energy, and this in a conscious or an unconscious way. As we have often said Life is not so much a function of *good* and *bad* but one of BALANCE; it is balance which is essential if the whole is to work as it should.

Therefore every planet needs to express that balance, within itself and with respect to what surrounds it. Insofar as any one planet is not in balance then it affects the rest of the Solar System, and from one point of view the whole of that System is then imbalanced — even if most of the planets are essentially in balance.

Because the contrast on Earth is quite acute the Earth has almost always been out of balance with the rest in some manner or other. There was a time when the Earth was reasonably balanced within its own sphere, but it was not evolving as fast as was the rest of the System — particularly planets like Venus and Jupiter. As it was lagging behind — not because it was at fault in so doing, but only because this was a condition which was developing into relative stagnation certain entities within the Solar System got together to discuss the issue and decide what should be done in order to bring the Earth into alignment with the rest of the System; this discussion had little to do with the pros and the cons of this situation; it had more to do with the dynamics of it. Eventually it was decided that the sister evolution on Venus would be allowed to somewhat interfere with the Earth's evolution so as to boost its evolutionary unfoldment. This took place, and what eventuated was that distinctions arose from out of the morass of uncertainty which the Earth's humanity had experienced thus far. This also brought about — eventually — great shifts in consciousness, and it became apparent that those who were becoming selfishly oriented were going to cause problems, particularly later in time, whereas those who felt in tune with the Spirit were trying to elevate their consciousness towards an all-encompassing state which might liberate them from the hard density which was then forming itself, or becoming *crystallised* (ie the physical plane was not as dense then as it is now).

In effect those who were trying to liberate themselves were refusing the opportunity to deal with the matter-state properly, and in balance with shifting conditions, whereas those who were becoming selfish in their orientation were becoming increasingly determined to rule over that matter-state. This polarity division only created a new kind of double imbalance, and we have seen this continue to this day. Traditionally this has been highlighted or spoken of as the *War between Light and Darkness,* yet it is more a question of imbalance than it is one of war; the Forces of Light and the Forces of Darkness in essence are One Force; yet the emphasis in polarity terms is archetypally opposite — the one seeks liberation still, and the other is seeking dominion over the dense states.

So your Earth Dream has been polluted by this schism, and for that matter it will continue to be polluted for as long as people think in terms of such opposites; until a resolution occurs and a new balance ensues there will always be that imbalance, there will always be *wars*.

Balance does not mean that both sets of views should be embraced at the same time; more that a new point of view needs to be evolved — one which takes into account that a balance is possible, and that out of that balance comes a new perceptual vision of what Life *is*. Once that much is sorted out then it is possible, or it will be possible, for the Earth to resume its Dream as it was originally designed to unfold.

Nevertheless the duress which has been experienced as a result of the imbalance will not go to waste; many millions of beings have incarnated here and learnt from this situation — learnt much which has been of great usefulness to them. Perhaps above all else it has really exemplified that balance is indeed really absolutely necessary, and that whenever something goes out of balance — in the ways that we have spoken of — that problems come into existence which need not have done so. These problems can be resolved, and indeed even at this time a great many people on your planet are working out these differences and are attempting to erase the imbalances which exist. This may seem like an enormous task strewn with unsurmountable difficulties, and yet it can be done — the main thing which needs to change is *consciousness;* the consciousness of the so-called average person in the street in particular; the secret of success lies almost entirely in this area, because those who become Initiates go on in time to other work, but it is the general humanity of the planet which effectively dictates the course of human affairs, regardless of which influences are at work on esoteric levels. Until this *general humanity* shifts in its point of perception, and tries to achieve a new balance within itself — and this world-wide — then there will still be wars of opinion, and sometimes military conflicts.

You should not have any illusions about the coming Age of Aquarius — there will still be *wars* and there will still be disputes — they may turn out to be different in character to those which hold sway now, at the present time, and yet they will be conditioned by much the same imbalance — therefore do not think of the Aquarian Age as an idyllic future-to-be. It will have its share of difficulties, and whereas certain troubles will be resolved over the years ahead, others will come into focus and will need to be resolved also.

One could say that the Dream of this planet is to achieve ULTIMATE BALANCE — indeed, having learnt from everything it has experienced over the thousands of years since it entered its phase of dualism it will be in an excellent position to do so; it has suffered more than most worlds in this respect, and it will therefore also gain more than most from setting the course of its destiny right.

Little is gained without effort; on this world you must always take into account that you *are* going to have to make an effort in order to achieve anything worthwhile — this may seem unfair, and it may seem even strange that any humanity of any kind should have to put up with conditions which are so adverse and so difficult to deal with — yet on the other hand you must also take into account that it is *you* — as humans — which create the conditions which you experience. These conditions have not been imposed upon you, even if way back in time the Venusians did come to Earth and did alter the flow or unfoldment of things — simply because the situation on Earth had been stagnating for such a long time that it was affecting the whole System in a way which could no longer be tolerated; ie the whole System was at risk because of this.

If humanity had responded in a balanced sort of manner to those forces which sought to alter the level of unfoldment here on Earth then you would never have experienced all the chequered history which has categorised the Earth as *the planet of sorrows*. There is no way of going back on all that now, therefore your main task is to move ahead and resolve your planetary differences without finding any more excuses not to do so.

This much applies everywhere on your planet. The exact conditions may vary somewhat from place to place, and yet the conflicts are much the same everywhere. Whether it be a conflict of ideology — for instance between capitalism and communism — or a conflict of basic character, or a conflict of apparent needs, all these things can be resolved, and indeed the Earth will not be able to Dream rightly for as long as these conflicts exist — regardless of what has generated these conflicts in the first instance.

The people of the Earth need to join together to face these matters; no one nation can impose its solution, as it perceives it, to the exclusion of what other nations may think or feel. Your United Nations may well be able to air certain views, yet for as long as there are divisions of opinion and interest there will be *wars* of all sorts — military ones, and ideological ones. We could say that you need to evolve a world government, neverthe-less these *wars* would not cease just because a world govern-ment might come into existence — it is not as simple as that. One should never forget that a government is a body of people which, ideally, actuates the needs of the people which it represents. It is a fact that few governments throughout your world ever really represent their people — they tend to represent their own self-interest instead. Therefore things need to change at this level, where each government actually represents the voice and needs of its people, and attempts to resolve differences of position or opinion between these people and the people of other nations. Then, and then only, can a real sense of peace emerge from out of the confusion of the past.

The Earth is indeed a small planet. In some ways there are far too many people presently incarnated on its surface, and there are many more who wish to incarnate — and there is simply no room for them at this time. There is a great need for balance, and this is exemplified by a need to settle old karmic conditions — which is also why there are so many people presently incarnate. It is a crisis period, and we will only see the sort of changes we are talking about if enough people make the effort to redress the wrongs which they have committed in other times.

This does not affect Initiates so much, since they are in a position to find their liberation from the dense states; it does affect them insofar as they find themselves surrounded by the same conflicts as everyone else, regardless of their particular state of evolutionary unfoldment. However, the Initiates of the Earth (or call them whatever you will) can be instrumental in affecting change, and indeed they should bear in mind that if they do not prompt themselves to help alter the conditions on Earth then they are denying themselves the insights which they need in order to progress beyond the periphery of the human state. One should not forget too that an Initiate is an individual who has progressively learnt from the planetary conditions which s/he has experienced over a period of many lifetimes, and that s/he is as responsible as is anyone else for the difficulties which exist; s/he has a duty of a kind to make sure that s/he eventually leaves the planet in a better condition than existed when s/he first entered it.

No one individual can set hirself up as a Christ or as a Messiah, and then sort it all out. This idea that the Christ is a being who comes into lower expression and goes about absolving other people of their responsibilities is also absurd; it is a scapegoat for those who do not wish to be responsible on behalf of themselves and on behalf of the planet. The Christ does not come to save, but to show the way towards balance — then it is up to those who listen to walk that way. We say this because there are many people who consider themselves Christians (a misnomer if ever there was one) who in fact refuse to see the way out of imbalance, and in fact contribute to it daily — even if that is not their perception of reality. The Christ is a Being (and a Cosmic Principle, it should be noted) whose impact is to sever the chains which keep people prisoner of their own illusions. The Christ is not a *somebody* who happens to manifest hirself every few thousand years in order to talk to people in parables — if the Initiate called by you Jesus did that on behalf of the Christ that is all well and good, yet one should never confuse the Christ with any given human individual — channels for the Christ emerge from time to time, and do whatever they can to help point out the way, yet most people refuse to *see* that way, and then go about calling themselves *Christians* (or whatever), which the great bulk of them are not — insofar as they do not exemplify or even mildly reflect the true nature of the Christ Essence.

If anyone thinks that Christ wanted churches and cathedrals and dogmatic *teachings,* s-he most certainly did not. S-he was only interested in showing the way towards a *world which could be* if those who were listening — through channels, or within their hearts — were prepared to assist it to come into being. The Spiritual Powers can only prepare the way; they cannot enforce a new kind of world on those who do not wish to make whatever efforts are necessary to precipitate it into reality.

There are those who will say that *God* is a Being who can do anything, who can impose anything, and who has every right to do so. But this is to deny that the inherent core of every human being is *of God* (or more appropriately of God-dess); that every human being must be a part of the act which might change things for the better.

Every religion has its perceptions of what God/Goddess (and less frequently, God-dess) really is, and abides by these percep-tions, usually erroneously. Pagans, for instance, speak of a Goddess and a God — this reflects the nature of Cosmic Duality; yet only in the Unison of Goddess and God can Truth be known. For as long as there is division that Truth cannot be apprehended, not fully. Nevertheless, having said that, the female polarity has its reality, and the male polarity has its own reality also. Put the two together and you get something far more dynamic and in keeping with Cosmic Truth — ie the Androgynous Essence of Life.

We have also said that if things do not change within the immediate future, and for the better, then we will have to force the issue; this is true, and we would. Yet what we would in effect be doing would be to increase the pressure — the energy-pressure — slowly, yet surely, so as to force you to act. That, if you can perceive it, is quite different to acting on your behalf, or saving you from anything, or imposing our will upon you. We have got a right to increase the pressure which bears upon you if you, as humans, create conditions of pressure (through ill-action) on the rest of the Solar System. We need change from you, because you are creating ill-effects within the whole Solar

System, and while we can appreciate that there many people today incarnate on your planet who are trying to make sure that things do change we will still have to force the issue if more of you do not respond in an appropriate sort of way — towards achieving balance, peace, and a dynamic sense of responsibility within and towards the rest of the Solar System.

You cannot say that we are not communicating with you — we are doing so here, and we are doing so through many hundreds of channels at this time, even thousands from one point of view. It is not a matter of which religion is right, or which government is best, or even which kind of path is chosen; it is a matter of finding ways of changing your situation so that all can feel free to explore their potential for harmony, for peace, and for well-being — in other words changing your sense of consciousness so that in effect you can be active participants within the Cosmic Reality, instead of *victims* of your own ignorance or your lack of will to be free.

Freedom is not a matter of being totally self-enclosed within your individual dreams; it is a part and parcel of opening yourselves up to ever higher levels of insight, so that you can then *see* for yourselves which paths towards that Reality are the most promising and the most effective.

There is no one path which is best, however; there are many paths, and all of these can take into account that there is such a thing as the Systemic Being, and that this Being in turn is only a part of an even Higher Being. Therefore we would never say, "Be this", or "Be that" — because what we are saying is that there are many roads to the same Centre; and each road has, or can have, its own beauty, its own relevance, and its own particular method of achieving or sponsoring the kind of freedom we would wish you to have — a freedom to contribute intelligently and intuitively, even willfully, to the affairs of the whole Solar System.

We could be accused of repeating ourselves endlessly, and yet we need to say these things over and over so that you may feel that you are indeed dealing with beings who are already on that path of freedom, and who want to help you to achieve a similar stage of evolutionary unfoldment. We are not elitist in our view, and we are only trying to make sure that you feel empowered to action — in such a way that you can effectively join us and begin to make those decisions which will make the Solar System a beautiful place to be, to visit, and to learn from; at present it is still marred by the one big problem which it harbours within its *body,* and that unfortunately is the Earth, and more specifically the people of the Earth.

In a future to come these things will be resolved, and yet for now we are concerned with the present situation and not so much with what will be. We can see ahead of you, and we know that eventually you will do those things which need doing, although it is not quite so easy to say with absolute certitude exactly *when* you will manifest the sort of changes that need addressing, that need to occur. We can see the cycles which govern the lives of planets, and yet we cannot be sure that anything will be thoroughly achieved by any given time — we can only try and make sure that they occur within a cyclic period which will be of use to the System as a whole.

Humanity will not find its freedom — as a humanity — overnight. We do know of some of your prophecies which indicate that almost unbelievable things will occur within a very short period, and yet these are only partial prophecies, and because they are incomplete they are not necessarily to be thought of as a total reflection of what will be. There is a battle going on in the ethers between those forces which are resisting change and those which want to make those changes come about, and the side of change is winning gradually, yet it has by no means won. It is a battle of minds, and to the extent that you — as individuals and as groups — begin to endorse the path towards change, then the battle will tilt towards change; yet, conversely, if too many of you either resist change or else cannot be motivated to change, or else fall prone to apathy and indifference, then the forces which are trying to negate the possibility of change will manage to hang on to a situation where there will be no clear outcome; a stalemate will ensue, where the forces against change will be pushed back for awhile, but will be able to come back into prominence later, instead of a situation where they will be driven out of this evolutionary cycle altogether, and thereby no longer affect the System as they have done — for so long.

The choice is yours; you are — each one of you individually — either for change or against it, and each one of you represents the power and the will to make it occur or else to hinder it; the battle we have spoken of is one which is happening within you. Whatever is happening without is only a reflection of what is happening within.

If you are to manifest a new sort of world based on principles of heart, of love, of consciousness — as distinct from lack of conscious focus — then the battle must be fought and won within yourselves; and then you will find it much easier to *dream* the world anew, and change it into a world where there is joy and challenge combined.

We will not speak of paradise, or of hell; these things are entirely relative to one's conscious state of being and attention. Lack of conscious focus tends to be hell-like, and a good conscious focus tends to feel good — in which case the world may well seem to glow with light in one's eyes. For this reason it is possible for two people to be side by side, one experiencing *hell* and another *heaven* — and yet it is the same world that they are dealing with; their feelings and perceptions are coloured nevertheless by what is happening within them. The world-to-be can be whatever you are prepared to make it, yet you should not fail to notice that, as a process, it is both beautiful and difficult to deal with, and that if you are prepared to change yourselves from within then it will reflect whatever it is that you are manifesting inside the sphere of your conscious thoughts.

The Earth Dream is your *dream;* the Planetary Being is a part of you, and you a part of Hir.

4 — *THE NATURE OF DREAMING*

We would like to impart something of how we *dream* ourselves — we *anticipate;* this is the best word that we can use. We visualise things, and we anticipate what could be if such and such was done.

Therefore in essence *dreaming* is very simple; what is not quite so simple for you to appreciate is that *dreaming* requires a constant application of one's intent — for without intent the *dream* has no energy to subsist on, to motivate it.

Intent in turn is derived from need — if one can perceive one's own needs, or the needs of the System one is dealing with, then one can formulate one's intent; the more precise one's perceptions are, the more precise one's intent will become.

This brings us back to consciousness — the higher one's state of consciousness is, the higher one's perceptions of things will be. Your task above all else is to enhance your consciousness, to perceive your real needs — and those of the Earth and Solar System — to develop your intent accordingly, and then to visualise or anticipate what needs doing; then finally to apply yourselves to the task of externalising or precipitating the nature of your *dream*.

Saying more than this is not absolutely necessary — this, if you like, is the *formula of dreaming*.

By degree you can discover what the Intent of the Earth is, then what the Intent of the Solar System is — then all you need to do is to *align* yourselves with these Intents (they are both similar and different, according to the point of view one cares to take at any one time — essentially the Earth's Intent, as we have already pointed out, is a subset of the Systemic Intent).

All this is best done in meditation, yet it can also evolve out of one's sense of direct application — meditation in this sense can be both receptive and active in its nature.

If you can visualise the sort of world conditions that you might want, or need, then you can precipitate them — the content of your *dream* is up to you, yet obviously the more you join together and agree with regard to what you want to bring about, the greater are your chances of success.

Simple, simple, simple — there is nothing more to *dreaming* than this; all the rest is detail, and not principle.

But you need power — the energy which will help you to manifest your *dream;* and this power can only be found within yourselves — you can borrow power in various ways for various periods of time, but the real power which you need to be able to access at will is there, within yourselves, waiting to be used.

It is the Power of Life itself, and it is what keeps you alive and conscious.

Its most potent expression is the Kundalini Force; towards this end your *dream* needs to become a *Kundalini Dream,* focused by perfect Will and perfect Love; and your minds must be clear and under your complete conscious control — always, moment by moment, and without fail.

Kundalini is not an easy Power to deal with, yet with more experience you will be able to use it in a viable manner — subject to the wisdom you will gain from your experience.

This is what *dreaming* is all about.

5 — THE EVOLUTIONARY RELEVANCE OF DREAMING

If there had not been a Cosmic Dream to begin with there would have been no Cosmos — that's also quite simple to understand, even if the measure of this Cosmic Dream surpasses anything which you can presently imagine. The Beings who were involved in the initial phases of that Cosmic Dream were powerful beyond anything that you can even begin to realise; they were the embodiment of *Power-through-Dreaming*.

They issued from a Source-of-Life on the Highest of the Cosmic Planes; in this respect they were essentially One Single Being. Yet, as supreme Archetypal Powers, they had to realise their differentiations; then unite their energy-forces as Cosmic Archetypes. This is a part of the Higher Devic Lore.

They even *dreamed* their own Power (at the Cosmic Astral level); they had to in order to manifest Themselves to Themselves, *separately* and unitively all at once. Then they joined up in Consciousness, and *dreamt* Life into being.

"In the Beginning there was One God-dess, who had to become several to Be."

This is an old aphorism which was given to students on another planet in another time so that they would be able to meditate on this and understand — now we present this same aphorism to you, for the same purpose. It is yours to mull over — there are Mysteries within Mysteries here!

The evolutionary relevance of *dreaming* is so profound that it takes an unusually elevated state of consciousness to perceive it for what it really is. Never, ever, confuse *dreaming* with mere astral cogitation.

The Cosmic Astral Plane is immensely beautiful and powerful — the Astral Plane can only reflect something of its Nature relatively dimly.

Stage by stage you will learn to *dream* on different levels — forget the Astral Plane — concentrate all your attention on the five Higher Planes within the Cosmic Etheric-Physical Plane: the Higher Mental, the Harmonic/Buddhic, Atmic, Monadic and Systemic Planes. From the highest of these Planes you will gain some small measure of insight into the Cosmic Astral Plane; you have much to learn and experience first, however. Full Adepthood does not occur by chance or very quickly — it takes time to *find* Itself.

"When the Singular Point is reached there is crisis; and crisis reveals only a sense of urgent need for a greater balance than has ever been known or required at any time before then. Strive to be at peace within yourselves — then you will *See*, then you will *Know*. The Path towards full Realisation comes in little steps, followed by greater steps, followed by steps which can no longer be measured by the common mind. That is all we can say."

"The Path towards the Centre of Being is a Path which you already know, for it is the Path down which you came at the beginning of Time."

"Everything is equidistant from the Central Core of your Inner Being — there is no distance, except the illusion of Space created by the Cosmic Dreamer."

"Make haste — there is no time left. You ran out of time and space before you even began! Make ado as you will and can — the Universe has already dissolved; only a shadow remains, a fading shadow..."

The last quoted comment is an allusion to the fact that the Universe was born, lived, and died in the same moment — only the appearance of manifested life exists; it is the *Momentless Moment* extended into Time-Duration, in other words slowed down so that it is perceived as Time, Space, Energy and Matter — the components of existence. You have time and no-time to express and fulfil your intent. Illusion and Reality are the two sides of a single Whole.

6 — CHANGING THINGS THROUGH DREAMS

Whether one calls it *dreaming,* visualisation or meditation, or whatever, the *act of dreaming* has a specific effect on various grades of ethers, and it is a way of ensuring that results ensue.

Your *dreaming* to date, if we take into account your humanity as whole, has been rather more reactionary to unconscious than it has been a conscious process the result has been if not disastrous at least somewhat erratic to say the least. Your *dreaming* over the millenia has lacked coherency, and has been subject to unconscious to semi-conscious changes without much by way of foreplanning or deliberate intent.

If we look at your civilisation as it stands it is full of different *bits of dreams* — many of which are in some measure of conflict with each other. If we were going to use your own psychological terminology we would have to say that it is the product of a schizoid, even schizophrenic expression. It lacks overall symmetry and does not partake of a common intent.

You can only change this by deciding what it is that you have in common that you wish to manifest on the lower Planes of the System. Where should you start? This can be answered thus: start with the highest possible denominator and then work your way downwards (and not the other way around).

Let us assume, as we would want to draw you into affinity with Systemic needs, that the highest possible denominator you can start with is the Spiritual Oneness of All Life (SOAL, we shall call it for short). This should be reflected in your society — not necessarily as a conventional-type religion, but as an insight into Spirit. If you affirm your dependence upon and solidarity with Spirit then this would become the prime focus of all your other affairs and activities — it would become the driving force behind any changes which you might wish to contemplate.

To be at-One with the Spirit implies a conscious state of Realisation, whereby you would be acknowledging your Essential Source of Livingness; you are (a part of) the Spirit; you are the Spirit expressing Itself in density — use that insight, and you will find that everything else will begin to fall into place quite nicely, if over a period of time.

If your civilisation was based on Spirit rather than on arbitrary material comfort, for instance, then you would be able to draw on the Spiritual Energies which make up manifestation at various levels, and these would do much of the work of changing things for you — all you would then have to do is direct these Spiritual Energies in the way that you want them to become fully manifest on the lower levels, including the dense physical plane.

The actual shapes or forms of the changes can be as diverse as there are minds to implement them — the external forms can be many, allowing for the full expression of creativity. The forms are not the most essential part of manifest expression, yet they can hold symmetries of shape and quality which do express something of the Essence of Spirit.

If you apply this to everything which you create — cities, towns, dwelling places, road networks, etc. — then the *organism* which your society would manifest would have an intended *imbedded* Spiritual Energy, one which would sustain you and inspire you. Thus forms do have their importance, insofar as they reflect Spirit. You could make those changes in a relatively short period of time, providing you found the will to implement them — consciously, with awareness and insight.

There are many different approaches to manifesting a dream; some are simpler, or else easier to understand than others. Let us make a list of some of the possibilities:

The fully structured approach: starting with the highest denominator we then go to the next highest denominator (one step *lower*), implement it, and move on to next highest denominator again, and implement that. In schematic form this could be represented by an inverse-tree, starting with the roots (Source-Spirit), followed by the trunk (Prime Denominator in expression), followed by primary branches (Secondary Denominators in expression, as related to Prime Denominator), followed by various grades of sub-branches, branchlets, etc. (Tertiary Denominators in expression, as related to Prime Denominator via Secondary Denominators). Power then flows from the highest through to the lowest; and it is One. Yet the Essence of Power itself is always beyond the structure that it works through; it must remain in a *High Place* so that it can *measure out* its infinite potency within Manifestation (otherwise it would destroy Manifestation instantly).

The unstructured approach: more intuitive in character, where expression acknowledges the Spirit, but where there is no specific structure to one's expression. This is the laissez-faire approach, the *Way of the Heart*. All the dreams and sub-dreams have one thing in common — the Spirit; in every other respect they move, act, and overlap in a relatively haphazard manner, yet achieve a type of intuitively-based balance with Love as a key-denominator. Each dream recognises and acknowledges any

214

other dream(s) as a part of the Spirit's expression, therefore has no conflict with it (them); there is mutual tolerance with regard to the forms of the dreams.

The semi-structured, semi-unstructured approach: a mixture of the two above, where the structure as described before exists, but where the dreams differ from the strict form in their implementation. This is often the easiest formula, because there is an inherent balance between structure and non-structure, which in turn allows for full flexibility without minimising the inherent strength of the overall expression. This is a formula which we favour ourselves as Devas, and permits us to depart from strict formulation processes so as to explore random processes and learn from them creatively.

These three approaches correspond to 1st, 2nd and 3rd Ray approaches.

We will mention four or five further approaches, which reflect the nature of the 4th, 5th, 6th, 7th and 8th Rays respectively, and finally conclude with a definition of a 9th approach, heralding something of the nature of the 9th Ray in the process:

The artform approach: expression through comparative levels of beauty-in-form. The definition of this approach, mathematically, is subjective in its potency. One starts with the highest expression of beauty, and then works downwards towards the nth expression of beauty-in-form. To understand this requires intuition and artistic flair, and though subjective is not as arbitrary as it might otherwise seem. What is the highest beauty-in-form? Definition: it is the closest form can get to Spiritual Essence, ie non-form. Brood on this, and this should become intuitively clear to you.

The scientific approach: expression through mathematical formulae. Definition: the highest mathematical formula is something in the order of $m = m^*0$, where m is the implied matrix of manifestation, and 0 (zero) represents the destructurisation of all forms (not the destruction, please note; there is a difference). Subsequent branch expression would read something like

$m = m^*1$, $m = m^*2$, $m = m^*3$, etc., reaching into complexities ad infinitum, including complex formulae as equations. The mathematical laws governing numbers and algorithms, etc, would govern creative expression.

The ideation approach: expression through successive stages of idea-emission. The highest stage would correspond the highest possible expression of a Universal Idea, followed by various stages of sub-universal ideas — ie progressively less likely to be a direct equivalence of the initial Universal Idea or Universal State, yet linked to it by direct implication; and this regardless of how removed a sub-idea may be from its Primal Source of Ideation.

The magickal approach: expression through rhythmical magickal application. The highest magickal stance is to be at-One with Source in consciousness; from this derives the various possible magickal formulae — as used by Devas of various grades, for instance. This approach is synthetic in its expression, and application is derived from a direct as well as an intuitive sense of expression-through-synthesis and cooperation.

One should not forget that the 4th, 5th, 6th and 7th Rays are all subsets of the 3rd Ray of Creative Mind-in-Expression (as Manifestation), which is itself an inversion of the 1st Ray; whereas the 2nd Ray is the "Divine Seer-ess who beholds the expression and effect of the 1st and 3rd Ray activities and *glues* them together so that war cannot be."

The eighth approach: expression through mutually forward and reversed interpenetrating flows of energy, best expressed symbolically by the figure of 8 on its side (a symbol used for infinity).

The ninth approach: expression through constant application of the Rod of Initiation. This is not an approach which has been in any way possible up until now, for you in particular as the human half life-stream. This approach is emerging into focus for you at this time, and more than that we will not say.

Rationalising, we will say this: there are Three Primary Rays, thus Three Primary Approaches (as defined above). There are between four and six Secondary Approaches, as identified by the 4th to 7th and 4th to 9th Rays.

Approach 1 is absolute, and difficult to express in a fully coherent way; this will be the objective of the next Solar Incarnation.

Approach 2 is conditional — i.e., it appertains to the level of Love and Intuition which can be brought into play, and in essence it conditions the present Solar Incarnation.

Approach 3 is *acquired* — this was the path taken by the 1st Solar Incarnation. It can be used with greater ease, from one point of view at least, since when using it one is reflecting a past state of expression.

One should note here that the 1st Ray epitomises Power-over-Form, whereas the 2nd Ray epitomises quality-through-flexible-response, and the 3rd Ray structural-identity-through-objective-precipitation, or Form-over-Power.

There are many, relatively simple, yet also complex Mysteries imbedded in the information given here, and you will have to use the full power of your intuition to access the true significance of these definitions. Each one of you uses these different Rays in various combinations of ascendant power, and each one of you may feel drawn to using one particular approach or another in your *dreaming;* seen overall, you as a humanity, are likely to reflect *shades in between,* with a predominant impulse to fulfil the second approach more specifically, since it is the one which rules over the current state of expression of this Solar System; as a secondary approach you are most likely to favour the 8th and 9th approaches combined eventually, since these concern the Earth in an important fashion.

7 — THE MYSTERY OF DREAMS

We have said much, and very little — you must understand that this form of communication, while it aims at elucidating abstruse subjects, is by no means as flexible as we might wish. We think, however, that you may by now be able to understand something of what we are *getting at*.

There are mysteries anent *dreaming* which we have not mentioned thus far — those concerning the multi-levelled evolutions which form part of the *Tree of Power and Love combined, and manifested through Mind;* there is also a view which holds that there are only TWO RAYS — that of Power, and that of Love-Mind. That the 3rd Ray is in fact an inversion of the 1st, and yet that the 2nd forms something of an esoteric counterpart to the 1st.

"Power beheld Love, and Love, not *knowing* Itself yet, created Mind so as to objectify Its very own Reality."

If you reflect on this sentence intuitively you may just grasp something of its true significance. In other words, the 1st Ray stands alone; the 2nd and 3rd are something of a single unit when seen from a particular angle, which may explain why:

The 1st Ray is structured in its approach (it must be); whereas the 3rd, which if it is an inversion of the 1st one would assume that it was unstructured, but it is in fact semi-structured, semi-unstructured. The 2nd Ray (unstructured) forms a bridge between the 1st and the 3rd, because Love Unites; and yet the 1st has also a direct affinity with the 3rd; and the 2nd has a mysterious affinity with the 3rd. Note the use of the words *direct* and *mysterious*, for they are intentional here.

There are other ways of looking at these things. Intuition and direct inner insight are the only things which can throw true light on all this — as words can only veil the real nature of these matters.

One last point, just to highlight this little, and yet Great Mystery: the *Key* is in the symbol for Infinity (one Point, two Loops; the figure of '8' on its side).

We, as Devas (of various degree and persuasion), are united in our efforts to bring you these words. Together we are U-MA; Mother Energy (and only Matter by way of by-product). We are

218

the Cosmic Mother; you, as human beings, are the Children of Power and U-MA (the Power cannot be given a Name). This Three-Part association of livingness is best represented by a diamond figure (upright) — two triangles base to base; we are the base (ie in the Middle). The Power is at the highest apex; you are at the lowest. Our resolution is in the Point in between.

Thus our message ends — for now.

U-MA in Light, Love, Laughter and Liberation!

Pleiades, Andromeda, K-El-La.

FOREWORD

The subject of psychic self-defense is perhaps one of today's most important issues or topics which we need to address and then to come to terms with. In orthodox terms it is often overlooked, however, or even dismissed altogether — yet in a complex world, which is very much under strain in many ways, some of which are obvious, and some not so obvious, it is easy to allow one's own natural defenses to become overwhelmed, either directly or else in a subtle manner — which is something which can or does happen to us all, either a part of the time, if not every day of our lives, and regardless of whether we acknowledge this or not.

The purpose of this booklet is simply to set out some guiding principles with regard to matters of psychic self-defense. It is particularly aimed at those who feel they need this type of information, perhaps because they have had one or several difficult psychic (or psychological) experiences where they found themselves unable to contain and/or annul the pressures which were brought to bear upon them, and this in some fashion or other.

If this includes yourself, then you should find this booklet very worthwhile. In fact it is highly likely to include yourself since it is equally improbable that you can genuinely count yourself as somebody who is entirely impervious to, or else free from what might be called psychic interference.

That interference exists all around us — consider these *mundane* examples alone: on Earth, at any one time, there are dozens of wars taking place, and therefore considerable blood-letting and misery; in some areas there is much famine and strife; the world over there are people dying, suffering, in pain, diseased, and physiologically, emotionally and mentally afflicted, or else even crippled; psychologically many people are near enough in tatters: strained, some barely holding on to a small measure of sanity, while others have succumbed to a fate which orthodox psychiatry often aims to subdue rather than cure, alone properly understand. All this suffering hangs on the energy-ethers, desperately requiring address, and yet we often do our very best to ignore all this; nevertheless it does not go away just because it is ignored.

It is very difficult to excuse any of this. Also we all know that there are enough atom bombs to annihilate all life and everything throughout the planet — not merely us as human beings, but all the animals, the plants, the insects, the fish... everything that lives, that breathes, that moves. There are other types of weapons which are just as disturbing and potentially equally as devastating: chemical weapons, bacteriological weapons, microwave weapons, laser weapons, sonic weapons, and even, it has been suggested, psychotronic weapons — not to mention conventional weapons. Then add to this scenario such items as pollution and the degradation of Nature, commercial pressures and advertising, credit debts and political self-interest, religious dogma and misplaced scientific experiments, and so on, and it is a wonder that we still manage to survive.

Our world is not an especially happy place to live in, and this despite any efforts which are being made to change things for the better. Nevertheless what has been said so far only covers the more or less *visible* tip of the proverbial iceberg; there are other dangers which lurk around, which are much less *visible* (or less consciously acknowledged), and which, generally speaking, come under the category of the psychic domain.

To our credit we have survived all these pressures thus far, although undoubtedly not without incurring many wounds; yet we can do better than merely survive — we can learn to deal with all these pressures on our psychological make-up, and these attacks on our psychic integrity, and thereby become stronger and more able.

... And as a result promote a better world to live in, in due course...

1 ⟶ *PSYCHIC SELF-DEFENSE AGAINST WHAT?*

The world that we live in is not just a physical world — it has many layers; and in the same way as there are dangers within the physical world, there are also dangers on these other layers.

This is not to say that we should become overly engrossed in fears with regard to unknown dangers, whatever they might be — we do not scare ourselves to death with fright every time we cross a street, therefore and equally, there is no reason why we should become totally and helplessly paranoid whenever we cross over a given boundary, into the psychic domain, and then find that we have to deal with whatever it is that we may encounter there.

Let's get things into some kind of perspective: we live, simultaneously, in the physical world *and* in the psychic world, and for that matter also in the Spiritual world. We are aware of each of these worlds, or aspects of the single world, to the extent that we are able to perceive and experience it. Should it be the case that we are unable to *view* the psychic (and Spiritual) world, either because our inner senses are dormant, or else because they are not sufficiently open yet to that kind of sight or perception, then that world may seem unreal, if not non-existent to us; but this does not mean that it does not exist, and that it does not affect us.

An analogy: throughout the world there are, at any one time, thousands if not millions of activities which are going on of which we have no personal knowledge. Some of these activities affect us in some manner, directly or indirectly, and this quite regardless of whether we know anything about them or not.

Furthermore: each action invokes its reaction — when a drop of water falls into the ocean, the ocean doesn't need to be conscious in order to react; there is a splash. In the same way, something may affect us, and yet we need not be conscious of our own reaction to it — subconsciously, however, we register the fact that something has affected us. Accumulatively our subconscious reactions may lead us to do something that we would not otherwise have done.

Much *psychic interference* is of this order. Action causing reaction, which reaction may cause further reaction, and so on. These things may happen at a physical, emotional-astral, and/or mental level, and beyond that, even at a Spiritual level (if in a different manner).

We still have a very myopic view of the psychic and Spiritual world. Religious dogma may infer this or that, yet by and large that dogma is usually about as sound as a dead fish — it doesn't deal with reality, but with arbitrary projections, with fears, with ignorance, with bigotry, and the like. The fact is, the psychic and Spiritual world is vast; and its parameters, if such they can be called, are not so easily defined as some esoteric books would have us believe. It is all well and good differentiating the world into etheric-physical, astral, mental, harmonic-buddhic, power-atmic, monadic-oneness and systemic Planes, as many of the Spiral Publications, amongst others, would have it, but there is more to all this than that; much more.

In order to come to terms with genuine Reality we have to deal with the whole, rather than with the various parts. First of all we need to acknowledge our place within that whole; then, and only then, can we begin to understand the nature of what really does surround us, within and without.

Because everything we do, feel and think causes energy to move, thereby effectively or at least potentially affecting others, we cannot exist in a vacuum and hope that what we do, feel or think will not invoke a reaction; whether that reaction stems from within ourselves or from without, in the end, is of no great consequence — there will be a reaction, and it will affect us.

Because we are psychic (and Spiritual) beings, as well as physical beings (to the extent that we are incarnate in physical, biological bodies), whatever we do, feel or think has an effect on the psychic domain; and in consequence the psychic domain will react to our input; and vice-versa.

The form of that reaction may be singular or else diverse, immediate or delayed, progressive or spasmodic, soft or sharp; its means of communicating its reaction may come along in a variety of guises.

It is usually the case that most esotericists, when psychically *attacked,* think of this attack as a literal one as initiated by some external psychic source or entities. Seldom do they interpret it as something which may be emanating from within themselves.

Nevertheless the one does not necessary exclude the other: one can be afflicted by one's own psychological projections, while simultaneously being *attacked* by external entities, whatever they may be in actuality. It is very important to realise that most forms of psychic *attack* are almost entirely dependent on the fear of the recipient in order to make their mark and thus achieve a *hit,* as it were.

Fear produces the *substance* on which psychic *attacks* thrive; eliminate fear, and the *attack* ceases. We'll get back to this later.

The next point is this: we are surrounded by an immense universe in which all manner of living beings exist. Even on Earth alone there are many beings which exist, in psychic space, of which we know practically nothing, if anything at all — yet everything we do, feel or think affects these beings, directly or indirectly, and to a greater or lesser extent.

Many of these beings are not overly preoccupied with us as humans, and therefore in the main do not specifically go out of their way to antagonise us, regardless of what we do ourselves. Yet there are others who are anything from playful to outright adverse with regard to our own output; some play with our feelings, inducing inexplicable moods; others *put thoughts into our minds,* and these thoughts may be creative or else destructive in nature; others chip away at our defenses, and

224

actually aim to harm. These things being so does not mean, however, that these beings are deliberately *at war* with us; we affect them, and they react to what we do, and thus they *do* things to us in turn.

Our greatest *enemies* are not beings of which we have little or no knowledge, but other human beings — some incarnate, and others discarnate. It requires scant observational powers to realise that, as human beings, we express anything from dire negativity to deliberate positivity, and anything else in between — including mixtures of both negative and positive traits and energies.

Of course there are human beings (again incarnate or discarnate) who are predominantly negative in their bearing, just as there are at least a few human beings who countenance very little negativity within themselves.

Each one of us has to come to terms with these things individually as well as collectively. The trick, unlike the expressed (if often hypocritical and contradictory) projections of many religions, is not however to be purely positive at the expense of negativity, or vice-versa, but rather to find or to achieve balance within oneself. When one is in balance with the life which surround us (again within and without) then one is free from the push-and-pull, action-reaction game, which otherwise will inescapably prevail. Subsequently things may tug at that balance, causing us to reach for an even better balance, and so on until nothing can affect us in any way adversely.

Ultimate psychic self-defense, thus, can be said to be balance. Nevertheless in this booklet we will also explore other forms of psychic self-defense which may help us to achieve that balance.

It is important when reading this to also read between the lines and exercise one's intuition. It has been said, and this quite rightly, that genuine truth cannot be conveyed with words alone — it has to emerge from one's own personal experience; if it does not do so then one can never be a *knower*. One can be a believer, by all means, and beliefs can sometimes be useful (and sometimes not); however they are of no great value when faced with a situation which remains inexplicable within the terms of reference that one is used to, or exclusively prepared to deal with. There are always surprises to be had, and to contend with, particularly when dealing with the psychic domain; therefore do not allow the information in this small booklet to become more important than your own personal experience. To the extent that this booklet may assist you in determining how best to achieve a flexible, responsive and unassailable balance, so much the better; yet to achieve that balance requires much work on oneself — inherently, that balance is there within oneself to be found or to be created; and yet there are many levels of balance — one can achieve one type of balance, only to be *thrown* by some event over which, it would seem, one has no control whatsoever.

To go over a previous point with slightly more emphasis, there are different kinds of *psychic attack* — and therefore more than one type of *psychic self-defense*. By way of analogy, once more, one would not defend oneself from an avalanche in the same way as one would from a flea... although in both cases one needs to be quick to respond, perhaps! By the same token, the bite of a flea is a nuisance, but the impact of an avalanche is quite likely to be severely damaging, if not lethal.

In an equal vein, some forms of *attack* may be fast and furious, whereas others may be so innocuous in their unfoldment that one fails to recognise them for what they really are, and yet they may be equally as dangerous.

Each kind of *attack* requires an appropriate response — and while on occasions there may be several options to choose from, in a given circumstance there may well be just one single way of dealing with things; and sometimes there may be no obvious way to defend oneself at all, leaving oneself, the defendant, naked, exposed, and highly vulnerable.

Sometimes one has to *fight;* sometimes one has to *close down,* and sometimes *let go.* Sometimes one needs to be serious; and sometimes humour will turn out to be the very best friend one has got!

Therefore there is no hard and fast *one* way of defending oneself psychically — psychic self-defense requires judgement, but above all else requires intuition; and in many instances, will — the will to do whatever is necessary, in whatever manner is most appropriate, at that particular time.

Lastly, for now: not all *attacks* are what they seem to be. It is easy to come to the conclusion that when one is *got at* psychically that this means that something is trying to kill oneself off, or at least trying to impart an injury of some kind, or attempting to possess one's psyche. Yet the *attack* may only be a test, whose aim is to teach oneself how best to deal with a given type of assault, and how to quicken one's response level. Yet test or no test, it may be just as difficult to contend with as an outright attack. And outright attacks most certainly do happen.

2 — BASIC PSYCHIC SELF-DEFENSE

There are different approaches to basic psychic self-defense — here, mind you well, we are talking about approaches, rather than about specific types of self-defense. For the sake of clarity let us list some of these:

— Entrusting one's self-defense to a *Higher Power,* whatever/whoever that *Higher Power* may be, according to the belief system one subscribes to (to a Pagan it may be the Goddess; to a Christian it will Christ or God, although in Latin America the Virgin Mary may figure somewhat more prominently; to a Mohammedan then it will be Allah; in Pantheistic and polytheistic religions there is often more than one protective-type god or goddess, or force).

— Entrusting one's self-defense to one's own *Higher Self,* which is, perhaps, the emerging popular *New Age* approach.

— Entrusting one's self-defense to some magickal entity, as invoked from time to time as needs may require.

The above three (which by no means cover all the possibilities of this kind) depend to a greater or lesser extent on belief.

Few people (bar Life-Initiates) have ever *met* a *Higher Power* face to face, as it were, that is, as a matter of personal experience; therefore their belief that such a *Higher Power* does exist, and that s/he is benevolent or agreeable to the act of personal guardianship, is often their only true recourse with regard to self-protection.

Then there are other approaches:

— The use of power-mantras, yantras, etc — effective ways of either surrounding oneself with powerful protective energies, or invoking protective principles.

— The use of power-symbols, such as pentagrams, circle-crosses, circles, triangles, and so on.

— The use of colours, or Rays, such as white, blue, indigo, violet, or green, and for some things yellow and orange.

In these instances the person is not specifically relying on any outside source, or even inner source, for hir self-protection. S/he is activating (or trying to activate) principles which are protective in their own right.

Then there are *Ways:*

— Shamanism teaches one to protect oneself, using any number of different devices as may be necessary

— Various magickal systems put emphasis on acquiring psychic skills which permit one to deal with all manner of different psychic events and circumstances.

— Starcraft teaches one to contact, then merge and fuse one's consciousness with one's Solar Deva, who is, arguably, the best possible source of self-defense in any circumstance — what is more, one's Solar Deva is an all-in-one defender-teacher-tester-inspirer-activator-empowerer, and sometimes humourous or practical joker as well! It's a very *live* relationship.

— The above constitute some of the better known approaches.

3 — CIRCLES AND SPHERES

Any form of psychic self-defense is based on a circle or a sphere, and this in many different ways. A circle or sphere is a dynamic, and very stable form — for instance, the reason a soap bubble retains its coherency is founded on the fact that the pressure of the air within is balanced with the pressure of the air without; again we are talking about balance here, you will note. Much the same applies in a psychic sense: when the pressure of an *attack* from without becomes greater, so does the one or the group within a circle or sphere of protection need to increase its internal pressure, thus ensuring equilibrium.

A circle or sphere, in itself, conveys a symbol of protection, and this symbol in itself has power — psychic power. It is not a coincidence that planets and stars are spherical; nor is it a coincidence that they maintain a balance between centripetal force (inward-pulling) and centrifugal force (outward-pushing), thus retaining their coherency as planets and as stars. A sphere is the perfect, dynamic, protective shape — as a power-form; and a circle is a two-dimensional representation of a sphere. The tension zone which is formed on the periphery of the sphere or circle relies on the equidistant relationship between all the points on its surface and the centre of this sphere or circle; therefore the internal pressure is equally distributed on the inner surface of the sphere or circle.

Again it is no coincidence that most types of magickal processes are based on working within a circle, or a mind-projected sphere (including Starcraft and Witchcraft, and the Amerindian Medicine Wheel, for instance). Going back in time one can imagine that single individuals and groups, who were sufficiently perceptive at a psychic level, therefore clairvoyant, realised that they were surrounded by a natural field of energy which effectively protected them from external psychic interference — which energy-field is now called the aura; from there it probably took them very little imagination to conceive of a circle or a sphere as a protective membrane of energy which would, in effect, symbolise the periphery of their auric emanations.

This field is not unknown to Science — which, when Science is disposed to acknowledge its existence, calls it the bioplasmic or bioplasmatic field; this field appears to be electro-magnetic in nature. Esoterically this field is known to emanate from the chakric power-points, which coincide closely with the endocrine glands.

To the extent that we all have auras, then each one of us is afforded a measure of natural protection against psychic interference — nevertheless, if a person's overall field is weak (temporarily or chronically), or else if any given area of hir aura is weakened (by stress, ill-thoughts, anxiety, psychological/emotional disturbances, ill-health, energy-damage, etc), then this natural auric protection will be endangered proportionally. Therefore hir field will require reinforcing, even healing — in other words it needs to be repaired and effectively restored to its natural protective state. One can effect these repairs oneself, through meditation and creative visualisation, and by working on one's psychological patterns, however this requires perseverance and much self-application — at least in most instances this will be the case; it all depends on what is actually causing the weakness or the auric disturbance(s).

Outside help from a creditable healer and/or a counsellor, is often very useful; s/he will be able to steer the afflicted person in the right sort of manner with view to repairing hir own field, and this primarily by addressing the causes of the disturbance(s) and then by helping that person to sort them out, hopefully decisively; and where appropriate a capable healer will be able to carry out many, if not all of the actual repairs by using hir own energies, or else those which s/he is able to effectively channel.

Some of these matters concern karmic situations, i.e. they concern long-term energy imbalances as inherited from previous lives — where this is so, a successful *cure* will often take longer; until what is imbalanced becomes balanced, then the causes will remain, and the auric disturbances will continue, and this usually regardless of how much healing is attempted — nevertheless this is not a hopeless condition, but it may need a lot of self-work as well as external support before adequate results are achieved.

Most people also leak energy through their auras, and thus loose some or else a great deal of their psychic strength as a result; these leaks need to be patched. If they are not patched and properly healed, then the energy-losses will usually contribute to an overall condition of auric weakness which may lead to vulnerability from *psychic attacks*.

Also, one of the most sensitive, and therefore most vulnerable points within our auras is in the area which extends from the solar plexus (above the navel) — therefore it should come as no surprise if most actual *psychic attacks* often focus the better part their impact on that particular area. Some of the ways of protecting the solar plexus are: to imagine a horizontal band of (white, blue or golden) energy around the body in line with the solar plexus; tying a silk scarf around that same area; visualising a circular energy-shield in front of the solar plexus; or placing one's hands, palms inwards, on the solar plexus. (Similar methods can be used for other sensitive or vulnerable areas, such as the top of the head, for instance).

The above has been mentioned because there is little point in talking about using circles and spheres as protective devices if one's aura is not adequately able to provide the energy-basis for these. Nevertheless, and having said that, a circle as delineated by a piece of rope (which ideally should only be used for that purpose, thus strengthening the mental association between that rope and its ability to protect), or a circle or sphere around one's body as delineated by one's visualisation, will provide a measure of extra psychic protection — particularly during meditation and magickal work.

One can go further than this (it is not absolutely necessary to do so, but the principle is here expanded): one can visualise circle within circle, or sphere within sphere, thus providing several concentric layers of protective insulation; each circle or sphere can be visualised in a different colour — for instance: the innermost circle/sphere as blue; the second as white; and the third as gold; etc. In effect each coloured circle or sphere will act as a specific barrier with regard to screening out particular kinds of adverse psychic interference. But they will not inhibit the passage of genuine Spiritual energies.

Cones, which after all have a circular base, can also be used — with the point of the cone facing upwards; a cone imparts the ability to access Spiritual energies from higher, more refined, and also more powerful sources.

These power-shapes — circles, spheres and cones — can also be associated with specific sounds. Ideally each sound should be in resonance with that of a given chakra, particularly the head, throat and heart chakras (on a more elaborate basis, then with the crown, ajna, alta major/throat, heart, solar plexus, spleen, sacral and base chakras — however it is usually only Life-Initiates who are able to *hear* the sounds of their different chakras, including that of their first para-chakra, which is above the head within the etheric envelope; getting it wrong can be more of a hindrance than a gain, therefore this should be practised with some caution).

Already we have here the essential basis for psychic self-defense as a whole. The remainder of this booklet will concentrate on various points which will enhance the ability of the person using these *devices* to either strengthen hir field, or else become as flexible as possible, and this with different circumstances in mind.

Obviously there will be instances when being too elaborate with regard to one's attempts at psychic self-defense will be impractical — for example, if one is walking about in Nature and something adverse should happen then one doesn't want to become too overly involved in visualising a mega-system of concentric spheres around oneself, all equally well balanced and poised for the worst. There are options to be chosen from, such as *feeling* and visualising a single sphere (say of blue light) around oneself, then walking on and away from that scene; or else finding a protective site, where harmonious energies prevail

— these can be found scattered around the countryside, however one needs to be able to *see*, or at least *feel* where they are located — and then sitting there for awhile; then one can elaborate on one's defenses if necessary.

Likewise if one is driving a car on a busy motorway one doesn't want to spend too much of one's precious attention setting up vast psychic defense systems! Once again it is all a matter of judgement, sensitivity, intuition and understanding, and need. In different situations one must do different things, as appropriate.

There are situations, also, where one cannot hope to fully contain powerful psychic *attacks* — in fact it is often the case that if one invests too much of one's consciousness in acknowl-edging the *attack* it will often become stronger (simple cause and effect; one ends up invoking it). Therefore it is sometimes better to ignore it altogether, and to be as *mundane* as poss-ible; and to preoccupy oneself with practical things instead. However, on occasions, and in turn, this may not work very well; and then one has to decide whether one is going to invest all one's energies in self-defense, or even whether one is going to counter-attack.

The problem with counter-attacking is that unless one knows, or *feels,* what one is truly dealing with one can make the mistake of harming or irritating an entity which is not really *attacking* at all — it may be curious about one's doings; it may be a nature spirit whose work one has disturbed. In the case of certain Devas its presence may be very powerful, and the proximity of its power may be disturbing; it may also be energising one's own energy-field to the point where this becomes most uncomfortable, and perhaps even alarming (this may be registered as heat, as magnetic forces, as electrical forces, or else a combination of any two of these, or even all three of them at once; or as tension within one's aura, or even within one's physical body; or as fluxes of energy in different parts of one's body; or as knots of energy — which usually indicate resistance on one's parts to the throughput of power).

233

Inwardly one can ask it to move away from oneself; and if it does not do so then one can erect defenses as one may feel the need. Yet it is usually best to be calm, to flow with the event as best one can, and not to turn defense into attack.

Then against that, in the case of dealing with truly negative influences, and given the power to do so, one may feel justified in counter-attacking — however it has to be an all-out attack; invoking and channelling White Light will annul the effect of the darker forces, one may hope (if one is well focused and without fear, it works).

4 — POWER SYMBOLS

It should be obvious by now that the subject of psychic self-defense is truly the province of the Shaman or Shamanka, regardless of style and persuasion. The great bulk of people who suffer from psychic interference are not even conscious that it is happening — even if various things are going wrong for them; even if they are inexplicably moody, angry, depleted, ill, or whatever.

Psychic *attacks* almost always focus on one's weakest points, or weakest traits those are the most probable *doors of entry,* of intrusion; which makes sense from two angles (from the *attacker's* point of view).

If the *attack* is a genuine attack, then there is little point focusing on the stronger points or traits — these will usually prevail against the attack. Therefore the *attacker* goes for the vulnerable points instead.

If the *attack* is a test of power, then the weakest points and traits need to be strengthened; therefore they need to be challenged — that is, one is challenged into responding appropriately to the kind of onslaught a given entity may be contemplating *on one's behalf.* Entities such as these, in Shamanic terms, are called *allies.*

In total terms, *allies* are neither black or white, positive or negative. If one does not deal with them properly, then they can inflict harm — potentially lethal harm. If one deals with them correctly, however, or else well enough, then the ordeal — if such it is — will impart a greater strength, and extend one's abilities. Given the power and the singular ability to focus one's energies at will then one may enter *into relationship* with one's *ally*. There are usually benefits in doing so, as well as possible, if not probable drawbacks (see the Carlos Castaneda books, for reference; yet there are other aspects to *allies* than those which are mentioned in these books).

The use of power-symbols in matters of psychic self-defense is often very useful, and in some cases quite necessary. We have already covered something of the effects of a circle or sphere as a power-symbol. Nevertheless one can also use a pentagram, either visualising and projecting it whole in front of oneself, or else tracing it clockwise from the apex (using white, blue or violet light). Likewise one can use an upright equilateral triangle in a similar manner.

The Christian idea of using a cross is in a similar category to the above — it aims to negate interference; however a circle-cross (ie an equal-armed cross within a circle) is far more useful, more powerful, and ultimately more Spiritual — and more balanced. The Christian cross as it is usually conceived, and in its more negative form, is a symbol of materialism or male dominance; and also of death — however one needs to extend one's understanding of death to encompass the principle of *Death-as-Liberator;* the 1st Aspect of Spirit, the *Destroyer-of-Forms* (Shiva).

Although these symbols can be useful in self-defense, they can also be useful in other ways — circle and triangles, for instance, can be used as doorways into order to access other levels of consciousness and existence (see THE PSYCHIC EXPLORER and THE POWER OF MIND & CONSCIOUSNESS). There are other symbols which can be used to summon energy, such as spirals, wave-shapes (undulations), zig-zags, laser beams... Symbols can also be used in association, thus covering several purposes at once.

5 — THE USE OF COLOURS

To an extent colours have already been mentioned with respect to psychic self-defense; yet one needs to understand what these colours truly represent.

They are Rays, or sub-rays of energy. White light diffracts into its colour components: red, orange, yellow, green, blue, indigo, and violet (and ultra-violets and infra-reds, which are normally invisible to the physical eye). However the Spiritual Rays are a diffraction of Spiritual White Light, or Cosmic Light, which is itself the expression of an *invisible* or transparent Essence. In any given Solar System certain Rays predominate; in the case of our present Solar System, Light Blue, and from another point of view Indigo, predominates. Furthermore, each Solar System (as a Spiritual Being) makes use of certain extra-systemic Rays, and then converts these slightly for its own evolutionary purposes; planets, likewise, evolve in accordance with certain cycles of Ray influence.

This subject is far too complex and metaphysical in nature to pursue it at length here. Nevertheless as soon as one begins to think of colours as Energy-Rays which have specific inherent properties, then it becomes easier to understand why white, blue, gold and violet colours, or Rays of energy, are useful in matters of psychic self-defense; or healing, inspiration, or whatever.

Red is energising, yet it can be destructive — using Rose-Red is a viable alternative; Orange is also energising or vitalising; Golden-Yellow stimulates the mind, and promotes a sense of well-being; Green is healing, and invigorating; Blue is healing as well, yet also protective, as is Indigo — although Indigo can be used for the induction of deep trance; Violet is cleansing, and it is practically always used in magickal processes.

This is the general effect of these colours. The Higher Spiritual Rays have superior effects, which are usually outside of our normal terms of reference. Suffice it to say that all life is made up of Rays in various combinations and potencies. Even our physical bodies are made up of Rays, or more precisely of their dense-energy equivalents.

When an aura lacks a particular colour, and more specifically when a chakra lacks a particular colour, or Ray, then it needs to be stimulated by and *fed* with what it lacks.

However one needs to *sense* what is really lacking — too much Red, for instance, can deplete one's energies, as can too little. Too much Blue may slow a person down, yet too little may leave one ill-equipped to deal with psychic interference; and so on. All this varies from individual to individual; therefore there are no completely universal formulae which can be given in order to cover everyone's needs at any one time. Nevertheless by and large the information which is given here can be used by anyone; and the actual effects will vary to a degree in accordance with a person's given circumstances and requirements.

While most people use colours as their personal preferences dictate — for example around the home — one can anticipate that the use of colour in the future will become a far greater preoccupation than it is now, both esoterically as well as scientifically. Colour is still very much under-rated medically, for instance; it is thought as too subjective a means, despite much research in this area by pioneers whose work has been largely overlooked.

6 — STRENGTHENING ONE'S ENERGY FIELDS

An energy field is only as strong as the throughput of power which activates it. We all have an energy field — an aura; nevertheless it is made up of several layers, or frequencies, of energy: etheric, astral, mental, harmonic, atmic, monadic, systemic. Yet as far as most people go only the first three are in any way developed, and not necessarily very well developed at that.

The etheric field, what Science calls the bioplasmic/bioplasmatic field, is formed out of the vital energy which keeps our physical bodies going. When that field is at low ebb people complain of feeling tired, depleted, devitalised; when it is at high tide people feel good, strong and healthy.

237

The bulk of human beings at present incarnate is, in a sense, polarised as it were in its astral field — which makes humans emotionally oriented; choices are made on the basis of feelings, desires, beliefs, infatuations, dreams. However, and increasingly, there is a tendency towards mental polarisation — this can easily be seen around us, and there is something of a battle going on between these two polarisations as the mental field is beginning to predominate or assert itself; this is best observed at political, financial and scientific levels, whereas *ordinary people* are still chiefly motivated by their emotions.

Nevertheless if one looks back a few hundred years then it is easy enough to see that humanity was chiefly emotionally oriented. Mind only figured lightly.

Those who are more evolved in their ways are becoming more conscious of other layers of energy — the higher intellect, intuition, and even Spiritual will figure as part of their personal traits and perspectives. All these things are represented at an auric level, and more specifically they can be observed in terms of chakric unfoldment — a capable clairvoyant can *see* these different layers and their stages of development.

Therefore when attempting to strengthen one's energy fields there are various layers which need to be addressed. To the extent that one feels full of energy, and more or less balanced at all levels, then one's aura shines brightly (if invisibly to most people's eyes) — and the colours are clear and vibrant. To the extent that one is consciously using etheric energy for the purpose of maintaining or else promoting body health, astral energy for the purpose of defining and activating one's dreams and harmonising one's emotions, mental energy for the purpose of turning ideas into concrete realities, higher intellectual energy for the purpose of exploring subjective concepts, harmonic (buddhic) energy for the purpose of exploring one's intuitional capabilities and also experiencing occasional ecstasy in the process, atmic energy for the purpose of asserting one's will in a creative manner, and monadic energy for the purpose of experiencing one's true Oneness with all Life — the God-dess within — then this·is the sort of overall energy field that a Life-Initiate would have — well developed, well nurtured, and dynamic in its impact on self and others.

Strengthening one's energy fields means addressing all these points, individually and collectively. The more one addresses them, the more one's fields become stronger, more alive, more vibrant, more colourful, and more able to intake and adapt to higher, more Spiritual energies.

One of the best ways of strengthening one's fields is to meditate, and to consciously breathe in energy into one's body and consciousness; then to express that energy, or multi-layered energies, in one's everyday output.

There are other ways of strengthening one's energy fields. Out in Nature there are places which are blessed with excellent energies; one can go to these places and absorb some of these energies into one's own energy fields — and providing one is then consciously prepared to work with these energies, then they will remain within one's aura; if one is not consciously prepared to work with them, then they will leak out, or even depart quite swiftly from one's aura. One's energy fields can only attract, absorb and retain energies of like kind — ie the kind one is working with or using.

As an exercise, try this: go to a place out in Nature which you feel very good about, that feels also powerful, either in a direct or a harmonious way (preferably both). Sit there for awhile and just become conscious of your breathing; then breathe more deeply, until your whole consciousness is invested in your breathing — slow, rhythmic breathing. Then address your etheric energies first: feel yourself to be intaking vital energy into your aura, and into your physical body, until you feel charged up with that energy, until it is vibrating serenely all over, from the top of your head right down to the bottom of your spine, and down into your toes. You can visualise that these energies are orange if you like, or white.

Then address your astral energies: breathe in as before, but this time look upon the world around you as a dream — a dream which has become dense and physical; look beyond the density, and allow yourself to see that the physical world mirrors the astral world — the dream world — if in a dense and somewhat imperfect manner. Allow yourself to perceive the finer essence of that dream world; and breathe in its energies, and consciously absorb them. Become an extension of that dream world.

Thirdly, after a while, when you have done the above and feel that you have absorbed as much of the finer astral energy as you need, then focus on the mental energy, which energy gives form to the world. All the forms that you see, including that of your physical body, derive their structures from the mind — it is the mind which conceives them — so breathe in these mental energies, and allow your mind to resonate with creative ideas.

If you have managed to do these three things, you can now move on. Become aware of concepts, refined concepts — allow your higher intellect to play with these, and breathe in those energies which will vitalise these concepts, and make them *live*, within and around you. Explore some of the possibilities here.

Then go beyond concepts, and allow yourself to *connect* with intuitional perceptions — *see* beyond the forms, and sense the living essence behind the forms; *see* yourself in a sea of essence-energy, allow yourself to become at-one with it, and then realise that you are entirely dependent on this essence for your life and your evolutionary expression as a human being. Now all around you, and within you, you can perceive harmonic-deva energies, suffusing all forms, blending them, interrelating them, giving these forms life, and sustaining them with their essence. Bathe in this essence, rejoice in it, feel high from it — allow the ecstasy of it to pervade throughout your whole consciousness and being.

Now try and feel those energies which are so potent and dynamic that they impart the ability to *will* — to *move* things directly; to act on all the other energies, and thus modulate them and direct them with Spiritual force. Allow yourself to channel these (atmic) energies, yet always in a creative, intuitive, and intelligent fashion.

Then, finally, breathe in and invoke your Higher Spirit, your Higher Self, your Monad — and *see* yourself, in full consciousness, as God-dess. As the One-Life. The Cosmic Being. You may or may not be able to do this, to Self-Realise what you *Are* — yet you can try and *connect* with that type of consciousness.

Should you succeed, on the other hand, should you, in all clarity of perception and with perfect love and perfect trust, *emerge* into Monadic consciousness and perceive yourself as a part of the Cosmic Oneness, then you will know that you have just experienced the first Life-Initiation.

This Life-Initiation can only occur when you have *bridged* the gap between your ordinary day-to-day consciousness and your God-dess consciousness — this involves enormous power; it practically always involves a measure of struggle, because one has to adapt to the higher energies within a fairly short space of time, and the power involved galvanises all one's lower energy fields — there is heat, there is magnetic power, there is electrical impulse. One's Kundalini force, from the bottom of the spine, rises dramatically, then floods the head chakras (as well as the other chakras in passing), and then *connects* with the first para-chakra — which is situated above the head. That Kundalini force is in fact activated by the power of this first para-chakra; when the two merge within the head centres, then one achieves God-dess/Monadic consciousness.

It is not comfortable to experience all this the first time round; yet later it becomes progressively easier to achieve this *connection* between personality consciousness and God-dess consciousness. In the process one strengthens one's energy fields immeasurably — providing one doesn't scatter (or distort) the energies involved out of fear or negativity (hence the need for perfect love and perfect trust).

The above exercise is designed to make the process easier and more approachable. You may not wish to go too far at first,

241

but you can use this exercise repeatedly over a period of time, or part of it at any one time, and gradually accustom yourself to the higher energies.

One of the effects of achieving Monadic consciousness for the first time, however, is that one establishes a new, far more dynamic rhythm within one's energy fields; in other words the energies of these fields become lifted to a higher overall frequency, and each field will now vibrate at a higher level. Perceptions in consequence become clearer; one feels more alive; one *knows* who or what one really is — a fragment of the Cosmic Essence. This transcends mere belief in Deity; belief is as nothing compared with *knowing* and experiencing *It*.

Nevertheless after this sort of experience, revolutionary as it is for oneself, one's energy fields settle down again — even if they are now vibrating at higher frequencies, they resume something of their normal rhythm. As a result one loses contact with Monadic consciousness, and gradually one drifts back down into normal personality consciousness. But the personality consciousness knows what it has *seen* and experienced — it does not forget that.

The more one *visits* the higher levels of energy in full consciousness, the more one's energy fields become stronger, more resilient, and more adaptable to powerful energy impacts — therefore they also become less vulnerable to lower grade psychic *attacks*.

By the same token one becomes more sensitive to the inner worlds around oneself, and as a result one experiences the impact of higher energies more often. One is simply now better equipped to deal with them — at an energy level, as well as a personal mental, emotional and etheric-physical level. One's consciousness become more flexible in the process; one begins to *know,* to intuit, how to *move* within the multi-layered world. One is not so likely to be caught out or adversely affected by any negative energies or negative projections on oneself; one can now deal with them with more equanimity than ever before, particularly if one does not indulge in fearing whatever comes one's way, or allow oneself to project negativity oneself.

Nevertheless it takes time for all this to produce the sort of peak experiences which will eventually lead to full, personal liberation from the *three worlds* or the etheric-physical, astral and lower mental planetary fields; which is something which happens when one has mastered the ability to deal with all energies, high and low.

None of this is easy, but these are the implications with regard to self-development and Self-Realisation (Self as in Higher Self). Which is why earlier it was mentioned that the subject of psychic self-defense is really the domain of the Shaman or Shamanka.

There are those who will read this, who may have obtained this booklet because they were looking for information which would permit them to deal with adverse psychic manifestations which may be impinging on the fringe, or even on the whole of their consciousness. Nevertheless there are no two ways around this — one has to make a leap, and grasp that in order to deal effectively with matters of psychic self-defense one must also come to terms with the fact that one is an evolving being who must do whatever is necessary so as to protect oneself from any kind of adversity; and when one cannot avoid that adversity then to deal with it in the best possible manner — yet one cannot do this if one does not have the flexibility or the resilience which will permit one to do so.

Those who, having read this, feel that they are not ready to make that sort of leap are best advised to contact a capable psychic counsellor, who will then be able to advise and guide them with regard to how best to deal with their problems in a manner which is most suited to themselves at any one time. There is an increasing number of such counsellors around, because there is an ever increasing need for these, and for services of this kind.

Nevertheless, as a warning of sorts: there are also those whose integrity is somewhat suspect who are cashing in on these needs, and who have very little to offer by way of adequate advice or proper, personalised guidance; and whose Spiritual awareness, if they are to be credited with having any, is maybe warped by either self-delusion or else religious dogma, or worst of all, both — not to mention those few who enjoy manipulating people for their own ends — whatever these may be. Whenever possible one should seek advice and guidance via recommendation from a friend, which, however, is not an entirely fool-proof way of finding what one needs; failing this, one is best advised to try the services of a given psychic counsellor, and if s/he appears to be the right sort of person to help oneself, that is if s/he *feels right*, then to avail oneself of hir guidance.

Also, orthodox psychiatry is often of very little assistance with regard to outright psychic cases or psychic events, as distinct from psychological disturbances and personality disorders (which may nevertheless be derived from psychic pressures).

In this world one has to be as courageous as possible, and wherever possible one has to sort things out for oneself — and, yes, it can be a challenge, admittedly. Conversely, seeking help from another or others is perfectly valid if one cannot cope with one's experiences. Most reliable psychic counsellors do not charge the earth for their services, and some even offer their help freely — nevertheless, like everyone else, they need to survive in financial terms, therefore even if they do not charge for their services it is at least reasonable to offer some kind of donation.

Then there are those who may find themselves in a most difficult situation: their Kundalini becomes stuck in *open mode*; they cannot close their energies down. Their perceptual abilities may far outstrip their aptitude to screen out consciously what assails them, what they *see*. They may find themselves unable to operate in a normal day-to-day fashion, at least a part of the time; their memories may suffer from on-and-off erasure, because the pressure of the energies which they are experiencing makes it nearly impossible for them to think coherently — their consciousness becomes fully preoccupied with events over which they often have no or relatively little control.

The orthodox way of dealing with people like this is to put them in a mental hospital, and then to drug them up with powerful sedatives — which is one of the worst thing one can do. With exceptions, these people are not in the least bit *insane;* they are merely overwhelmed by their experiences.

What is needed are places where these people can go to, where they will receive proper and caring help from people who understand what they are going through, who know what it is like to experience the Kundalini force, and who know of various ways of *switching it off,* or at least of moderating its impact on one's consciousness.

These places scarcely exist at present, and those which do are badly in need of external funding — one cannot expect people who are experiencing these things to always pay for the help which they *need.*

Nor can one do as did the Incas, who (amongst others) trepanned the top of the skull so as to "let the energy out". Far too many people died that way, although some survived for awhile. But they did know of the problem, and they did try and do something about it.

We are at the beginning of a new Age, a new cycle of human exploration and of evolutionary self and collective development — and we need new ways of dealing with the unusual... and what may not be quite so unusual in the times to come. What is needed in this context is not hospitals, but places where people can go to relax, to progressively deal with their experiences, and then come to terms with them — places which have a harmonious *atmosphere,* run by people who are at least partially enlightened to these sorts of conditions; places where people can learn to balance or moderate the energies which course through them; and also places where these people can work at a practical level, whenever possible, which will help them to *ground* their energies in a viable manner.

Such changes herald something of the nature of what we need to manifest for ourselves as a human culture and civilisation. The planet's energy fields are being increasingly galvanised through evolutionary development, as well as by extra-planetary energies (see STARCRAFT and THE STARCRAFT HANDBOOK). If our societal priorities continue to be as myopic as they are at present, then our present civilisation will burst apart or else become utterly chaotic — nevertheless if we change along with what is happening then we will see the emergence of a new culture and civilisation — one which is in tune with, and for that matter, an extension of our growing needs.

We do need to change our priorities — life on Earth is not just about surviving, making money, or making money for others should we be debtors; it is about evolving and participating in the planet's growth, in the Spiritual sense in particular, since the Spiritual includes matters of culture, of ecology, of international and global aid and support, and so on. We can only go forward if we *do* change our priorities.

Much of the ambient to specific cases of psychic *attacks,* as they may be interpreted, are caused by our present inability to adjust and adapt ourselves to higher levels of energy, as a humanity. The increased energy threshold is *stirring the pot,* as it were, and everything which is both or either negative or positive in nature is being brought to the surface, where we dwell — in consciousness; therefore we are being confronted by events which as yet surpass our immediate ability to cope with them properly. We can only come to terms with what is happening if we communicate, that is if we exchange views openly and without fear, and then move things towards their resolution — regardless of our personal persuasions, politically, religiously, commercially, or otherwise.

There may be those (there are undoubtedly those) who think that they will be able to impose their pattern of priorities on the world for the foreseeable future; the fact is the world's evolution is going to impose its priorities on them — and if they cannot see this, then the energies of the world as they change will render their efforts at mass manipulation to zero.

What is happening is an elemental revolution — an elemental revolution of energy; one which in a few years time will tend to annul any negative activity, automatically, if not instantaneously. This will have far-reaching consequences; ones which we can perhaps only just begin to anticipate clearly in any way.

Essentially it means that anything that is based on negativity will cease to function; which means that people who predominantly embody negative energies and refuse to change, will die — their energy fields will collapse, as a result of which their biological functions will grind to a halt (heart-attacks may figure prominently). The systems which they endorse will fall apart; which is why viable, balanced alternatives need to be not only encouraged but brought into expression as soon as possible — in a concerted and collective fashion at that.

If some should find these notions alarmist, others, without doubt, will welcome them without reservations. Nevertheless what we need is genuine alternatives — and not hypocritical, reactionary, or ill-conceived efforts, which in effect amount to little more than the former pattern(s) in a different guise.

It would seem that we have now gone a long way from considering the subject of psychic self-defense, and that we have enlarged our periphery of vision to encompass matters which are more planetary in context. From dealing with personal psychic self-defense as a would-be Shaman or Shamanka, we are now confronted by the whole issue of our survival as a species, on the one hand, and the evolutionary and Spiritual impetus of the planet as a unit, on the other. In the process we have, if briefly, reviewed certain energy events as pertinent to the subject of energy fields, and how these can affect us.

What has not been discussed so far, even if it has been somewhat implied, is the fact that there is a Planetary Spirit — or what the ancient Greeks called a Logos (there is in truth a shade of difference between the Planetary Spirit and the Planetary

Logos, as the Logos forms a focus through which the Planetary Spirit can express itself).

When perceived or acknowledged as an Entity in its own right, the Planetary Spirit, or Planetary Logos, must be viewed as a Being who has Hir own evolutionary aims, which far outstrip those of humanity, yet to which humanity contributes in some way — it has been suggested that we as human beings in effect are like individual brain cells, the brain being the planet, or Planetary Spirit; the Planetary Logos is the focused consciousness within that brain, the *mover* who uses that brain for its own planetary, evolutionary purposes.

If we can but understand something of this, and ally ourselves to the purpose of the Planetary Logos, then we would find that each and every one of us would become an extension of that Logos, in expression — at least up to the level at which each one of us individually could function at any one moment. Collectively, then it would be as if each brain cell was able to communicate directly with every other brain cell, and this would then speed up the unfoldment of viable alternatives considerably. This may be a big notion to take in at face value, and yet it is neither new or beyond our grasp to understand — if we are open to it.

7 — THE INVOCATION OF PROTECTIVE DEVAS

All energy is Devic energy; Devas are those beings who generate, and to a great extent embody energy — regardless of grade and essential quality. Yet energy in itself is neutral; in polarity terms, positive and negative energies are still essentially neutral as far as *good* and *bad* are concerned — that is, they are functional in electrical and magnetic terms; from that point of view they are not neutral, but dynamic or responsive.

The fact that there are beings, particularly human beings insofar as we need be concerned, who (on the lower Planes) tinge that energy with *good* and *bad* attributes or qualities is something else. *Bad* energy is energy which has been distorted

248

and imbued with adverse attributes (usually emotional-astral and sometimes lower mental ones), such as fear, anger, malice, and whatever. *Good* energy is energy which has been imbued with creative, harmonious attributes.

Since we have explored much to do with energy fields, and considering that energy is Devic in character, it should be obvious enough that the best beings to address and invoke when seeking the protection of one's energy fields will be Devas.

But which Devas in particular? There are countless different types (see STARCRAFT). A great many Devas are small nature spirits who can, given the inclination, sometimes assist human beings, directly or indirectly, as can certain other Devas, such as Dryads (or tree spirits). Nevertheless it should be obvious enough that if all energy is Devic in nature, and if we have energy fields, then our energy fields are already generated and maintained, and repaired when necessary, by the Devas who actively create those fields in the first place. In other words we are human beings, but our fields are Devic, which by implication means that behind the veil of appearances we are also Devas — and this regardless of whether we are conscious of that fact or totally unconscious of it; and regardless of the fact that we represent, as human beings, one life-stream, and Devas represent the complementary-opposite life-stream — there was a time when both life-streams were *one single life-stream,* in consciousness, as well as otherwise.

This is why balance in one's life is so critical; if one is in balance with Life then one energy fields will be balanced (in truth it is mostly the other way around: if one's energy fields are balanced then one will be in balance with Life). As soon as we become out of balance, or our fields become out of balance, then our fields become vulnerable to *attack.*

This is what *Karma* is all about — balance; energy balance. So-called *bad karma* indicates that one's fields (ie one or more of them) have become imbalanced by some self act which has effectively distorted them (not to mention those of others, possibly); until the distortions have been put right by another, opposite self act, or an *external* act which is somewhat imposed on oneself and which puts matters right on one's behalf, then the imbalance will prevail — for seconds (*instant karma*), hours, days, years, or whole lifetimes (in most cases one's *bad karma* will consist of several different types of distortions, each one of which was caused by a different self act; different types of self acts will affect the etheric, astral or lower mental energy field).

So-called *good karma* is a little different — this also represents an imbalance, yet it is not one which will weigh adversely against oneself. There are those who think of it as some kind of *energy-credit,* and in one sense it is; nevertheless it is an excess — which can be neutralised by an opposite self act of a similar kind, but not necessarily by an opposite act of a different kind.

Since all natural living organisms, including energy fields, automatically strive to remain in balance, any imbalance which occurs also automatically invokes its own remedy — hence *Karma.* Whatever distortions one produces in one's fields, one's fields will attempt to neutralise; and sooner or later they will succeed in doing so — and if not in the current lifetime/incarnation, then in the next one, or the one following that, and so on, until balance has been achieved.

This matter of balance brings us once more to the subject of the two life-streams — Human and Devic. Before we explore the Devic side of ourselves something needs to be said about our Human side — as human beings we are not just physical persons; we are human spirits — that is, each one of us is composed of a human soul, which as it were presides over a human personality, which is itself composed of a lower (structural, organising) mind, an astral/dream self, and an etheric-physical vehicle, ie the biological body plus its vital force (or etheric *blue-print*), which in combination one uses during any given incarnation.

At the end of an incarnation the etheric field diminishes in strength, and at some critical point it becomes too weak to sustain the physical, biological body, which body then dies — ie it ceases to function (unless of course the physical body is lethally damaged by an accident, and therefore dies before the etheric field has lost all its functional strength). For a short time one finds oneself conscious on the etheric layers, then the etheric field ceases to function and dissipates, and one then finds oneself conscious on the Astral Plane, within one's astral field, or *dreambody*. Some more time passes, during which period one recuperates somewhat from the strain of physical incarnation, then the astral field diminishes in turn, and disintegrates, and then one finds oneself conscious on the lower Mental Plane, within one's lower mental field. Finally this field diminishes as well, and one's personality self is absorbed into one's human soul — which resides on the higher Mental Plane. One's soul then *debriefs* the human personality self, that is it absorbs all the gains and experience of the last incarnation.

In effect the human personality self is a fragment or projection of the human soul. To the extent that the personality self fails to be conscious of its soul, then they can be spoken of as two distinct beings; yet if the personality self is conscious of its soul, then there is much less distinction to be made; and if the personality self is fully conscious of and at-one with its soul, then there is no distinction to be made between the two. Nevertheless very few people are fully conscious of and at-one with their souls — except, that is, for third degree Life-Initiates, and to an extent 1st and 2nd degree Life-Initiates.

When a new incarnation is required one's soul then projects part of itself back down through the Planes — in effect it projects a single point of force, which embodies all the previous incarnational developmental patterns. As this point of force travels *down* through the lower Mental Plane it activates lower mental energy, gathers some of it to itself, and recreates a lower mental energy field in this it is assisted by certain lower Mental Plane Devas. Then as it travels further *down* into the Astral Plane this point of force, which is now *coated* with one kind of energy field, activates astral energy, gathers some of this to itself in turn, and then recreates an astral/dream energy field — this time it is assisted by certain types of astral Devas. There for a time it waits, although the process of reincarnation is in fact continually in progress — the personality self at this stage is alive as an astral human being, and therefore participates in astral activities, and this more or less consciously. To a given extent s/he then establishes what s/he needs to do and learn from hir next incarnation in physical density, and in this s/he is advised by other human beings, who are more evolved than s/he is, and who for all intents and purposes are specialised in giving this sort of advice — these have the ability to *view* what is happening on the physical plane, and can therefore inform hir of the best possible courses of action; and can make certain *arrangements* on hir behalf as well. Then it is a matter of choosing the most appropriate dense conditions in which to unfold hir plans, and then finding a suitable physical vehicle in which to incarnate.

Finding the right vehicle is perhaps not so very easy; yet finding any kind of vehicle is not particularly all that difficult. At any one time there are thousands of impregnated ova in existence around the world — which are all spinning anti-clockwise, and thus creating downward-drawing vortexes of energy (courtesy of those Devas who specialise in such things); and these vortexes can be seen adequately enough from the vantage of the Astral Plane whenever they are sought.

Various interesting choices may be in evidence; nevertheless for one reason or another they may not actually be *right*. For example, the personality self will be seeking parents who can provide the required sort of genes or chromosomal mix; furthermore s/he will often be seeking parents, as human spirits, with whom s/he has karmic matters to sort out; or else affinitive links. In fact the *right* choice can be very difficult to find as ideal conditions are very rarely encountered. If the chromosomal mix is right, then the parents, as human spirits, may not be; if they are then the area of the world may not be appropriate; if it is then the local cultural conditions may be inadequate; and so on.

When the right (or the best possible) physical vehicle is finally located, then the personality self projects a line of energy into the fertilised egg, and thereby attaches hir energies to it; yet s/he does not actually incarnate immediately or directly into the egg. S/he waits a while for things to progress further, and monitors the developments. S/he can still withdraw the connection which s/he has made if necessary, at least within a given period. Eventually the egg travels into the uterus, becomes an embryo, and gradually grows into a fully fledged foetus — and to an extent the sex of that foetus can be influenced by the would-be incarnating self; then after about three months of gestation sexual differentiation occurs. Bit by bit more and more of hir energy becomes invested within the foetus, and then close to the moment of birth the vortex sucks the rest of hirself (as a soul fragment) down into incarnation. In the process all past memory is erased from hir consciousness (but not from hir subconscious).

This much is said to briefly illustrate this process. Yet at the other end of things, when the personality self found itself progressively stripped of its energy fields, and then was finally absorbed by its human soul, there it encountered its Solar Deva — one's Solar Deva is the complementary (and opposite) half to one's human soul; from one point of view they are one and identical — and from another angle they are two distinct beings, each operating on two distinct life-waves, or life-streams — Devic and Human.

It is one's Solar Deva who oversees the process of recreating the energy fields lower mental, astral, then etheric — by guiding other types of Devas to do the required work at these various levels. The Solar Deva has a life of hir own, and yet s/he is also inextricably in touch with what the Human soul half of hirself is doing, and therefore with the projected fragment — which becomes the personality self. While the Solar Deva does not spend hir whole time monitoring what is happening to that fragment, the personality self can call upon hir Solar Deva at any time, and providing the personality self calls or invokes hir in the right manner, then s/he will respond to it. The level at which that response is *felt* or is otherwise perceived will depend on one's clarity of consciousness at that particular moment.

The Solar Deva is also known as the *Guardian Angel;* s/he is more in tune with the projected fragment/personality self than any other being can be, since that fragment is actually a part of hirself, via the Human soul. One's Solar Deva, in consequence, is the most appropriate being one can invoke with regard to one's protection (and one's inspiration, also).

How does one invoke one's Solar Deva (Soul-ar Deva; effectively, Sun-God-dess)?

One can simply call out, vocally or sub-vocally, "Solar Deva"; or "Dæva". Yet s/he will most readily respond to a sound pattern which approximates the sound of hir own nature and expression as a Deva — or a name, one which is symbolically *descriptive* of hirself (s/he will usually have more than one name, however). How does one find out hir name (or at least one of hir names)?! There are various ways: one can do this in meditation, subsequent to having invoked hir as mentioned above; one can invoke hir before going to sleep, and the answer may come in a dream — or just after waking.

On a more elaborate, and more distinctly magickal basis, one can do a ritual. Surrounding oneself in a circle one can invoke hir while facing the North; then turning clockwise one should invoke hir while facing the East; then the South, and then the West. Then one should sit down (or stand) in the centre of the circle, facing the North anew, and wait for hir answer. If that answer is not immediately forthcoming, then one should do the ritual again, and again — at intervals, even over a period of days, weeks, or months — until the answer finally comes (it may have been given, but was it *heard?*).

Before your Solar Deva gives you a name by which you can invoke hir s/he will usually wait until your motives are sufficient pure, or sufficiently heartful — s/he will not give out any of hir

254

name until s/he is reasonably sure that you will not abuse it, magickally or otherwise.

When a name is finally forwarded — in some way — that will not be the end of the matter: at other times s/he may offer other names, usually superior ones — these will be designed to help you access new perspectives.

Over a period of time your Solar Deva will advance new names by which you can invoke hir. Sound them in your head, and try and identify yourself with their symbolic reality. In the case of a Life-Initiate s/he will begin to suggest names which are more powerful — and some of these s/he will use to draw attention and consciousness to certain archetypal Devic principles or processes. Further in time s/he will announce names which are not specifically hir own, but those of hir own Higher Devic Aspects.

The purpose of gaining insights into these Devic perspectives may not be apparent to everyone who reads this, and yet to *know* one's Solar Deva is a joy to be able to identify with hir world-view by merging one's consciousness with hir own is to open a door on a beyond which has no conceivable limits.

If the information which is given here is cross-referred with that which is given in this bundled book, in THE PSYCHIC EXPLORER and in THE POWER OF MIND & CONSCIOUSNESS, then you will find that it forms a pattern; each publication contains part of that pattern, or puzzle. It is a puzzle which is still *coming through,* and in order to understand it fully, to resolve it properly, one's intuition is required.

BLESSED BE!

APPENDIX I

THE SEVEN PLANES & THE SEVEN COSMIC PLANES

Each of the Seven Planes is composed of seven sub-planes; and the Seven Planes collectively form the lowest of the Seven Cosmic Planes. Therefore one can say that there are 49 sub-planes within the Seven Planes, and 49 Planes within the Seven Cosmic Planes (or 343 sub-planes).

This system of Cosmic Planes is therefore absolutely vast, in fact well beyond our present comprehension: however the actual principle involved is relatively simple.

These are some of the names which are given to these levels (which names have been used in this book):

7th Plane: Adi (Systemic)

6th Plane: Monad (Seed-Self/One-Self)

5th Plane: Atma (Spiritual Will)

4th Plane: Buddhi (Harmonic; Spiritual Love)

3rd Plane: Higher Spiritual Mind, & Lower Mind: (Manas)

2nd Plane: Astral (The Dream Plane/emotional energy/sentiency)

1st.Plane: Etheric-physical Plane (the incarnational plane).

On the etheric-physical plane, dense solids, liquids and gases represent the three lowest sub-planes of matter.

The ancient Tibetans counted these Planes from the top.: ie the 1st Plane was the Adi; likewise with regard to the Cosmic Planes:

7th (1st) Cosmic Plane Of Adi

6th (2nd) Cosmic Plane Of Monad

5th (3rd) Cosmic Plane Of Atma

4th (4th) Cosmic Plane Of Buddhi

3rd (5th) Cosmic Mental Plane

2nd (6th) Cosmic Astral Plane

1st (7th) Cosmic etheric-physical Plane: i.e. the Seven Planes.

From one point of view all these Planes are in fact a spectrum: an infinite Spectrum! There are Meta-Cosmic Planes beyond the Cosmic Plane of Adi.

ESSENTIAL BIBLIOGRAPHY

Carlos Castaneda:
THE TEACHINGS OF DON JUAN (Penguin)
A SEPARATE REALITY (Penguin)
JOURNEY TO IXTLAN (Penguin)
TALES OF POWER (Penguin)
THE SECOND RING OF POWER (Penguin)
THE EAGLE'S GIFT (Penguin)
THE FIRE FROM WITHIN (Century Publishing)
THE POWER OF SILENCE (Simon and Schuster)

Alice A. Bailey:
ESOTERIC ASTROLOGY (Lucis Press)
A TREATISE ON COSMIC FIRE (Lucis Press)
ESOTERIC PSYCHOLOGY — I (Lucis Press)
ESOTERIC PSYCHOLOGY — II (Lucis Press)
A TREATISE ON WHITE MAGIC (Lucis Press)
THE RAYS AND THE INITIATIONS (Lucis Press)
LETTERS ON OCCULT MEDITATION (Lucis Press)
ESOTERIC HEALING (Lucis Press)

Vee Van Dam:
THE PSYCHIC EXPLORER (Skoob Books Ltd., Spiral Publications)
THE POWER OF MIND & CONSCIOUSNESS (Skoob Books Ltd.,Spiral Publications)
STARCRAFT (Skoob Books Ltd., Spiral Publications)

Richard Bach:
A BRIDGE ACROSS FOREVER (Pan)

Barbara Hand Clow:
EYE OF THE CENTAUR (Llewellyn Publications)

Steve Richards:
INVISIBILITY; MASTERING THE ART OF VANISHING (The Aquarian Press)

Robert A. Monroe:
JOURNEYS OUT OF THE BODY (Corgi)

G.M. Glaskin:
WORLDS WITHIN (Arrow)

Fritjof Capra:
THE TAO OF PHYSICS (Fontana)

Lyall Watson:
SUPERNATURE (Coronet)

Neil F. Michelsen:
THE AMERICAN EPHEMERIS FOR THE 20TH CENTURY (ACS Publications)

G.A. Briggs and F.W. Taylor:
THE CAMBRIDGE PHOTOGRAPHIC ATLAS OF THE PLANETS (Cambridge U. Press)

Josef Klepesta and Antonin Rukl:
CONSTELLATIONS (Hamlyn)

Timothy Ferris:
GALAXIES (Sierra Club; Stewart, Tabori & Chang)

Michael Tobias:
DEVA (Avant Books; Fiction)

Ingo Swann:
STAR FIRE (Sphere; Fiction)

Jane Roberts:
THE EDUCATION OF OVERSOUL SEVEN (Prentice-Hall Inc.; Fiction)